Playwriting

Fraser Grace's published plays

Perpetua (1999)
Gifts of War (solo play), in *TWO into War* (2005, with Naomi Wallace)
Who Killed Mr Drum? (2005, with Sylvester Stein)
Breakfast with Mugabe (2005)
Frobisher's Gold (2006)
The Lifesavers (2009, reprinted 2010)
King David, Man of Blood (2010)
Kalashnikov: In the Woods by the Lake (2011)
(all published by Oberon Books)

Clare Bayley's publications

Blue Sky (2012), Nick Hern Books
The Enchantment (2007), English version of the play by nineteenth-century Swedish writer Victoria Benedictsson, Nick Hern Books
The Container (2007), Nick Hern Books
The Enchantment is included in *100 Great Plays for Women* (2013), ed. Lucy Kerbel, Nick Hern Books
Contribution in *My First Play* (2013), Nick Hern Books
'Guatemala Moon' in *The Asham Award: Reshape Whilst Damp* (1999), ed. Carole Buchanan, Serpent's Tail

Playwriting

A Writers' and Artists' Companion

Fraser Grace and Clare Bayley

Series Editors: **Carole Angier and Sally Cline**

Bloomsbury Academic India
An imprint of Bloomsbury Publishing Plc

BLOOMSBURY
NEW DELHI • LONDON • OXFORD • NEW YORK • SYDNEY

BLOOMSBURY INDIA
Bloomsbury Publishing India Pvt. Ltd
Second Floor, Building No. 4
DDA Complex LSC, Pocket C – 6 & 7
Vasant Kunj, New Delhi 110070
www.bloomsbury.com

BLOOMSBURY, Bloomsbury Academic India and the Diana
logo are trademarks of Bloomsbury Publishing Plc

First published in India 2020
First published 2016

This edition published with permission from Bloomsbury Publishing Plc,
50 Bedford Square, London, WC1B3DP, UK

British Library Cataloguing-in-Publication Data
A catalogue record for this book is available from the British Library.

Library of Congress Cataloging-in-Publication Data
A catalog record for this book is available from the Library of Congress

ISBN: 978-93-89351-87-3

For Sale in the Indian subcontinent only

Series: Writers' and Artists' Companions

Typeset by Integra Software Services Pvt. Ltd
Digitally Printed and bound in India by Replika Press Pvt. Ltd. In 2019.

Bloomsbury Publishing Plc makes every effort to ensure that the papers used in the manufacture of our books are natural, recyclable products made from wood grown in well-managed forests. Our manufacturing processes conform to the environmental regulations of the country of origin.

To find out more about our authors and books
visit www.bloomsbury.com and sign up for our newsletters

Fraser Grace
for Ciaran and Lewis

Clare Bayley
for Felix and Laurie

Contents

Preface

Playwriting is the ninth and last in our series of writers' Companions – and what a finale! From the Foreword by the Artistic Director of the National Theatre, through the authors' every word, to the essays by their famous guests, it flashes with passion for the theatre and the thrills (and spills) of playwriting. For of all literary genres, only plays are created together with other people, born in the presence of yet other people, and different every night.

But *Playwriting* isn't merely exciting. It is a clear, authoritative, accessible guide to everything you need to know about being a playwright. It offers an original theatrical history from the writer's point of view, and a minute analysis of the playwright's craft, from writing to rehearsal, performance and after. It considers how you write for every kind of theatre, from the oldest proscenium stage to the newest site-specific and promenade forms; how you deal with character, dialogue, plot and setting, with stage directions, acts and scenes, and with the layout and formatting of scripts. For all of this, the heart of the book, it provides detailed exercises for use in classes, or for anyone working alone in their garret. During the rehearsal period it gives precious (and sometimes hilarious) advice on how to deal with actors, directors and new panjandrums such as dramaturgs; and finally on how to behave during and after the run, including – perhaps the most useful advice of all – about reviews. It concludes with a summary of how to deal with the industry as a whole: finding theatres and agents right for you, and getting your plays published.

We're certain that you will not find anywhere a more knowledgeable, practical and entertaining companion for your playwriting journey. In theatre parlance (though stealing it from another place) we recommend it to the House.

Carole Angier and Sally Cline
Series Editors

Foreword

Writers are the most important artists in the theatre world. They hold a clear, crooked, chaotic or glorious mirror up to humanity. It is through their imaginations that we are drawn into a deeper understanding of ourselves and are confronted with the moral, intellectual and spiritual questions of our age. They allow us to stand in the spotless or shabby shoes of others and understand what we are, what we could be, and what it is to be alive and kicking now.

But it is a marathon. Stamina, sensitivity, fortitude, eloquence, dynamism, a deep quality of hearing – the characteristic wish list goes on and on for the absolute playwright.

There is one facet of the playwriting craft, however, that is more important than all others. It might be blindingly obvious and want obscuring, it might be incredibly elusive and need digging out – either way, it is the nucleus of the endeavour that is indisputably yours: why does the realm you are exploring need *you* to reveal it? What is your umbilical link to this story? By this I don't mean an autobiographical ownership. I mean why, on a profound level, will anyone give a damn? That, for me, will almost inevitably come down to you – your deep connection to the material and your courage in mining that connection.

The craft – structure, believability, character definition or what you will – can all be practised but for me, as a director in this most collaborative of art forms, understanding this personal anchor is the key: to liberating your interpreters to encourage or challenge you to go further, to growing our collective form from your personal content, to celebrating it in the theatrical medium we inhabit.

The cost is high, in terms of conquering inhibition and the layers and layers of work it takes to shape your truth. But the prize can be higher. Playwrights are the arrowhead of our culture, and there is no more worthwhile aim than to sharpen that point with a commitment to what you personally hold to be worth saying.

This book is intended as a whetstone to that purpose. It'll help you see your work in the context of the dramatists who have gone before you, as well as containing words of wisdom from some of the finest contemporary playwrights. It offers companionship not only in the craft of writing, but also in navigating your way through the industry and into the rehearsal room. Whether from a historical perspective, from the advice of your fellow writers featured here or from the practical guidance offered up, I'm sure you will find fuel for your marathon and a sharp prompt in these pages.

Rufus Norris
Artistic Director, National Theatre

Acknowledgements

Fraser and Clare would like to give special thanks to all those playwrights who contributed their tips and tales to this book.

We are also very grateful to our editors, Carole Angier and Sally Cline, and to David Avital and Mark Richardson at Bloomsbury.

Fraser would like to acknowledge a debt to the work of David Edgar and Steve Waters, particularly in Part 3 'Action and plot' and 'Units'. He would also like to thank Ezra Barnes, Josh Costello, Ciaran Grace, Anne Hogben, Professor Russell Jackson, Lucile Lichtblau, Linda Muirhead, Susan Sellers and Sue.

Clare would also like to thank Andy Lavender for meticulous reading, David Benedict for helpful comments, fellow writer and teacher Vicky Grut, and Fraser for getting her mixed up in all of this. And to Chris.

All errors remain our own.

Introduction

> Let us stand here and admit that we have no road.
>
> William Empson

The idea that the work of a playwright is a craft that can be learned and honed is well established – the clue, at least in the UK, is in the spelling: wheelwright, cartwright, shipwright, playwright.

That said, we would like to propose that William Empson's homage to the British Library – you'll find it over the entrance – be tattooed inside the eyelids of every writer setting about the writing of a new play. Reflecting on it will get us all grounded, accustomed again to the idea of not knowing – which is 90 per cent of the writing process.

In the rest of life, 'knowing what's what' is the trick that helps us survive; it's how we dodge the bullets, keep all the balls in the air, carve out time to write at all. But when writing a new play, be prepared first of all to not know. Get yourself into a state of frenzy, or calm, whatever works best – but give the path time to show itself. The road you are looking for is the one that will lead to the summit of this far-off (but unique) play that so far you sense more than see.

We cannot tell you how you should pursue this road. How could we? This new play of yours has never been written, it's unique – the path that leads to your summit didn't start in the same place as our paths; your destination lies somewhere else entirely.

That is the premise of this book. It's not a map, not a rule book; it's a penknife, a bit of string, and at times, if you're lucky, it'll work as a compass. Write till you're lost, then wait till you know what's next. In the meantime, maybe consult your Companion – read a chapter, consult the notes or diagrams you made yourself before beginning, reflect and go again. When you get to your summit – to the end of your own unique playwriting process – give us a wave. We need the encouragement.

Oh, and by the way, a playwright is someone who is *in the practice* of writing plays (if you've written one play, you're a playwrote). That summit you're striving towards – when you reach it – is just in front of the next one.

Now, that one really does look steep.
Good luck.

Clare Bayley and Fraser Grace

Part 1
Reflections

Reflections

Fraser Grace

It has often been observed, but is nonetheless true, that writing for the theatre makes for a precarious existence. It is bound to, because theatre itself is such an elusive art form. Consequently, we optimists who engage in it do our best to develop a strong streak of pragmatism. As Winston Churchill had it, success is going from failure to failure with no loss of enthusiasm.

That said, the best of the failures in my own playwriting have been transforming. Good theatre can be an almost mystical experience. If you've ever inspected stage props when the stage lights are down – when cruel house lighting reveals all those hastily daubed surfaces – the stuff theatre is made of is often very basic, even tawdry. If ever there was an activity that relies on something to make the whole greater than the sum of its parts, it's theatre.

But what is that 'something'? At what point does a pale game of 'let's pretend' shift into the transcendent mode every theatre worker or theatre lover hopes for? That's very hard to nail, and it's even harder to predict when it's going to happen. You're just very grateful that it did.

The rules of theatre don't help here. In fact, theatre writing has barely any rules at all, and the most exciting theatre writing arguably thrives on renegotiating whatever rules it began with, finding new ways to break old lore, seemingly with every project.

Here's what we know for certain about how the drama works. Frankly, it's not much to go on.

A group of people gather in a space, and are divided – knowingly or otherwise – into two groups. We could call these performers and audience, except that like all divisions in the theatre, even this is porous. Better to say, that some of those assembled have made a plan in advance – a proposal for what is going to happen – and have agreed to work broadly in pursuit of it. Most people in the space have been granted no such warning. Those with the privilege of seeing the plan beforehand – nowadays the plan is called a script – actors, directors, designers, technicians (the list of these specialisms has grown over time) – lead those without the script (they may have bought tickets and a programme in lieu of a script) into an act of usually willing self-deceit. The deceit goes something like this: 'For the duration of the performance, we will all believe ourselves to be wherever the action takes us, to observe what it is we are shown, to allow ourselves to feel whatever emotions the events evoke, and we will try to discern what of importance, if anything, is being alleged about it. During the performance and after – whenever our reason is at its strongest – we will attempt to draw a few conclusions that might help us understand our world and our place in it a bit better. Armed with these insights, we might possibly begin to question the way the world is, why we put up with it and what we would have to do to change it.'

A deceit perhaps, but on such things revolutions are founded.

So the playscript (like the ticket) is a powerful thing.

The script can be created by a team, either of writers working together, or of performers acting as originators. More often the script is the creation of a single individual, of a single powerfully focused imagination. No matter how the script was originally created, it's only the beginning – it's a plan, after all – and any script clearly has its work cut out. First, it has to carve out an area of interest. Second, it has to determine how that interest will be interrogated – there will be actors, almost certainly, but what parts will they play? What will these 'parts' do in their world? How will they express themselves? What will be the pattern in which the playing out of these parts is observed?… and so on. Third, the script has to hook and stimulate the imagination of all those whose imaginations are needed to complete the act of theatre and, through them and with them, the imaginations of the observers or audience. Without all these co-conspirators, the act of theatre doesn't take place. But without the script, no one knows what the act of theatre will coalesce around, or how the act will be prosecuted. Even with a script, no one knows for sure what the effect on everyone will be – positive or negative; will it inspire joy or despair? Will its effect be long-lasting or forgotten by the time we reach the bus stop on the way home?

It is, as I said, an unpredictable business, but viewed in this light, the script – humble, tawdry, hastily daubed – is the first step towards transcendence.

Why a play for the stage?

Every playwright surely pokes at this elephant in the writing room on a regular basis: why, in this age, write a play for the stage at all? In the age of the digital revolution, and of falling theatre attendances; in a time when TV and film offer so much bigger financial rewards, and such exciting prospects in terms of exposure to mass audiences, plus many tantalizing creative possibilities, why does writing a stage play make sense? Isn't it odd that any talented writer should expend their energy in this least hi-tech, most exposing and least commercially rewarding of activities?

That theatre, and especially new plays in the theatre, are under threat, is not in doubt. When the playwright Finn Kennedy published his report *In Battalions* in 2012, the surveys he conducted painted a grim picture of the situation in the UK. In spite of huge and conspicuous successes like *A Servant of Two Masters* or *Jerusalem*, recessionary pressures were hitting this industry hard, and the playwrights' corner of it especially so. Theatres reported fewer new commissions for new plays being offered; cancelled productions; new plays being produced for shorter runs; and in some cases, reduced commission fees for playwrights. The situation is even worse if the playwright is female. The British Theatre Consortium's Interim Report (2015), in fact found that the programming of new work in the UK recently overtook that of revivals for the first time in a century, a certain cause for celebration. However, a Supplementary Report, published later that year, shows that the benefit falls disproportionately when anaylsed according to gender. When a new play is programmed, it is 14% less likely to have been penned by a woman. What's more, when the playwright is female, the play is more likely to be produced in a smaller theatre, and for fewer performances.[1]

[1] British Theatre Repertoire 2013, Supplementary Report, Still Looking Through a Glass Ceiling? – distributed British Theatre Conference, Saturday 25 April 2015.

As for those at the 'receiving end', in 2012 ACE reported that attendance figures for theatre as a whole fell from 14.1 million in 2009 to 13 million in 2011. Outside London, audiences had fallen by 10 per cent over this same period.

In the USA, *Variety* magazine likewise found that audiences for theatre in 2012 were dwindling, although in the much smaller not-for-profit sector there was evidence that figures were steadily recovering to pre-recession levels, from a low in 2010.

Against this, Live Analytics' document 'State of Play: Theatre UK' reported in September 2013 that 63 per cent of the UK population had been to at least one theatre show in the previous year – a figure that seems astoundingly high, beating any sport or other pastime. More tellingly the report also reveals that if the total audience is becoming smaller, there is some evidence that it is also growing younger: a 71 per cent increase in attendance at the theatre among 16–25-year-olds since 2009. This stat again seems remarkable – isn't this age group supposed to spend every waking hour plugged into computers, downloading their cultural fix?

It seems that, instead of being displaced by digital activity, theatre is yet again adapting to its time. The same survey found that the increased percentage of young people attending theatre had frequently been drawn to the event by new media, and were using the same to disseminate their views of the experience. With the development of simulcasts of big theatre productions in regional cinemas, and live streaming of theatre and opera online, it seems the relationship between the digital relaying of experience and the live physical enactment of theatre might be becoming more symbiotic than oppositional.

Nor is writing for the stage always and only an end in itself. One reason given for the boom in the quality of TV drama coming out of the US is the east–west drift of its best playwrights. TV looks for 'proven' talent to fill writing teams on blockbusting serials; cut your teeth off-Broadway, and LA beckons. Theatre is, as it has been since the advent of film, a recognized training ground for dramatic writing across all dramatic media. It gives even the most timid of writers the opportunity to begin with what they have, and to answer the call from Hollywood only once some confidence and dramatic know-how has been gained.

For the playwright, there is also the draw of theatre as a workplace. Unlike other kinds of writing, playwriting shifts its practitioners by necessity fairly quickly out of splendid isolation and into a more sociable sphere. Now the playwright meets other artists and practitioners, inventive and challenging, determined to be the best they can be, and bending and transgressing the boundaries of this common medium to innovative effect – while at the same time continuing to address issues of the day, of the planet and of our species. A play is an end in itself, but writing one is also a passport into a working life of collaboration, exploration and adventure, perhaps in part precisely because it is a less commercially defined art form.

My own experience of that life began almost by accident. Childhood holidays with my factory-working dad and postwoman mum always began with packing a large cardboard box full of library books before heading off to a caravan on the east coast. Once inside, head deep in a rabbit burrow or my feet planted firmly on the deck of a three-master, I would pray for the rain outside to continue, and give me more hours of reading. I soon began writing stories and poems – it was the one thing I got praise for at school – and then finally I discovered Samuel Beckett. Now I understood that theatre could not only take you to other worlds, but *is* another world – unique, mysterious and profound.

Still, it wasn't until I went to university, intent on becoming a social worker, that I fell among actors; immediately, I began writing plays for them – us – to perform. We took the first long play I wrote to the Edinburgh Festival Fringe. We got one review. It was a good one. We formed a company and toured for seven years, us against the world until, exasperated with writing the next play in the back of the van, I decided I had to give this thing my proper attention. I still thought the world needed changing, but I had discovered that writing a play for the theatre, was a glorious end in itself.

I still find it astonishing that in the twenty-first century, there are so many people who love to sit in a room with a crowd of strangers, to see or rather feel the lights go down, and to be transported by imagination and a few emblematic props and characters, light and sound, to other times and other cultures. There they see something *seem to happen*, live, which challenges, delights and disturbs.

Depending where they live in the real world, this audience may well find issues raised and leaders mocked in a way it would never encounter outside the space, or in other, higher-profile media. As a dramatic medium, theatre often travels under the radar, the least shackled by either commerce or censorship, free to experiment with ideas, as much as with form. When the houselights come back up, the act of theatre has disappeared. No other dramatic art form can pull off that particular trick; nothing digital – as we are learning – ever disappears forever. Theatre is little more than a wisp of smoke, remembered long after it is gone.

And all this, more often than not, begins with a script created by a single playwright, alone or with a gang of collaborators, on a piece of (sometimes virtual) paper.

Did I mention this is also available as an e-book?

Clare Bayley and I intend this *Companion* for all those who wish to embark on this ancient, and very modern, adventure. In addition to Clare, I owe thanks to many fellow travellers, not least the students who have patiently and sometimes impatiently listened as I've scratched around to find a way of analysing the alchemy that goes into making a play, and tried to explain, however unconvincingly, why it seems to me to be the best of all trades.

To my family, I owe apologies; you're right, I wasn't listening. I was somewhere else.

Reflections

Clare Bayley

The most skilful writing in any form looks effortless, and many people make the mistake of thinking that writing plays is easy. For some people, perhaps, it is – but not for most of us. David Hare has described how 'the strange, necessary combination of vitality on the surface and power below – wave and tide, if you like – is harder than it looks'. And because playwriting is by necessity a collaborative process, the playwright's work has to be robust enough to survive the interventions of the rest of the creative team, but supple enough to absorb their input.

Anyone who aspires to write plays does so because he or she loves the theatre. For some they were inspired by seeing a performance at a formative age – for Caryl Churchill it was seeing *Cinderella* when she was three, and the impression that Buttons' red clothes made on her. For David Edgar at a similar age it was the masked figure in *Beauty and the Beast* which led to his being escorted screaming from the theatre (and yet wanting to go back). Other people are captivated by the taking part. In my case it was being cast against type as the drunken Chief Weasel in *Toad of Toad Hall*. It was my first experience of theatre's ability to let you step into someone else's shoes – whether they are naughtier, crueller, more dangerous, more oppressed than you. It's both transgressive and transformative, and that's why it's so important in our culture.

I always loved the rehearsals more than the performances, though, and so it dawned on me that perhaps I wasn't cut out for acting. Instead, after university I started writing reviews of theatre shows I was seeing, and sending them off to publications. It led to paid work as a theatre critic, and for the best part of a decade I was immersed in theatre: seeing shows up to five times a week and interviewing the writers, directors, actors and designers during the day. It was an excellent apprenticeship, constantly watching, absorbing, discussing and thinking about theatre. Every writer should see as much as they possibly can, especially at the start of their career. What you love inspires you, and what you hate helps you define your own dramatic aesthetic. A critic doesn't necessarily choose what to review, so I was exposed to work I wouldn't otherwise have seen. Some of the productions I was most dreading (five and a half hours of *Julius Caesar* in German, anyone?) turned out to be the greatest experiences of all.

Choose your theatre as you would your religion

George Devine famously said: 'Choose your theatre as you would your religion'. Saturating yourself with other people's work is one way to know what you want from theatre as a spectator, and need from it as a human being, and so to understand what you can offer as a writer. The skill is to find the unique form for your ideas. It's a craft, and there are technical aspects that need to be mastered. But as we've said, there's no formula, and how you choose to fashion and arrange the elements depends on your intention and artistic vision.

If you write down on a piece of paper the five most memorable moments you've experienced in the theatre (do it now, before you read the rest of the paragraph), it gives you an indication of the type of theatre which is yours. As a writer it can be disconcerting to realize that it isn't the words you remember, but the images and the emotions invoked. From the shaven-headed, beaten-up young Russian conscripts falling through the ice in Lev Dodin's *Gaudeamus* for the Maly Theatre of St Petersburg, to the Giant shaking Johnny Rooster's hand in *Jerusalem* (I really think I saw that), to Helena Lymbery in a parka as the gruff and curious 7-year-old in Wink Theatre's *The Art of Random Whistling*. It's rarely the words that stay with me – the notable exception is from Brian Friel's *Faith Healer*, performed by the late Donal McCann intoning the names of the villages like an incantation:

> Aberarder, Aberayron,
> Llangranog, Llangurig,
> Abergorlech…

Theatre allows us to witness and to tell every kind of story, as Chekhov said, 'internal and external truths'. The frisson comes when the experiences of, for example, teenage boys in the Russian army, or a down-at-heel charlatan, become alive to you, and affect you personally. The radical nature of theatre is that it is empathic. It is not just intellectual, or sensual or emotional, but combines all of these at once to allow you a new insight into the experiences of other people.

It's a lifetime's work to find out what kind of stories you are compelled to write, and yet somewhere we all know it instinctively. It is something that needs to be investigated, and questioned. Why do we want to tell them? Is it for our own benefit, or for others'? And having considered this comes the hardest thing of all: how to tell them. What form will they take?

Learning the craft

Tom Stoppard reminds us in Part 2 'Tips and Tales' that 'Theatre is an event, not a text.' But the script is often the beginning and without it, for the playwright, there is nothing. So after the process of defining your theatre necessarily comes the need to practise your craft. It's no accident that so many playwrights are former actors (Sam Shepard, April De Angelis, Harold Pinter, Wallace Shawn, Rebecca Lenkiewicz …). Acting takes you inside the form and teaches an almost somatic understanding of dramatic structure. When something in a play isn't working, it's often the actors who can identify the moment that needs fixing.

Howard Brenton once likened the rehearsal process to Russian roulette: 'You have three or four weeks of rehearsal and then, bang! It either works or it doesn't,' he said, chuckling gleefully. Those three or four weeks are the crucible for a script, when the heat of other people's talent turns it from words to event. It's a time of intense learning for a writer, the first of three key stages when you start to see your script from the outside, and learn its true mettle.

First the director reads it and gives you his or her opinion; then the actors get their hands on it, and you see and hear your words being spoken; finally, you sit in the audience, watching the audience responding to your work. None of this can be learned in any other way.

On second chances

The good news is that despite the Russian roulette nature of the rehearsal process, in theatre there are second chances. However well or badly the first night goes, the second night's performance is going to be subtly but discernibly different. There may be rewrites between the two, or adjustments to the direction. The third night is different again, and so on through the run. A performance is a living, breathing thing; it's not static, or fixed. You have to be there, and something about the audience informs the performance. The version that each audience sees is in some tiny ways unique.

And while a production can vary from one performance to another, one script can have many incarnations. If you feel that a production didn't bring out something you hoped for in your play, there's the chance that a subsequent production will.

Likewise, if you send your script off to a theatre and it's rejected, send it to another. Personal taste affects these decisions, and your script has to find the person who will love, cherish and promote it. The screenwriter Anna Symon has likened this process to finding homes for an orphanage full of unruly children. If one doesn't get adopted, it's not the child's fault – it's just that that family wasn't looking for a cute little girl with sticky-out ears, they wanted a boy with a quirky sense of humour.[1] My play *The Container* was rejected by the Tricycle, who commissioned it, and for nearly five years I thought it was dead and buried, until it finally found its champions, won two awards and has gone on to further productions in London, Cardiff, Baltimore, Melbourne, Toronto; it's been adapted for radio and there's a screenplay in the pipeline.

Posterity and ephemerality

One of the many pleasures of working in the theatre is knowing the backstage world – walking into an empty theatre from the wings, knowing how the magic trick or the fight scene is choreographed, seeing the actors as ordinary people moments before they are transformed into something

[1] From the Script Consultant blog, http://www.script-consultant.co.uk/ (accessed: 29 November 2014).

else on stage. In the spirit of theatre, the audience willingly colludes with the illusion. It's the roughness that makes the magic, to paraphrase Prospero. The phenomenal success of *War Horse* and the emotion that those snorting, stamping, whinnying horse puppets inspire is because, not in spite, of seeing the puppeteers manipulating them. Theatre is alchemy, magic, unpredictable and above all, ephemeral.

Each performance of a play is unique and once it's over, that's that. A published play text keeps the play alive, but apart from your memories, a poster and some production pictures maybe, your play as an event cannot be immortalized. Theatre is symbolic of our mortal life that happens, then is over; you have to be present to witness it. But it's also very annoying when everyone refers reverentially to a production that you missed. Whether that's because it sold out too quickly, or because you were still in nappies when it happened, every theatre maker feels a sense of frustration at the defining moments of theatrical history that they didn't see.

The first night of *Waiting for Godot* in London is one of those that rankle for me, along with Peter Brook's *Midsummer Night's Dream* at the RSC in 1970. This is one of the crucial functions of serious theatre criticism. It's not about telling you what's good and what's not – it's about passing on to succeeding generations what it looked, felt and sounded like, what it was like to be there. The *Guardian*'s Peter Fiddick, writing about *A Midsummer Night's Dream*, amusingly gives us a sense of the outrage the production's modernity caused: 'Do you seek gossamer love? Peter Brook will give you a phallus the size of a man's arm. Do you crave the sweet-sounding lute? Mr Brook … will give you music from India, from the machines, and from the most raven throats this side of the Isle of Wight.'[2]

The voice of experience

Hindsight is a beautiful thing. There are many things in this book that I wish somebody had been able to tell me when I was starting out. The first of

[2] *The Guardian*, archive review, http://www.theguardian.com/stage/1970/aug/28/peter-brook-midsummer-nights-dream (accessed: 12 May 2014).

these is to have self-belief, without arrogance. Accept criticism, but don't let it destroy your belief in yourself.

Second, expect rejection. Every writer encounters it; you have to accept that, and persist. It's the easiest thing in the world for someone in a position of power to say 'no', or just not to get around to answering your email. It's their job to have a relationship with you, so persist until that happens.

Third, talent isn't necessarily enough. The world isn't going to come to your door to discover you, so you need to get out there and make it happen for yourself. Hardly any successful writer has just sat there and hoped for the best – they have all had to develop sharp elbows. You're going to have to compete, and sometimes that means fighting for your work. That can feel undignified, but it's your work you're defending. Sam Peckinpah, the wild man of 1960s Hollywood, allegedly made a point of always going into meetings with the studio executives (who had massacred his early film *Major Dundee*) carrying a pet snake curled around his cane. He wanted to intimidate them, to prevent them from curtailing his artistic vision. You will need your own metaphorical snake in your career as a playwright.

Reflections on the history of playwriting 1: The Ancients and after

Fraser Grace

A brief history of playwriting

Any brief history is a plot full of holes. In that spirit, what follows is a pocked and pocket guide to the history of theatre in the English language – and to the shifting fortunes of the working playwright.

Playwriting in the ancient and classical worlds

The very, very first dramatists were almost certainly priests.

The text fragments we have from Egypt's Middle Kingdom don't reveal much about what their cultic drama looked or sounded like, but we know it had a sacred, ceremonial function. The Ramesseum 'Dramatic' Papyrus, dating from 1250 BCE, talks of the enthronement of a king, a ritual in which priests appeared dressed to represent various deities. The papyrus records their short, dialogue-like utterances, which they accompanied with gestures.[1]

In Europe as early as the sixth century BCE, dancers in rural Greece were donning animal masks and performing in their own religious rituals[2] – though again, the origins, circumstance and style of their delivery are not entirely known.

---

[1] H. R. Hall, *The Ramesseum 'Dramatic' Papyrus*, The British Museum Quarterly, Vol. 4, No. 2 (London: British Museum, Sept 1929), pp. 37–38.

[2] Peter Levi, Greek Drama, in John Boardman, Jasper Griffin and Oswyn Murray (eds), *The Oxford History of the Classical World* (Oxford: Oxford University Press, 1985), p. 157.

Ancient Greece

By the end of the fifth century BCE drama in ancient Greece had left both temple and village behind. It was now playing a role in service of the political machinery of the day. The Athenian experiment in a new kind of god-ordained governance – democracy – required responsible citizens, literate in the moral debates of the day. One school of thought is that the drama developed to fill this gap. It was certainly the civic duty of citizens to attend the theatre, and it was the sacred duty of the dramatist to serve up stirring dramas – usually based on myths previously kept alive by lone storytellers like Homer. The aim of these dramas was to entertain but also to challenge: What does it mean to be a good ruler? When is a war justified? What are the dangers of overweening power, or the proper limits of revenge?

The earliest complete plays that we possess are those of Aeschylus and of Sophocles. Aeschylus, the older of the two, is known to have written more than seventy plays and Sophocles nearly twice that many, but only seven plays from each survive in their entirety. Aeschylus' earliest play, *The Persians* (472 BCE; and therefore, our earliest playwrights' earliest work), celebrates a great Athenian victory at Salamis. The play is remarkable, first, because it describes actual historical events, only eight years after those events took place. This is rare by Greek standards – almost all Greek tragedies are based on myths, tackling contemporary issues only indirectly, by implication.

Second, and even more stunning, is the fact that Aeschylus, who himself may have fought in the battle, chooses Xerxes, commander-in-chief of the hated Persian army, as his central character. Aeschylus' ability to slip into the shoes of this 'barbarian', and his willingness to do so, is an act of empathy (though hardly sympathy) that sets a remarkable precedent.[3]

The surviving plays of Sophocles – the most famous being the Theban trilogy of *Oedipus at Colonus, Oedipus Rex* and *Antigone* – continue the tradition set by Aeschylus' other work: retellings of great myths for tragic effect.

[3] For more about *The Persians*, and for a potted account of the origins and development of the Tragedy in general see Nancy Coffelt and Edith Hall, *Inventing the Barbarian: Greek Self-Definition Through Tragedy* (Oxford: Oxford Classical Monographs, 1989).

But Sophocles introduces an important innovation: where Aeschylus had split the solo voice of Homer into a dialogue between two actors, Sophocles introduces a third character to the scene. Now there is not only the possibility of conflict and debate, but also interruption, genuine dilemma and perhaps a loyalty to be fought over.

In ancient Greece the plays of Aeschylus and Sophocles – and those of Euripides and Aristophanes who followed – were performed only after careful vetting, and crucially, in annual competitions. Originally there was a tragedy festival called the City Dionysia held in spring, and a comedy festival called the Lenaea in winter.[4] It remains a comfort to many playwrights to know that a tragedy as great as Euripides' *Medea*, when it was presented in 431 BC, only came third in competition.[5]

There were strict rules governing these competitions. In the Dionysia, every playwright had to produce three tragedies and a satyr play (a kind of mythological burlesque), and each tragedy had to be performed by a maximum of three speaking actors.[6] If the playwright was entering the comedy competition – and both Greeks and 'resident aliens' were allowed to enter the Lenaea – he could add another speaking actor, making four in all. As the last sentence indicates, all the playwrights we know of in ancient Greece were males, as were all the actors.[7]

Enter the critic

The date 468 BC is particularly important in Greek theatre. This was the year that the upstart Sophocles – then aged twenty-eight – was first accepted into competition, and scored an immediate hit, defeating the old master Aeschylus. But it's not just his innovations, or winning the Dionysia, that sealed Sophocles' reputation. A later play, *Oedipus the King*, was chosen as

---

4 The Dionysia was at first a festival of tragedy; eventually both festivals would be mixed.

5 The competition was won that year by Aeschylus' son Euphorion, with Sophocles in second place – the titles of the plays in question are not known.

6 Plus chorus and child actors. 'Barbarians', speaking broken Greek, were also allowed as additions.

7 Levi, *Greek Drama*. See also Alan H. Sommerstein, *Aristophanes: Lysistrata/The Archarnians/The Clouds*, Introduction (London: Penguin Classics, 1973), p. 24.

the optimum tragedy by someone who would shape playwrights' thinking about the drama for centuries to follow – not always for the better.

This shaper of thoughts – Aristotle – wasn't a playwright at all but a respected political analyst and biologist. He was also born the year after Aristophanes died, so by the time he was writing, 'the big four' Athenian dramatists had all made their exit.

As the first theorist to consider poetry as a distinct subject, Aristotle anatomized the plays he saw being performed in the theatre. Possibly his most fundamental observation identifies *mimesis* as the thing that makes art, art. This mimesis is not defined very clearly, but a workable definition is that mimesis is the act of imitation or representation. The drama, a painting or a sculpture is different from historical works or facts, in that it does not attempt to present what *is* – that is the subject itself – whether that's a family, a flower or a sequence of events. Instead it offers a *version* of it; the only rule is that the version presented must be recognizably related to the subject.

What's more, in the case of drama, these events must be enacted, and unfolded over time. This has massive structural implications for the play, as we'll see in Part 3.

Aristotle's other fundamental observation is that the drama of his day fell into two distinct types, recognized in the annual competitions – the tragedy and the comedy. The two were distinct and had their own rules. His favourite tragedian, as we've seen, was Sophocles, and he chose Aristophanes for laughs.

Aristotle determined that in tragedy, plot was the most important element – the way a story is unfolded, the sequence in which we learn. The best sauce for tragic meat, according to Aristotle, is dramatic irony; a father tells us how much he loves his son, how determined he is to make amends with that son for their estrangement – only AFTER we, the audience, have begun to suspect that something dreadful has happened to the son. All hope for reconciliation is therefore in vain – at least in this life – but only we, the audience suspect that. This is the root of the tragedy, for now an audience anticipates the impact of the coming news, before the blow is delivered – and felt – by the father.

This simple trick of ordering events to control the flow of information creates an emotional effect – fear or pity – a holding of the breath, a shudder as the dreaded truth looms. When the blow is delivered, we see the fallout, and the drama concludes. Others are dead but we have been spared. Awaking from our involvement, we realize how lucky we are. The audience leave the auditorium a wiser, more understanding bunch of people – and better citizens. This experience Aristotle called 'katharsis' – another concept that has entered our everyday thinking – a kind of moral release or purging.[8]

By contrast, in comedy it's not plot but character at the centre, and the losses incurred by these characters are much more trivial. The project of a comic play is not irrevocable change, but the ironing out of recognizable, if exaggerated, human foibles.

The targets of Aristophanes' comedies – the acme of the form, according to Aristotle – include real-life rulers, notably Cleon, in *The Knights*. But Aristophanes' plays often seem remarkable less for their satirical power, than for their wicked crudity. In plays like *The Frogs* or *The Knights* the playwright never misses an opportunity for a bawdy line or an obscene sight gag. The drama of ancient Greece may have maintained its concern with the gods, but with Aristophanes' stirring the brew, by the end of the fifth century BCE the comedy was using the bluntest of instruments to bring its leaders down to size. This power to outrage through sheer filth has proved a useful weapon for playwrights ever since.

A further analytical perception that we owe to Aristotle is that the beauty of a play – comedy or tragedy – lies in its completeness; it should be appreciable as a whole, possessing a beginning, middle and end, and it also needs to attain (great word, this) 'amplitude', often translated as 'magnitude'. A drama should have heft, or be of consequence.

To be classed among the best, a play should also have coherence, which is secured largely by its unity of action – a subject we'll return to in Part3. Finally, a tragedy should also contain a pivotal moment of 'recognition' or reversal – the moment when the truth is seen, alas too late.

---

[8] For a fuller discussion of Katharsis – and other concepts in Aristotle's work – see Penelope Murray, Introduction, *Classical Literary Criticism* (London: Penguin Classics, 2004).

Aristotle abused

In the seventeenth century Aristotle-ites added Unity of Time to the idea of coherence (Aristotle mentions this 'unity' only in passing) and went even further to insist on 'Unity of Place', which as Nicoll notes, Aristotle doesn't mention at all.[9] A doctrine of 'The Three Unities' was forged in Aristotle's name, and used as critical cudgel. Resentment towards these 'Aristotalitarian' restrictions abounds even today. But leave aside his misrepresentation, and take into account the nature of his approach – like the scientist he was, describing only what he saw – and Aristotle's 'laws' seem more a challenge than a diktat.

Lives of the Greeks

What the lives of playwrights in ancient Greece were like, or how their production processes worked, is hard to say. An 'Archon' was appointed by the authorities to run the Dionysia or Leneae festivals each year, and he was responsible for appointing rich men (choregoi) to act as producers for each play. He also chose the dramatists on the basis of submitted plays or outlines.[10] Most dramatists directed and perhaps appeared in their own work, with the exception of Sophocles, whose acting ambitions are said to have been thwarted by a weak voice. Only Aristophanes is known to have recruited others to direct his plays, probably because he was underaged according to competition rules.[11]

The backgrounds of the ancient playwrights also varied. Like Aeschylus, Sophocles had been a public servant and also a soldier – a general, in fact – but Euripides held no such posts; his mother was a greengrocer, while Aristophanes was the son of a minor official of the city. All, as poets of the drama, were seen to be serving the democratic system. This might suggest that theirs was an establishment role, but if so it was a potentially

---

[9] Allardyce Nicoll, *The Development of the Theatre* (London: George G Harrap & Company Ltd, 1966), p. 25.

[10] T. B. L. Webster, *Life in Classical Athens* (London: BT Batsford Ltd, 1969), p. 90.

[11] Sommerstein, *Aristophanes*, p. 21. Officially, dramatists had to be eighteen years of age.

dangerous one. Phrynichus, a near contemporary of Aeschylus, had been fined 1,000 drachmas for his (now lost) *Fall of Miletus* as early as 494 BC, and banned from ever producing it again;[12] Aristophanes was censured by Cleon, the ruler of the city-state, for anti-Athenian propaganda when his second play *Babylonians* won the comedy competition seventy years later; and Euripides probably fared worse still. He went into exile (how willingly is debated) at the age of seventy-three, spending the last seven years of his life many miles from Athens, in Macedonia. Playwrights in ancient Greece could clearly find themselves on the wrong side of power, and what put them there was their critical voice.

For all that, playwriting in ancient Greece was clearly a trade like many others, passed through generations. All the writers mentioned above had sons who also became playwrights – Aeschylus also had a nephew in the trade – and some of these sons, like their fathers, met with great success in competition.

Roman theatre

The plays of the big four writers of ancient Greece – Aeschylus, Sophocles, Euripides and Aristophanes – were still being revived, in either extracts or as whole plays, alongside new works in the Roman theatre of the second century AD. The Romans' use of masks and symbolic costumes, and the obsession with the gods (now given new Roman names) likewise recalled the theatre of Athens. The context however was radically changed – physically, politically and economically.

In the Roman world, theatre was still associated with festivals but it had few religious associations.[13] Nor, in Imperial Rome was there any experimental democratic process to support. There was though, a new pressure of competition, not from other plays, but from other forms of popular entertainment. In Rome itself, the drama's competitors were the Colosseum,

[12] Graham Speake (ed.), *Penguin Dictionary of Ancient History* (London: Penguin Books, 1995) p. 496.

[13] There is evidence that temporary theatres were used, with a covered area, and may also have introduced what we would recognize as backcloths – see Nicoll, *Development*, p. 19.

with its gladiators and executions, and the Circus Maximus, home of exotic dancers and chariot races. Given all this, it's not surprising that popular comedy began to dominate, winning out against the austere concerns of the tragedy, or the bite of genuine satire. The playwright whose work was most revived in this period was a writer of social comedies, even if he was a Greek. Menander (c.342–292 BCE), a poet from a well-to-do family, wrote over one hundred plays, all of them classed as comedies. None of his plays now exist as complete texts, but we know that his was a comedy of manners, holding up a mirror to the audience's foibles, rather than to the crimes of a political system, or its rulers.

A century later, Roman playwrights like Plautus were still taking their cues from Menander's New Comedy, pushing the form in an even more popular direction. A stage-hand and actor before he became a playwright, Plautus added what was effectively musical underscoring to leaven his big speeches, and loosened the dramatic structure to create a more freewheeling comedy. Manic puns and broad characters were preferred to dramatic situation or irony. Only in his bawdiness does Plautus really echo Aristophanes.

Other writers of comedies like Terence, who followed Plautus as one of the home-grown names of Roman drama, strained for a gravity – amplitude – that seemed to be slipping away in Plautus' work. The six plays that survive show that this ex-slave was much more of a structuralist in the Greek mould, with plot and consistent character again delivering the comic goods. And tragedy also remained a force. New versions of the Greek masters, now rendered in Latin, were presented, along with works from Roman playwrights like Pacuvius (220–c.130 BCE) hailed by Cicero as the greatest tragedian of all.[14]

Whichever theatrical tendency or genre dominated at any one time, the drama in ancient Rome was now firmly regarded as an entertainment, rather than a necessary part of civic life.

---

[14] Speake, *Dictionary of Ancient History*, p. 457.

Roman Britain

Although little evidence exists for a vital theatre tradition in pre-Roman Britain, it would be a mistake to assume that drama was completely unknown in the British Isles before the Romans arrived. The legends consolidated in the seventh century as the epic poem *Beowulf* began somewhere, and Caesar himself noted in his journal the immense feats of memory via which the Druids kept safe their stories and histories.[15] It's likely therefore that storytelling and epic poetry were common features of life in ancient Britain. As elsewhere in Europe, they may have been delivered by both individuals and travelling bands of players. Nonetheless, this tradition was inaccessible to the Roman invaders (the word 'barbarian' is believed to be derived from 'baa-baa', a derogatory rendering of the native Britons' impenetrable tongue). On their arrival in the first century AD, the Romans set about building theatres in England.

Traces of large Roman-style theatres have been found in several English towns of the time, including among others St Albans, Canterbury, Colchester and Bath, some equipped with orchestra pit and a stage.[16] In addition there are remains of perhaps twelve amphitheatres, where dramas might have shared the programme with other entertainments. Theatrical masks have also been found.[17] According to Trussler, this amounts to evidence for the development of 'a broad-based tradition of performance in Roman Britain, stretching from Yorkshire down to Kent and from Caerlon in South Wales across to Essex'.[18]

Nonetheless when the Romans left in the fourth century AD, it seems that the practice of putting on plays in a theatre, and of going to the theatre to see plays, vanished completely.

Branigan attributes this to British apathy; perhaps the locals were just not that taken with drama. It's also possible that theatre was resented as

[15] http://heritageaction.wordpress.com/reclaiming-prehistory/ (accessed: 13 August 2014).

[16] Keith Branigan, *Roman Britain: Life in an Imperial Province* (London: Reader's Digest, 1980), p. 108.

[17] These masks may have belonged to travelling players, rather than actors in the formal theatre.

[18] Simon Trussler, *The Cambridge Illustrated History of British Theatre* (Cambridge: Cambridge University Press 1995), p. 2.

the art form of the imperial conqueror, but the truth might be slightly more complicated.

By the third century AD, the Roman Empire was officially Christianized, and most forms of popular entertainment fell under suspicion. The theatre probably suffered for its association with beast-baiting and dancing, 'low' entertainments that interspersed the dramas, while the players' habit of directly mocking Christian practices did nothing to help. Throughout the Empire, members of acting companies now found themselves excommunicated, and Romano-British actors were probably no exception.[19]

Whatever the direct cause, theatre, like many other aspects of 'civilized' Rome once the Romans left Britain, was first abandoned as an organized public event and then forgotten. What remained of the drama was probably once again in the hands of those strolling players whose peripatetic entertainment pre-dated the built theatres. They would continue their craft for the next 600 years almost unmentioned in official histories, only noted when the church authorities took offence.

It would take inspiration from another, rather surprising source, to spark the beginning of an organized theatre in the English language.

Medieval theatre

After being driven almost out of existence by the religious intolerance of Christianized Rome, theatre remerges in early medieval England independent of the Greco-Roman tradition. But when it does emerge, ironically its roots are drawing from the very authority that had found the drama wanton in the first place.[20]

Put another way, the earliest formal drama of the period is in Latin, and in church. *Quem Quaeritis?* is a liturgical dialogue based on the gospel account of the resurrection of Christ. Introduced into the Catholic Mass sometime in the tenth century, the *Quem Quaeritis?* focuses on the question posed by the angel unwittingly encountered by Mary, sitting by the open tomb:

[19] Ibid., p. 4.

[20] Nicoll, *Development*, p. 49.

'*Quem Quaeritis?*' (Whom do you seek?) asks the angel.[21] What follows in the drama is a relatively simple question-and-answer sequence, but the parts are attributed, the words function as dialogue, stage directions are given, it was performed before an audience, in costume, and it was intended to move emotionally – and it proved popular.[22]

Over the next 200 years, this and other 'tropes', proliferated, adding stock characters like Doubting Thomas and The Seller of Spices along the way. Whether these dramas inspired or merely coincided with other popular, vernacular dramas that emerged in this period is debated – but simple plays in Latin and in English were soon being performed in towns and cities across England.

The Mystery plays, as the vernacular plays were known, were presented annually, especially during the feast of Corpus Christi in spring. Putting on the plays drew on the energy of a whole town, and their production was abetted by skills learned in the presentation of royal pageants.[23] They also depended on the writing talent of clerks, schoolmasters and priests employed to devise the plays.

The surviving Mystery cycles of Wakefield, York, Chester and Coventry vary in content, but all present scenes from, or associated with, the Holy Bible.[24] Each story was the responsibility of a different group of tradesmen in the town.[25] As Woolf notes, the link between trade and story could be ironic – watermen might be given responsibility for presenting the Flood, and so on.[26] The overall form was expandable as required, as many episodes of the Biblical scheme being presented as there were groups of tradesmen to present them, though the 'essential' points of the narrative – Creation, Fall, Nativity, Passion and Resurrection – were always honoured.

---

[21] The question itself doesn't appear in the canonical gospel accounts, though it is implied.

[22] See Nicoll, *Development*, p. 49; Trussler, *Illustrated History*, pp. 18, 19; also Christopher Hibbert, *The English: A Social History 1066–1984* (London: Paladin, 1988), p. 89.

[23] The pageant was perennially permissible pomp; celebrating coronations, military victories and royal arrivals had remained popular throughout the period formally known as the 'dark ages'.

[24] Versions of the mystery play arose also in Spain and France at this time, seemingly independently.

[25] One view is that it is the Latin word for craft – *ministerium* – that gives the form its name.

[26] Rosemary Woolf, in W.F. Bolton (ed.), *Sphere History of Literature: The Middle Ages* (London: Sphere Books, 1987), p. 303.

Standards in these productions were maintained not by vetting of the play beforehand (though this might have taken place) or the awarding of prizes in competition, but by fines for guilds producing substandard work, or even for actors forgetting their lines.[27]

It may have been to avoid these fines, and the notoriety that came with them, that the writers of these plays worked anonymously. More likely, the concept of authorship as a professional status was simply not so prevalent at the time.[28] Like the costumes and the scenic embellishments, the scripts were paid for by the town, and became civic property, to be reworked and patched together each year.

The nearest we come to an identifiable playwright involved with the Mysteries is the 'Wakefield Master', believed to be responsible for six of the thirty-two plays in the Wakefield Cycle. Who this Master was, and how he came to write his scripts, we don't know – but his work, and the other Mysteries, are still in use (most grandly by Bill Bryden's company at the National Theatre in the 1980s), and the same spirit can be seen in the community plays of Dorchester, Chester and elsewhere.

The advent of the Mystery play – along with the closely related Morality play[29] – meant that the drama as organized public entertainment was back, even if it was mainly a seasonal or occasional activity. Crucially, it had crossed the language divide into English. Towns spent handsomely on their annual civic theatre binge – but this was nothing to the sums spent on a form emerging at the other end of the social scale.

Behind the masque

Not much genuinely dramatic literature graced the courts of English monarchs prior to this time, but their courts were never devoid of theatricality. In the Middle Ages this produced a form known as the masque (or confusingly, mask). These one-off court entertainments, like private mini-pageants, often

[27] Hibbert, *The English*, p 92.

[28] Janette Dillon makes this argument, in her *Cambridge Introduction to Early English Theatre* (Cambridge: Cambridge University Press, 2006), p. 109.

[29] Epitomized by *Everyman*, Morality plays were intended as instruction, rather than celebration.

had ostensibly religious or mythological subjects but were always, as Ewbank notes, essentially on the same theme: the glorification of the monarch.[30]

Thus there were now two traditions of theatrical production in the land – the dramatic and the emblematic (to use Wickham's helpful distinction). These would eventually flow together to produce an entirely new phenomenon – the professional theatre of the Elizabethan Age, with a new cadre at its core – professional playwrights.

Diverse duckers and dodgers

According to Wickham, at the beginning of the seventeenth century, Thomas Middleton was paid £282 for his work on a pageant for the Grocer's Company.[31] This single fact tells us quite a lot about Middleton, and a good deal about the working lives of dramatists in the period, for Middleton was by that time an established playwright.

In the latter part of the sixteenth century, at least in London, companies of actors and their audiences had outgrown their regular performance spaces in the courtyards of inns, graduating to purpose-built theatres. The Theatre, the Curtain, the Rose, the Swan and the Globe were just some of those built at this time. Unfortunately for those involved, this was also the age of the puritan.[32]

Seeing the theatre as a moral threat (as well as a risk to public order and public health) in 1598 the Privy Council determined that just two companies would be allowed under licence: the Lord Admiral's Men and the Lord Chamberlain's Men. These rivals were to slug it out under the censorious gaze of the Lord Chamberlain. The rest were to be suppressed. In fact, the law was never rigorously or consistently enforced, so competition for an audience was always fierce; and despite the constant threat of closure because of fire, censorship or the plague, it is reckoned that at the beginning

[30] Inga-Stina Ewbank, *Masques & Pageants*, in Boris Ford (ed.), *The Cambridge Cultural History: 17th Century Britain* (Cambridge: Cambridge University Press, 1992), p. 113.

[31] Glynne Wickham, *Early English Stages Vol. 1*, quoted Hibbert, *The English*, p. 88.

[32] See, Owen Chadwick, *The Pelican History of the Church, Vol. 3: The Reformation* (London: Pelican Books, 1972), pp. 178–179.

of the seventeenth century, up to 15,000 people in London visited the theatre every week.[33]

A few lucky playwrights were virtually resident writers or 'ordinary poets' to the companies attached to these theatres, but most shuttled between one company and the next on a commission-by-commission basis.[34]

Each company also had its star actors, and a large number of plays in repertoire, but most plays were produced for only one or two days.[35] A theatre manager like Philip Henslowe at the Rose Theatre (home to the Admiral's Men) would pay £5 or £6 for a new play, increasing to around £10 in the time his daybook was recording his transactions.[36] But once delivered, the play became the manager's property – the playwright had no copyright, and would earn no royalties from his work. Even in those times, £5 was quickly spent.[37] In comparison, the standard wage for an agricultural labourer was 8d per day, or around £20 a year.[38] Clearly, a playwright needed to turn out at least three or four full-length plays a year to survive – or even more, given city prices. This led to the practice of theatre managers contracting playwrights to produce a number of plays over a given time in return for a weekly wage, plus, perhaps, a single benefit performance of each play.

As Thomas Middleton's employment by the Grocer's Company shows, the professional theatre of London didn't supplant other forms of dramatic entertainment, but added to them.[39] Most playwrights patched together a living by traversing a variety of forms and the different social

[33] Hibbert, *The English*, p. 241.

[34] William Shakespeare was unusual in having a stake in his company, the Lord Chamberlain's Men (renamed the King's Men by James I). This was the probable source of the wealth that allowed his retirement in 1612. He was also unusual in never having worked for their rivals, the Admiral's Men.

[35] The nine-day run of Middleton's *A Game at Chess* in 1624 – before it was suppressed for its satirical attack on the Court's pro-Spanish policies – was an exception. Bryan Loughrey and Neil Taylor (eds), *Thomas Middleton: Five Plays* (London: Penguin Classics, 1988), p. xxii.

[36] Dillon, *Early English Theatre*, p. 111.

[37] A quart of ale at this time cost 4d, and an hour with a prostitute 6d: Hibbert, *The English*, p. 240. Meanwhile, a night at the theatre might cost as little as 1d in a rough playhouse, but rise to 2s6d at an indoor theatre like Burbage's at Blackfriars. Ibid., p. 245.

[38] http://www.langhaminrutland.org.uk/pdftemp/col.pdf (accessed: 15 January 2015).

[39] Loughrey and Taylor, *Five Plays*, p. xxix.

'worlds' from which they were commissioned, turning their hands to pageants, court masques and even pamphlets as well as dramas, as the opportunity arose.

While the writers were no doubt scrabbling to land these commissions, the period is also marked by playwrights working in collaboration. Rowley, Dekker, Beaumont, Ford, Jonson, Fletcher, Webster, Marston, Marlowe, Shakespeare and Middleton (to name a few) all worked together in varying combinations as well as producing sole-authored works.[40]

This co-writing method – not so far removed from the practice of today's Hollywood screenwriters – perhaps speeded up the production process. It may also have spread the risk (financial and legal) and shared out the gains, thus helping the playwrights to at least even out their precarious existence.[41] Nonetheless, a playwright of repute like Middleton, at the peak of his powers, could command a very significant fee if he was willing to take on a civic commission – though out of his fee the playwright was expected to sub-contract many of the other tradesman involved. Here again, partnerships – particularly with 'artificers', whom we would recognize as designers – helped share the risk and increase the creative energy. The most famous of these teams is Ben Jonson and Inigo Jones, but Dekker and Middleton also had their regular artificers, and these collaborations could clearly lead to lucrative commissions.

This variety of output from playwrights also resulted in inevitable cross-pollination, between comic and tragic writing, and between forms – elements of the masque thus appearing in drama. Shakespeare, for instance, introduces masque-like elements into *The Tempest* and *Henry VIII*, as well as affectionately mocking them in the Rude Mechanicals of *A Midsummer Night's Dream*.[42]

---

40 This is one basis for the modern argument that Shakespeare is unlikely to have been the author of all the plays attributed to him. According to Stanley Wells and Gary Taylor (eds), *Complete Oxford Shakespeare* (London: Oxford University Press, 1986), *Timon of Athens* (with Middleton), and the last three plays (with Fletcher), are the most likely of his plays to have been co-authored, to which other scholars have added *Titus Andronicus* and *Henry VI*.

41 In this way, Thomas Dekker was able to earn £35 in 1599 – Hibbert, *The English*, p. 246.

42 Trussler, *British Theatre*, p. 98. In time, elements of the pageant and the masque would further enrich theatre, as with the innovation of moving scenery after the Restoration.

With the advent of the indoor theatre, such as that at Blackfriars, the opportunities for playwrights increased, but also made even more demand on their flexibility. In Jacobean times a playwright had to write plays that could flourish in 'private' performances – that is indoors, to a more select clientele paying handsome ticket prices – as well as in 'public' performances in the older, cheaper playhouses open to the elements, such as the Globe.[43]

Versatility, pragmatism, determination and resilience – a playwright needed all of these to complement his vision and passion. These playwrights also shared similar backgrounds. They were all men, most obviously, and most were the sons of tradesmen-made-good – good enough to afford their sons a university education anyway. Ford and Marston were lawyers (and the sons of lawyers); Webster also entered the Middle Temple, but his father was a coachmaker, and Webster himself combined coachmaking and playwriting for most of his career. Marlowe was the son of a shoemaker, and Jonson's step-father – like Middleton's natural father – was a bricklayer. Shakespeare's father was famously a glovemaker-cum-local dignitary, though after a grammar school education, Shakespeare may only have been a schoolteacher, rather than an undergraduate.[44] Thomas Dekker's was probably the most humble background of all; his father's trade is unknown, but Dekker himself spent a good amount of time in debtor's prison – including a stretch of more than six years – quite a glitch in any playwright's career.[45]

All these playwrights, in addition, were drawn to London. Middleton, Webster and Ford were native to the city, but Marlowe came from Canterbury via Cambridge, Shakespeare from Stratford-upon-Avon, Philip Massinger from Salisbury via Oxford and Fletcher from Sussex via Cambridge. If you wanted to be a playwright in the professional sense, clearly you had to be where the work was – and that was in the capital.

---

[43] Webster's *Duchess of Malfi* is the prime example of this, as the frontispiece from the 1623 edition of the play shows; see Elizabeth M. Brennan (ed.), *The Duchess of Malfi* (London: New Mermaids Edition, 1977), p. xxxi.

[44] Margaret Drabble (ed.), *Oxford Companion to English Literature* (Oxford: Oxford University Press, 1985), p. 888.

[45] Ibid., p. 264.

Given the precarious nature of life in the theatre, and the at-best ambivalent legal and religious attitudes to the play, the playwright's life was, finally, never a respectable one.[46] Most writers seem to have abandoned playwriting as soon as they could: John Webster on marrying a rich widow (though John Russell Brown puts his cessation down to a 'failure of artistic confidence'[47]); Shakespeare once able to retire to his land in Stratford-upon-Avon; Thomas Middleton when he finally landed a respectable job – aged forty – as City Chronologer.[48]

Yet out of this tumult of energy, productivity, insecurity and disreputable enterprise came new forms of drama. Tragedies were now written to include moments of low comedy, and comedies could dip into tragedy.[49] As befits a drama that had to survive in the market place, these were highly theatrical and tonally varied plays, plays that could shock and amuse as well as move, plays with something for every section and mood of the audience. But even this self-preserving evolution of the play could not save the theatre when the country tilted decisively in the Puritans' favour, when the theatre's royal patrons were swept from power (and from life itself in crucial cases), and Britain's theatres were closed for eighteen years – a period we can with some justification, call a genuine dark age.

The distracted state

On 2nd September 1642, the English Parliament issued its famous decree: actors appearing in 'Stage Plays, Interludes or other common plays' were to be 'punished as Rogues, according to the Law'.[50]

---

46 William Rowley was subject to a court case alongside Dekker, Ford and Webster at the time of his death, for the dramatizing of two contemporary scandals. Ibid., p. 852.

47 John Russell Brown (ed.), *The White Devil* (Manchester University Press, 1966), p. xxv.

48 A position to which he was succeeded by Jonson.

49 As George Parfitt asks with good reason, 'in what sense is *Merchant of Venice* a comedy for Shylock?', see Ford, *Cultural History*, p. 125.

50 Cecil A. Moore (ed.), *Twelve Famous Plays of the Restoration and Eighteenth Century*, Introduction (New York: The Modern Library, 1960), p. vii.

It's clear from the proclamation itself that for Cromwell and his allies, the distractions of the playhouse were at least partly to blame for the outbreak of ungodly hostilities that had riven the country:

> While these sad causes and set times do continue, Public Stage-plays shall cease and be foreborne, instead of which are recommended to the People of this land the profitable and seasonal considerations of Repentance, Reconciliation and Peace with God, which probably may produce outward Peace and Prosperity, and bring again times of Joy and Gladness to this Nation.[51]

Most histories of theatre break off at this point, implying that like the monarchy, the drama came to a full stop as the theatres closed, only to begin afresh after the Commonwealth ended. But what happened to the playwrights?

In fact the 'golden age' of the professional playwright was pretty much over by the time the closure came about. Marlowe, Shakespeare, Beaumont, Fletcher, Rowley, Middleton, Dekker, Webster, Jonson, Ford and Massinger were all dead. Of the next generation, many were Royalists by instinct if not breeding (the monarchy having been patrons of the theatre). Some of these were now caught up in the civil war. The despairing poet Lucius Cary, Lord Falkland, was one of these, killed in battle in 1643; William Cartwright, author of *The Royal Slave* (1636), died of camp fever in Oxford, without making it as far as the battlefield. Sir John Suckling, a poet and dramatist (albeit chiefly at his own expense), took his own life while exiled in Paris, though it's believed this was to avoid a charge of high treason for his actions in the war, rather than because he missed the theatre.

Other playwrights, though, survived the war and kept at their craft, despite the closed theatres and threat of persecution. Two who did so, with varying degrees of success, were James Shirley and William Davenant (aka D'Avenant).

[51] Chad Thomas, *Negotiating the Interregnum: The Political Works of Davenant and Tatham* in *1650–1850: Ideas, Aesthetics, and Inquiries in the Early Modern Period* (2004), https://www.academia.edu/530241/ (accessed: 4 June 2014).

The survivors' club

James Shirley was originally an Anglican priest, whose conversion to Catholicism probably triggered the loss of his teaching post in St Albans and his arrival in London in 1624. The following year his play *Love Tricks, or the School for Compliment* played at the Cockpit Theatre – a private or indoor venue, where Queen Henrietta-Maria's Men played. The play was a hit; Shirley became a regular playwright there, and would write a total of about forty plays in a career that earned him a considerable reputation. Eventually he succeeded Massinger as 'ordinary poet' for The King's Men, based at the Globe, but when the theatre was closed just two years later, the playwright was obliged to drop his pen for a sword, fighting with the Earl of Newcastle with whom he had previously written a play. Finding himself on the losing side, Shirley meekly returned to London, and slipped into another teaching post. While his professional playwriting career was thus shelved at the age of forty-six, Shirley nonetheless continued to write, putting his energies into masques, into plays for school performance and into a dramatic pamphlet, the *Contention of Ajax and Ulysees* (1657), which was widely read.

Slightly more impressive as an artistic survivor is William Davenant. Having lost most of his nose to syphilis at an early age (and thus perhaps his hopes as an actor) Davenant was unable to follow up initial successes as a playwright by the forced closure of the Phoenix Theatre in 1642. He kept himself in the game during the Interregnum by writing his dramatic works as proto-operatic, musical entertainments – which placed them outside the scope of the censors. Like their author, these pieces are often dismissed by modern commentators, and certainly Davenant was no political firebrand. But Chad Thomas offers a good defence of the idea that by setting his plays – with titles like *The Cruelty of the Spaniards in Peru* (1658) – in exotic, distant locations, and wrapping them in an all-embracing English nationalism, Davenant was able in fact to critique the intolerant cruelties of those who had closed the theatres around him.[52]

Davenant's new-form dramatic operettas were also radical in a more fundamental (and lasting) way – he was the first to reintroduce women actors

[52] Ibid., p. 232.

to the stage – smuggled in, under cover of music. As the Interregnum wore on, and the power of the Protectorate faltered, Davenant slowly returned to writing 'straight' plays, but the women remained. When Charles II legitimized the theatre, female actors – a common place in continental theatre – would finally become an established part of the theatrical scene in London. In the next century, they would be joined by female playwrights.

Restoration theatre

By the time of the Restoration of the English monarchy in 1660, the prohibition against theatre had pretty much crumbled: when the theatres were officially reopened by royal decree, playwrights, actors and especially actresses must have breathed a huge sigh of relief at their newfound legitimacy. But although Charles II was a firm fan of the drama (and of the actress) he was to prove about as firm a fan of criticism as any other 'divinely appointed' ruler. He granted only two theatre licences in the capital – and those to proven 'friends' of the crown. Thomas Killigrew had been something of a wit in the circle of the Prince in exile, and William Davenant had combined his subtle criticisms of Cromwell with the role of emissary to the Prince during the civil war. Charles II was clearly keen to reward these loyalists, but he was also determined to avoid a free and independent theatre. This was reflected in the terms of his warrant, calling for a programme of 'innocent and harmless divertissements'.[53] While the new order was less censorious about sexual matters, political criticism was clearly not going to be tolerated.

The programming of Davenant, licence holder of the newly formed Duke's Men, and especially of Killigrew, his rival at the King's Men, therefore began, unsurprisingly, in cautious mode. Rights to the canon of existing plays had been arbitrarily divided between the two companies, and it was revivals of old, mainly Jacobean plays that reopened the theatres. The introduction of women actors was likewise tentative, beginning with an unnamed actress playing Desdemona in a production of *Othello* by the Duke's Men in 1660.

[53] Warrant granted by Charles II 21 August 1660, quoted by Peter Thomson, *The Cambridge Introduction to English Theatre, 1660–1900* (Cambridge: Cambridge University Press, 2006), p. 10.

When the casting of women seemed to get the royal nod, it quickly became a selling point. This peaked in 1672 with Killigrew's King's Men (despite their name) mounting a series of three plays performed entirely by women. The use of movable scenery, and the advanced role played by music and spectacle, hangovers (at least in Davenant's case) from survivalist tactics during the Interregnum, likewise proved popular.

As for the life of playwrights, it is often asserted that this was changed beyond recognition; no more the hurly burly of the Elizabethan and Jacobean scene, in which professional dramatists touted for commissions from competing 'roughhouse' theatres. What's true is that the social origins of playwrights now reflected the polarized backgrounds of the men who held the licences: courtier-cum-amateur-producer Killigrew, and the professional man-of-the-theatre, Davenant.

Given the licensing situation, no playwright of the Restoration could really prosper without good social connections – not to mention a show of monarchist sympathies – but it was now quite possible for a courtier with no theatrical experience (but a reputation as a wit) to write a play and get it produced. The important thing was to achieve this while maintaining what Sir George 'Easy' Etherege referred to as a 'noble laziness of mind'.[54] Etherege and his fellow knights Buckingham and Sedley were among the rakes who rose to this challenge, as it were, and celebrated their libertine values not only in the plays themselves, but in their work ethic. The meagre output of Etherage (three brilliant and successful comedies,[55] followed by retirement) was positively prodigious compared with Charles Sedley's (just two plays, almost twenty years apart).

Running in parallel with this trend for the gifted, feckless amateur, the life of the professional playwright (albeit one with good connections) was in many ways little changed from Elizabethan times. For writers like John Dryden and Aphra Behn, the skills of industry and adaptability which the wits decried, remained vital. Dryden, a future poet laureate, is known to have produced

[54] Moore, *Twelve Famous Plays*, p. xiii.

[55] These include the much-performed *The Man of Mode* (1676) featuring the character Dorimant, largely based on Etherege's even more dissolute fellow rake and poet, the Earl of Rochester.

approaching thirty plays in around thirty years writing for the stage, while Behn is notable not only for being one of the first female playwrights,[56] but also for writing at least sixteen plays in a career lasting only twelve years. That she had turned to playwriting as a way out of debt may partly account for such an Elizabethan-like work rate.

Both Behn and Dryden also acquired contractual arrangements that the likes of Shakespeare and Massinger would have recognized. Dryden was contracted in 1668 to produce three plays a year for the King's Men, in return for shares in the company.[57] Aphra Behn seems to have had a similar arrangement with the Duke's Men.[58] The range of plays Behn in particular could turn her hand to is remarkable, embracing political tragedies (*The Roundheads*, 1881), sex comedies (*The Lucky Chance*, 1686) and musical farce (*The Emperor of the Moon*, 1687). Dryden too demonstrated the need and ability to shift with the times. Having originally aspired to rival French dramatists like Racine and Corneille for sophistication, Dryden reluctantly abandoned heroic verse drama in the face of increased demand for more populist fare.

This adaptability and application of craft was also clear in the number of revisions of old plays that these two writers embarked on. Behn's greatest play, *The Rover* (1676), is in fact a cut-and-shut job performed on a two-part play *Thomaso*, first written by Killigrew in 1654 while in exile in Spain.[59] 'Revisions' or 'polishings' of Shakespeare plays were also meat and drink to professional writers of the period: Dryden's *All for Love* (1677) may only have been inspired by the same story as *Antony and Cleopatra*, but his rewrite of *The Tempest* (also 1667, in collaboration with Davenant) similarly aimed to 'regularize' the original. Nahum Tate (in)famously did a similar job on Shakespearean tragedy in *The History of King Lear* (1681). In all these cases, the aim was to improve on both the form and the conclusions of the original, better organizing the drama (in line with Aristotle's supposed

[56] The very earliest, such as Elizabeth Griffith, were primarily actors.

[57] A work rate he in fact failed to accomplish.

[58] Freelance writers, however, had to rely on income from the third performance of the new play, and later also from the sixth and ninth productions, if the play was a success.

[59] Trussler, *British Theatre*, p. 127.

'Unities') to provide a more streamlined structure, together with a more 'moral' distribution of rewards and punishments. Such 'improvements' are apt to be condemned by contemporary critics; but if nothing else they demonstrate that these playwrights had an enterprising attitude to recycling 'found material' not so different from Shakespeare's own magpie tendencies.

By 1682, the King's Men had passed to the control of Killigrew's son, and the company fell on hard times. As the two companies were merged into the United Company, revivals and reworkings dominated the programming to an ever greater degree. There were still new plays, but as Trussler notes, these declined in number from around twelve a year in the later 1680s, to around four a decade later.[60]

The merging of the two companies lasted thirteen years, but by the end of the seventeenth century, there were again two companies in London. Following a dispute over feeble management of the United Company, a breakaway group led by the veteran actor Thomas Betterton was allowed by the Lord Chamberlain to set up business in 1695 as the Actors' Company. This proved an auspicious choice of name, for in the century following it would be actors who replaced the wits of court as the celebrities of the day. And it would be actors who would increasingly dominate affairs in the theatre.

Eighteenth century

The mid-late eighteenth century in British theatre is generally referred to as the age of the actor-manager – and of one actor-manager in particular. Through the efforts of David Garrick, it also marked the first age of theatrical respectability, and the advent of the cult of Shakespeare. Ironically, given this elevation of Shakespeare to the epitome of taste and decency, it was to be a tough period for living playwrights, many of whom, like Henry Fielding, were eventually forced to look to essay writing or to the emerging field of popular prose fiction as an outlet for their talents.

The London theatre had begun the century in some foment, characterized by commercial frenzy, artistic dispute, the collapse of the licensing system

[60] Ibid., p. 134.

and, for a short period, an explosion of opportunity for new plays and new formats. It was the project of one particular working playwright that briefly ignited these opportunities, before the iron fist of censorship and the programming of Garrick and others combined to severely restrict the opportunities for living playwrights.

The collapse of the patent system had been a long-time coming when, in the early years of the century, Italian Opera with all its grandiosity became wildly popular among the chattering classes of the English capital. Panic-stricken programmers in the licensed theatres responded to this new challenge by developing programmes of entertainment offering much greater variety, including music and dancing to leaven the shortened dramas, and adding comic after-pieces.

Surveying this changed scene, for once playwrights and critics agreed. Letters to the newspapers bemoaned a loss of faith in the spoken word, and despaired at the taste for spectacle and emotionalism shared by both Italian Opera and the new programming. There was a xenophobic edge to some of this – shades of 'Italians coming over here and stealing our audiences' – and a chauvinist assertion of the obvious superiority of the English theatre. It was a jobbing writer, John Gay, who came up with a solution to the impasse, in the shape of *The Beggar's Opera*.

Gay was a West Country poet who had dabbled in playwriting before publishing a successful collection of verse in 1720, and then blowing the proceeds in unwise investments. *The Beggar's Opera* (1728) somehow met the needs of both Gay's pocket and the times. This new 'ballad opera' reflected the variety format offered by the licensed theatres, but within an overarching (if rather loose) plot. By incorporating operatic arias alongside a love story, tragic parody and a crime plot satirizing contemporary politicians, it manages to take a swipe at Italian Opera while also swiping its audience. It also breached the class gap, drawing interest from the less fashionable audiences of the spoken-word theatre. Despite having been rejected by Colley Cibber, manager at Drury Lane, and accepted by John Rich at the Lincoln's Inn Fields only after an intervention by Gay's patron the Earl of Queensbury, the show (for that's what it undoubtedly was) was wildly successful. Rich was even able to build a new theatre in Covent Garden on the proceeds. Pirate versions of Gay's play proliferated, and the Lord Chamberlain found himself unable to keep a grip on the situation.

Ever responsive to public appetite, the licensed theatres now abandoned their composite programmes in favour of plays in the new mould. These plays were increasingly spiced with topical allusions to current constitutional issues, other targets including fops, foreigners (including anyone who was not English) and clerics of every hue. For a brief period it seemed that plays could be presented anywhere, saying anything, about anyone, with impunity.

The opera houses now, in turn, had to find their response. The oratorio, and in particular those written to English verse by the adopted Londoner, George Handel, offered beautiful music on elevating subjects, while also ticking the patriotic box. It was cheaper to produce than grand opera, too. The oratorio was almost immediately popular, both with its intended audience and with many who also enjoyed ballad operas. Its success sparked the development of further new venues, in particular the Pleasure Gardens in Vauxhall, an open-air space where people of all sorts could, for a modest sum, stroll the pathways and listen to this elevating music.

London was now awash with new plays and new music, constantly spawning new venues, all seemingly beyond the reach of the law. So, naturally, a new law was called for.

The 'Bill to restrain the number of playhouses' of 1735 not only aimed to reverse the intrusion of new theatres into respectable districts, but also proposed a board of censors to clamp down on political content. The Bill failed, but was followed two years later by a scandal. A play called *The Festival of the Golden Rump* – which made scatological reference to the King's farting and haemorrhoids – was quoted in Parliament as an example of the typically obscene fare offered by the unlicensed theatres.[61] This time a Bill was passed emphatically, and Britain entered a new phase of licensing: every new play must now be submitted to the censor two weeks in advance of opening. Furthermore, only two theatres for the spoken word would be tolerated in London.

[61] Trussler for one casts doubt on the authenticity of the script, suggesting that Walpole, the Prime Minister, may even have had a hand in soliciting it. Ibid., p. 172.

At a stroke, the prospects for playwrights, who had recently enjoyed such a boom, were now bust – at least in London.[62, 63] For the first time, producing a new play was considered by actor-managers to be far more trouble – commercial and political – than it was worth.[64]

There were, though, some positives. With a huge audience newly developed, the licensed theatres had the opportunity and incentive to expand and improve both their companies and their buildings. By the end of the century, Drury Lane Theatre could accommodate an audience of 3,500. And if a bigger house inevitably conspired with difficulties over censorship and matters of taste to encourage conservative programming of classic plays from the past, the training of actors and the general standard of production were raised to a new level – at least while there was a man of Garrick's capabilities at the helm.

The age of Garrick

David Garrick was a former law student turned wine merchant, who became both a dramatist and an actor, and whose stewardship at Drury Lane would span twenty-nine years. He began triumphantly, when a rival production of *Romeo and Juliet* folded in favour of Garrick's superior offering. Garrick now set about establishing Drury Lane as the bastion for spoken-word drama. At its centre were the plays of Shakespeare, backed up by Garrick himself as resident dramatist. Garrick, however, presented himself as a figure of unimpeachable character, a quality he was as keen to project on stage as in his private life. While the stage was set for a golden age of acting, led by

[62] Henry Fielding, for instance, had written twenty-five plays in the previous decade, most of them satirical romps, several staged at the unlicensed Little Theatre. After 1737, he wrote no more plays for the stage, and became known mainly as the author of *Tom Jones*.

[63] The Act had no writ in provincial towns and cities, where theatres were licensed by local authorities.

[64] Brewer quotes the seemingly timeless words of Garrick's biographer Thomas Davies in this connection: 'The time bestowed in rehearsing the piece, and the expense of new scenes, dresses, music and other decorations, make it often ineligible to a director of theatre to accept a new play; especially when it is considered that the reviving of a good play will answer his end of profit and reputation too perhaps.' John Brewer, *The Pleasures of the Imagination: English Culture in the Eighteenth Century* (London: Harper Collins, 1997), p. 392.

Garrick himself, it was also based on texts shorn of their racier aspects. What new plays were produced – many, again, by Garrick himself – were likewise carefully apolitical and seemly. It was not until the last quarter of the century that Drury Lane would find a more dashing playwright in control.

Enter (and exit) Sheridan

In 1775, after an early life beset by scandals, a penniless ex-Harrovian, Richard Brinsley Sheridan, enjoyed a massive success with his first stab at playwriting, *The Rivals*. Three years later he was able (with partners) to buy out the retiring Garrick's share of the theatre in Drury Lane, and install himself as manager. His next move was to enter into partnership with Thomas Harris, licence-holder of the Covent Garden theatre, buying the King's Theatre in the Haymarket. This put the two managers in control of all the legitimate drama and opera in the capital. Although finances were never secure enough to press ahead with schemes for newer, bigger theatres – probably due in part to Sheridan's extravagant lifestyle – the latter's success as a playwright, especially with the universally lauded *The School for Scandal*, meant that vigorous new writing was again pulsing through the veins of London's theatres.

Sadly, RBS was by his own confession never a lover of theatre; his real ambitions lay in politics, in which he made some progress. Nonetheless, this distraction from his business responsibilities, plus the misfortune of having the Drury Lane theatre first condemned as unsafe and demolished, and then destroyed by fire, meant that he amassed debts at an unstoppable rate. In 1811 he lost his seat as MP, was barred from any hand in the theatre's management and was arrested for debt. Friends saved him from prison, but he ended his days five years later in squalid circumstances. By then, however, he had raised a huge public subscription to rebuild Drury Lane.

The new century was less than twenty years old, and the efforts of an outstanding actor and a reluctant playwright had ensured that playmaking and theatre-going would remain vital activities, at least in London. With the passing of Garrick, and now Sheridan, there was room for a new dynamo in British Theatre. But the craft of playwriting was for the time being secure, and even semi-respectable.

Reflections on the history of playwriting 2: Modern and contemporary

Clare Bayley

The nineteenth century

In America, theatre's disreputable reputation was sealed when Abraham Lincoln, emancipator of slaves and saviour of the union, was assassinated by an actor, John Wilkes Booth, during a performance in 1865. The nineteenth century was not a distinguished time for theatre on either side of the Atlantic. Melodrama, light comedies, Victorian burlesque, pantomime, farce and operetta were the order of the day.

The groundbreaking theatre at that time was going on in Scandinavia: in particular in the capital of Norway, then known as Christiania, where a seismic artistic movement known as the Modern Breakthrough was underway. Writers, artists and actors were flocking there to wrestle with a new aesthetic for the moral and social questions they urgently wanted to address. Women writers flourished in this culture of experimentation and politically progressive debate, and they did not shrink from writing about inequality, oppression and other taboo subjects that society expected respectable women to be ignorant about: free love, prostitution, even rape. Notable among these was the novelist and playwright Victoria Benedictsson, a formidably intelligent woman whose progressive father gave her a man's education, and who was widely believed to have been the model for Ibsen's Hedda Gabler, and possibly also Strindberg's Miss Julie.

While the reputation of the Modern Breakthrough women didn't travel outside of Scandinavia, the influence of Ibsen and Strindberg spread to the rest of the world and changed the direction of drama forever. **Henrik Ibsen**

(1828–1906) is now regarded as the father of realism and credited with having redefined the nature of modern European drama. But he did not have an easy time of it, and it's worth remembering (especially when things are not going well in your own career!) that despite a huge output of plays, it wasn't until he was forty-nine that he began to achieve some recognition.

Ibsen's affluent merchant father was bankrupted when Ibsen was only seven, and at fifteen he had to leave school to be apprenticed to an apothecary. While there he had an illegitimate son, and for the next decade or more he had to pay for the child's upkeep. He failed his university entrance exams, and his first play, *Catilina*, written when he was twenty-two, was published but never performed. It did get him a job in a theatre, however – first in Christiania, then in Bergen – where he worked on more than 145 plays as writer, director and producer. A travel bursary in 1864 allowed him to travel widely, and he didn't return to Norway for the next twenty-seven years. From his exile he began to find some success in Scandinavia, beginning with the Stockholm production of *Brand* in 1865. His great characters – from Hedda Gabler to Nora and Oswald – reflect the tensions in his own complex and difficult background. They are not natural rebels, yet strive for a kind of emancipation which will cost them something precious to them: their place in society.

With critical success came controversy, because of the questioning nature of his work, but his next twelve plays (including *Hedda Gabler, The Wild Duck, Ghosts* ...) secured his reputation as a writer. It wasn't until the 1890s that his reputation travelled to Europe, but when it did it provoked cultural debate across Europe and America. By the time Ibsen died in 1906 he was celebrated for his enormous influence on theatre. As Raymond Williams puts it: '[M]ore than any other man, Ibsen created ... the consciousness of modern European drama.'[1]

August Strindberg (1849–1912) was an almost direct contemporary of Ibsen's in Scandinavia, whose influence also spread throughout the world; but his plays were significantly different in outlook and aesthetic. Even

[1] Raymond Williams, *Drama from Ibsen to Brecht: A Critical Account and Revaluation* (London: Penguin Books, 1998), p. 77.

though Ibsen's later plays were known to be symbolist, and Strindberg's early play *Miss Julie* is considered a key text in early Naturalist drama, the dichotomy between their two approaches to theatre continues to hold sway over European playwriting today: Ibsen representing realism, and Strindberg experimentation and expressionism.

Strindberg's shipping merchant father died young, resulting in a poor and unhappy childhood for his son. Poverty forced him to leave university before graduating, but in 1877 he married the divorced baroness and actress Siri von Essen (the first of three doomed marriages) and started writing plays and short stories. His early plays gained little attention and, like Ibsen, he travelled abroad between 1883 and 1896. In France he was influenced by Zola's call for reform against the theatre of 'patent-leather shoes and patent-leather themes',[2] the rallying call which led to naturalism. During this period Strindberg's plays (including *Miss Julie* in 1888) were harsh and neo-realist. Later, he became interested in the Symbolist movement and began actively searching for new dramatic forms as well as themes. After a mental breakdown (following a painful divorce from his second wife in 1895) he started to delve into alchemy and the occult. This led to a new, lyrical style of writing, and his work became more experimental in form, leaving realism far behind – culminating in *The Dance of Death* (1900), *A Dream Play* (1901) *and Ghost Sonata* (1907). Although these plays are not performed nearly as often around the world as Ibsen's greatest successes, their influence has played out in the work of artists ever since, especially in expressionism, surrealism and the Theatre of the Absurd. In America his influence was seen in the plays of Eugene O'Neill; in England *A Dance of Death* was given a celebrated revival at the National Theatre in London in 1967, with Laurence Olivier playing the Captain.

The next great non-English language playwright to definitively influence the English-language theatre was the Russian doctor, short story writer and playwright **Anton Chekhov (1860–1904)**. In 1895, at the age of thirty-five, Chekhov was already a prolific short story writer. He was also consumptive, though not yet fully aware of the fact, and still working as a doctor, frequently

[2] Ibid., p. 80.

complaining of the lack of money and the time to write. His one-act comedies (*The Bear, The Proposal, Swan Song*) were successful, but he was as dismissive of them as he was of his stories. 'All I have written hitherto is trash in comparison with what I would like to write. I would write exultantly', he wrote to his friend the newspaper editor Alexei Suvorin in 1888.

He was much less flippant about *The Seagull*, his first full-length play. It was born out of a frustration with the theatre of the day ('mere routine and prejudice') and striving for a new form of theatre fit for the times he lived in: 'we must have new formulas. That's what we want. And if there are none, then it's better to have nothing at all'.[3]

But the first performance was a disaster, as he vividly described in a letter to his brother Mikhail Chekhov: 'The play fell flat and flopped with a bang. The audience was bewildered. They acted as if they were ashamed to be in the theatre ... The moral of the story is: I shouldn't write plays.'[4]

The incomprehension and hostility of the audience when faced with radically new work is something that has been experienced by groundbreaking playwrights across the centuries (for instance, Beckett with *Waiting for Godot*, John Osborne with *Look Back in Anger*, Sarah Kane with *Blasted*). In each case the work found its defenders, and in Chekhov's case they were the producer Vladimir Nemirovich-Danchenko and the director Konstantin Stanislavsky. When they opened their Moscow Art Theatre the following year, *The Seagull* was its opening production; and with their radical approach applied to this new work, the production was a resounding success. 'It is a significant moment, in the history of modern drama, for it shows a writer of genius beginning to create a new dramatic form, but in ways so original and so tentative that ... another kind of art has to be invented to sustain it',[5] said Raymond Williams.

After the rehabilitation of *The Seagull*, Chekhov's great plays followed in quick succession (*Uncle Vanya* (1897), *Three Sisters* (1900), *The Cherry Orchard*). Chekhov's consumption finally killed him in 1904, the same year that *The Cherry*

---

[3] Ibid., p. 108.

[4] Anton Chekhov (Lillian Hellman, ed), *The Letters of Anton Chekhov* (Bungay, Suffolk: Picador), p. 193.

[5] Williams, *Drama from Ibsen to Brecht.*

Orchard was produced. In the UK and US it took a little time for audiences to catch on, and for directors to disentangle the question of whether Chekhov's plays are comedies or tragedies. It wasn't until the 1920s that his plays started to gain traction in the UK and the US, but they have been consistently in the repertoire ever since. The fact that successive waves of commentators claim that previous interpretations of Chekhov's work have been false, and that *their* new way is the true way, proves how durable and profound those plays are – they continue to surprise, reveal and confound us to this day.

The early twentieth century

If the great influences on nineteenth-century theatre came from Scandinavia and Russia, those on the early twentieth century came from Germany and France respectively – Bertolt Brecht and Antonin Artaud.

From his first award-winning play *Drums in the Night* (1922), produced when he was twenty-four, **Bertolt Brecht**'s path to success was clear. He was to become one of the most influential figures in modern theatre, and one of the few dramatists whose theories were widely taken up by playwrights of his own and succeeding generations. As a theorist his works are still key texts on any drama course. And he achieved the rarest of honours when in 1949 he was able to found a theatre expressly to produce his own work – the Berliner Ensemble.

In 1924 Brecht went to Berlin to assist Max Reinhardt, but found that the approach of director Erwin Piscator was much more compatible with his own artistic ambitions. Piscator was already reacting against the prevailing naturalism, developing a concept of theatre as a means of education, and not mere distraction for audiences. Piscator's productions used newsreel, machinery, film clips and audio recordings to present a Total Theatre, and Brecht immediately began to absorb these ideas[6] and then to take them further and develop his ideas about Epic Theatre.

6 Piscator was exiled under the Nazis and worked in America, where he influenced both Arthur Miller and Tennessee Williams. He later returned to Germany and in 1962 became artistic director of the Volksbuhne in Berlin.

'Art is not a mirror with which to reflect reality, but a hammer with which to shape it', Brecht later wrote. The aim of Epic Theatre was to appeal to the audience's reason, not their emotion, and to provide them with the tools for a sober analysis of their condition, and the construction of informed opinions about it.

To achieve this, the dramatist and actors must not 'cast a spell' or draw attention to their powers of transformation. For Brecht the 'engendering of illusion' is not desirable. In his essay 'The Street Scene – A Basic Model for an Epic Theatre', he likens a play to an eyewitness account of a traffic accident, retold so that bystanders can form an opinion about the cause and decide on the culpability of the players. The performance is not pretending to show the accident itself, but is simply a representation of it, so that the spectators' critical faculties remain engaged throughout. In order to ensure that this happens, Brecht's famous '*verfremdungseffekt*' or alienation effect employs a number of devices, such as the use of choruses, documentary projections, direct address to the audiences, songs and placards. The structure of the play is episodic, the characters are defined by their actions, and the subject matter is ultimately nothing less than class war: 'a way to portray social processes as seen in their causal relationships'.

Man Is Man (1926) is considered the first play to attempt to embody these theories of Epic Theatre and the alienation effect. But as his work developed, Brecht became more concerned with the question expressed in his essay 'On Experimental Theatre': 'How can the theatre be both instructive and entertaining? How can it be divorced from spiritual dope traffic, and turned from a home of illusion to a home of experiences?'

The answer came in the plays of his mature period, *Mother Courage and Her Children* (1941), *Life of Galileo* (1943), *The Good Person of Szechwan* (1943) and *The Caucasian Chalk Circle* (1947).

At almost the same time in Paris, another experiment in dramatic form and purpose was being conducted by the writer and director **Antonin Artaud (1896–1948)**. His books *The Theatre and Its Double* (1938) and *Theatre of Cruelty* (1933) proposed his theories, which combined the influences of surrealism with Eastern dance drama to form a violent and ritualistic theatre. It used exactly the techniques which Brecht avoided: magic tricks, elaborate sets and costumes, which were employed to hypnotize and overwhelm spectators. The intention was to shock audiences into an awareness of their basic savage nature.

Leading audiences into the early part of the twentieth century were the wit and comedy of Oscar Wilde and Noel Coward on the one hand, and the heirs of Ibsen producing serious social commentary on the other – George Bernard Shaw, Sean O'Casey and Eugene O'Neil.

The Abbey Theatre in Dublin, the first Irish national theatre, was founded in 1904 by the poet W. B. Yeats and Lady Gregory to be a 'People's Theatre' and to promote Irish writers. Writing to Lady Gregory, Yeats described his pride in the Abbey as 'the first doing of something for which the world is ripe, something that will be done all over the world and done more and more perfectly: the making articulate of all the dumb classes, each with its own knowledge of the world, its own dignity, but all objective with the objectivity of the office and the workshop, of the newspaper and the street, of mechanism and politics'.[7]

The Abbey became a home for some of the greatest dramatic writers of the century. There was a political imperative: Ireland was preparing itself for self-rule, and the theatre's role in defining a national culture and identity was crucial. The work was urgent and progressive, but not always what we would call 'politically correct' today. The first production of J. M. Synge's *The Playboy of the Western World* in 1907 caused riots among serious-minded nationalists. The story of the Christy Mahon, the anti-hero who claims to have murdered his father and is feted and admired, trounces the very idea of heroism, at a time when Ireland wanted to see itself in a noble light.

Some objected to the fact that the Abbey produced work in the language of the colonizer, not in Gaelic. But all the Abbey's great playwrights – J. M. Synge, Sean O'Casey, Tom Murphy, Brian Friel, Frank McGuinness, Marina Carr – have written in a version of English which is unmistakably Irish.

The Abbey cannily toured work to the US from early on, ensuring that those writers gained an international reputation, and pointedly bypassing London. Yeats perceived Synge's controversial genius, and was vindicated

[7] Bentley, E. (ed.), *The Theory of the Modern Stage* (London: Penguin Books, 1992), p. 327.

when the play later found supporters in literary heavyweights as diverse as Antonin Artaud, Bertolt Brecht and Jean-Paul Sartre.

Yeats also backed Sean O'Casey's early works, the so-called 'Dublin trilogy', *Shadow of a Gunman* (1923), *Juno and the Paycock* (1924) and *The Plough and the Stars* (1926). But his 1928 play *The Silver Tassie* took a new approach and was highly stylized. Yeats rejected that play, and O'Casey left Ireland in high dudgeon – finding homes for his increasingly symbolist and expressionist work in London and New York.

Compared to the ferment in Ireland, in Britain the theatrical scene was somewhat tamer, powered by the regional repertory system. There was a rep theatre in most major towns which churned out a regular diet of popular plays using a resident company whose actors had to act in one play at the same time as rehearsing another and learning lines for a third, to allow the programme to change every week. Between the wars there were over 100 rep theatres in operation in Britain. They provided a harsh but rigorous training for actors, and several writers learned their craft from their time as actors in rep – notably Harold Pinter and Howard Brenton.

In New York the number of theatres grew from forty-three in 1900 to eighty by 1928, but that was the time that Broadway became synonymous with lightweight, commercial fare. The Washington Square Players, the Provincetown Players and the Neighborhood Playhouse were lone voices in presenting classic plays and modern European works. Eugene O'Neill almost single-handedly took on the considerable task of cultivating audiences' appetite for contemporary American playwriting. Otherwise, comedy was the order of the day.

In the '30s Lillian Hellman, John Steinbeck and Clifford Odets flew the flag for challenging modern American drama. In the '40s Tennessee Williams and Arthur Miller were the twin leaders of the serious drama. But aside from playhouses attached to universities, New York remained the focus for theatre, until Margot Jones spearheaded the Regional Theater Movement. She founded Theatre 47 in Dallas in 1947, Nina Vance founded the Alley Theatre in Houston in 1948 and Zelda Fichandler the Arena Stage in Washington D. C. in 1950. More followed, so that there were soon established homes and growing audiences for new plays outside New York, creating greater opportunities for an increasing number of American playwrights.

The fifties

'If you want to understand the social history of Britain since the war, then your time will be better spent studying the plays of the period ... than by looking at any comparable documentary source.' So writes David Hare in his book *Writing Left-Handed.*

After the sense of national unity and purpose brought about by the Second World War, the 1950s saw a withering of that clarity about right and wrong, a questioning of the need for restraint and austerity. There was a dawning realization that for all the sacrifice and change, and despite a Labour government, the old guard were clinging onto power and dominating bourgeois morality. In social terms, progress was stalling, while in other ways everything had changed.

This malaise found expression on our stages, and marked a high watershed in the theatre. Samuel Beckett's groundbreaking *Waiting for Godot* premiered in London in 1955, and a year later John Osborne's *Look Back in Anger* burst into the public consciousness. From then on, the French windows of the drawing-room comedies were decisively shattered. The wit and urbanity, the cocktails and aristocrats of Noel Coward, the restrained passions and thwarted ambitions of Terence Rattigan – all these began to fall out of favour. On both sides of the pond, audiences were becoming disenchanted with seeing the leisured classes on stage. In came salesmen, caretakers, faded beauties, drunks and bums, housing estates and liquor stores, overt politics and unromantic sex. A vibrant and opinionated new generation was pushing at the boundaries of content and form, and the young trailblazers Arthur Miller and Tennessee Williams were to become the granddaddies of them all.

The Royal Court

Up to this point, the great productions of the British theatre were the classics, and the great giants were the actors – John Gielgud, Lawrence Olivier, Edith Evans. But in 1956 George Devine founded the English Stage Company at the Royal Court and became its first artistic director. Devine was an actor himself, as well as a director. He had already founded the Young Vic Theatre

Company, and been instrumental in furthering John Gielgud's career. But on founding his new company he declared, 'Ours in not to be a producer's theatre, nor an actor's theatre ... it is to be a writer's theatre.' His intention was to make theatre part of the intellectual life of the country, by inviting and welcoming writers who had something to say about the state of the nation – 'hard-hitting and uncompromising writers'.

Ann Jellicoe recalls the Royal Court Writers Group meetings with Arnold Wesker, John Arden, Edward Bond, Maureen Duffy and others. 'We recognised each other's talent and supported it. This is said to be rare among writers. The meetings had all the fun of a party, and none of the boredom.' She describes the fragility of even those inspired writers' egos, and the fact that they were selective about who was allowed in, because 'anyone too argumentative or destructive would upset the balance'. They all shared a common idea of Direct Theatre: 'a theatre of action and images rather than words'.[8]

John Osborne was not in that group. But when Devine placed an ad in *The Stage* newspaper calling for submissions, among the 700 responses was Osborne's *Look Back in Anger*, which had already been rejected by the theatre establishment of the day: Laurence Olivier, Terence Rattigan and Binkie Beaumont.

Look Back in Anger was the English Stage Company's fourth production, and the first of what were known as 'kitchen sink dramas'. The night of its premiere is considered another landmark in modern theatre, and not without controversy. Devine went on to fight a long-running battle with the theatre censors.

Until 1968, the Lord Chamberlain had the power to withhold or withdraw a theatrical licence, with no legal obligation to disclose the reasons. Three Royal Court plays were originally refused a licence to be performed at all (Osborne's *A Patriot for Me*, Edward Bond's *Saved* and *Early Morning*). In other cases the offending lines or speeches were indicated, and it was up to the writer and director to decide how far to compromise their work. Devine cleverly managed to get many plays past the censor, including Bond's *Saved*,

[8] Richard Findlater, *25 Years of the English Stage Company at the Royal Court* (Derbyshire: Amber Lane Press, 1981), p. 55.

complete with its scene depicting the stoning of a baby to death in its pram. When he couldn't, as with *Early Morning*, he turned the theatre into a private Theatre Club.[9] These battles with the Lord Chamberlain, and Devine's stalwart defence of his writers, eventually led to the demise of theatre censorship altogether.

At around the same time, over in East London, the charismatic director and actor Joan Littlewood had taken over the Theatre Royal, Stratford East in London, for her Theatre Workshop. A card-carrying communist (she was allegedly under surveillance by MI5 for years, and banned by the BBC) her commitment was to a popular theatre for and of the people. The company put on classics and original plays which were often devised by the company, a radical idea for British theatre at the time. Joan Littlewood is probably best known for her 1963 hit *Oh What a Lovely War*, a satirical anti-war piece about the First World War created as a song-and-dance revue; and for the fact that Brecht himself sanctioned the British premiere of *Mother Courage* at Stratford in 1955, in which Littlewood both directed and played the title role.

But she also championed the work of writers, including Brendan Behan, Lionel Bart and **Shelagh Delaney**, one of the few women writers to break through during this time of the 'angry young men'. Delaney left school at fifteen and took casual jobs (cinema usherette, salesgirl) in her home town of Salford. At the age of eighteen she went to see Terence Rattigan's *Variation on a Theme*, and was so inspired to write something more meaningful for people like her that she wrote *A Taste of Honey* in six weeks. She sent the script to Joan Littlewood, accompanied by a letter which shows her remarkable bravura, and a beguiling mixture of arrogance and lack of confidence.

'I set to and produced this little epic – don't ask me why – I'm quite unqualified for anything like this. But at least I finished it and if, from among the markings and the typing errors and the spelling mistakes, you can gather a little sense from what I have written – or a little nonsense – I should be extremely grateful for your criticism – though I hate criticism of any kind',[10] she wrote.

---

9 Hay and Roberts (eds), *Bond: A Study of His Plays* (London: Eyre Methuen, 1980), pp. 67–68.

10 Quoted in the National Theatre programme for Bijan Sheibani's 2014 production.

In 1958 every aspect of the play, from single mothers to mixed race relationships, homosexuality and teenage pregnancy, was taboo at the time. Plays were not generally considered to be written by women – let alone an uneducated, northern, 18-year-old one. As Dominic Sandbrook writes,[11]

> although we often think of the Angry Young Men as anti-establishment rebels, much of their anger was actually directed at their wives and girlfriends ...

A Taste of Honey is funny and moving. It was championed by Joan Littlewood, praised by Kenneth Tynan (though many other critics found it hard to handle), made into a film (starring Rita Tushingham as Jo), was a hit in New York in 1961, and has enjoyed a lasting success ever since. However, Delaney's second play, *The Lion in Love*, was panned by the critics, and she didn't write for the stage again for twenty years. The stage's loss was the screen's gain – among many others she wrote the screenplay for *Dance with a Stranger* (1985), about the last woman to be hanged in Britain, Ruth Ellis.

Into the midst of all this kitchen sinkery, **Samuel Beckett** arrived from Paris, bringing with him a wholly different artistic sensibility. When *Waiting for Godot* premiered in London in 1955, it had already caused a storm in Paris the previous year as *En Attendant Godot*. But it was so different from any stage play that London audiences had seen, with its disregard for conventional plot, its poetic, fractured dialogue and seemingly meandering mixture of lyricism, vaudeville, whimsy and profundity, that it was met with incomprehension and hostility. Only a few lone voices recognized its game-changing brilliance, among them Kenneth Tynan, theatre critic for *The Observer*.

'*Waiting for Godot* frankly jettisons everything by which we recognise theatre', he wrote in his review. 'It forced me to re-examine the rules which have hitherto governed the drama; and having done so, to pronounce them not elastic enough. It is validly new, and hence I declare myself, as the Spanish would say, godotista.'

[11] Ibid.

The play premiered in New York the following year, staring Bert Lahr (father of the critic John). In the *New York Times*, Brooks Atkinson echoed Tynan:

> The point of view suggests Sartre – bleak, dark, disgusted. The style suggests Joyce – pungent and fabulous … Theatre-goers can rail at it but they cannot ignore it. For Mr Beckett is a valid writer.

It seems amazing now that both critics felt they had to positively assert Beckett's *validity* as a serious writer; but such is the shock of the new, and the general population's wariness of experimentation. In this respect, Beckett's avant-garde credentials were impeccable: born in Ireland in 1906, he went to Paris in the 1920s and worked as James Joyce's secretary. He settled in Paris permanently in 1938, and established his literary reputation, writing first in French and then translating his own work into English.

It's for his plays that he is now most remembered, and for which he won the Nobel Prize for Literature in 1969. Starting with *Godot*'s extreme reassessment of dramatic form ('no plot, no climax, no denouement, no beginning, no middle, and no end', as Tynan said) Beckett continued to push further and harder at the limits of drama for the rest of his career. *Not I* features only a disembodied mouth, and draped, shadowy figures; the late Billie Whitelaw, Beckett's frequent collaborator, described it as like 'falling backwards into Hell, emitting cries'. [12]

Beckett resolutely refused to explain his work, saying only 'I meant what I said.' Equally, he was (and his estate still is) famously intractable in the matter of staging – his stage directions are there to be followed to the letter, and no deviation is permitted. Beckett's artistic vision emerged fully formed and unnegotiable.

Despite the impact made by *Godot*, the Theatre of the Absurd never took hold in England or the US as it did in Europe, and Beckett staunchly refused to become its flag-waver and figurehead. He did, however, befriend one of the English language's most influential writers, Harold Pinter, who freely

[12] Trevor R. Griffiths and Carole Woddis (eds), *Bloomsbury Theatre Guide* (London: Bloomsbury, 1991), p. 30.

acknowledged the influence that the older playwright had on him. In his 'Wake for Sam', Pinter reads from a letter he wrote in 1954 to a friend about Beckett; it serves as a kind of manifesto for the kind of work he himself admired and indeed wrote:

> He is the most courageous and remorseless writer going … he leaves no stone unturned and no maggot lonely. He brings forth a body of beauty.[13]

The vision of the world that Pinter presents is harder edged than that of his spiritual mentor, revealing a violent and peculiarly English masculinity – not without its bleak humour, which finds poetry in 'the banalities, the repetitions, the evasions and even the hiatuses of everyday speech' (as Michael Billington says in his biography of Pinter).[14] His early plays were written while Pinter was working as an actor in rep, living an itinerant life and staying in down-at-heel boarding-houses. All charting the menace in relations between marginal but powerful men, they include *The Birthday Party, The Dumb Waiter, The Caretaker* and *The Homecoming. Betrayal* tells the story of an adulterous love affair with the deceptively simple dramatic device of starting the story at the end and working backwards. In later life Pinter's plays became more explicitly political (*Mountain Language*, for instance, was inspired by a trip to Kurdish communities in Turkey with Arthur Miller in the early 1980s).

The sixties

George Devine retired from the Royal Court in 1965 and died the following year, but his legacy remains not only in the plays and playwrights that he nurtured, but also in the generously endowed and highly prestigious George Devine Award for new plays.

William Gaskill, who had been Devine's assistant, succeeded him as artistic director. He continued to champion the work of the so-called 'angry

[13] Available at: http://www.youtube.com/watch?v=-N99S8n2TiA (accessed: 12 May 2014). It was broadcast on the BBC in 1990, available at: http://www.apieceofmonologue.com/2011/08/harold-pinter-samuel-beckett-wake.html (accessed: 10 December 2014).

[14] Michael Billington, *The Life and Work of Harold Pinter* (London: Faber and Faber, 2007).

young men', including Osborne and Bond, Howard Barker and John Arden, and alongside Littlewood helped to introduce the work of Bertolt Brecht to British audiences.

In the early 1960s the young writer Tom Stoppard was having some success with plays for radio and TV, when in 1966 his play *Rosencrantz and Guildernstern Are Dead* suddenly became a hit. He recalls 'getting the telephone call which can change a young writer's life'[15] and from then on his witty, clever, inventive plays earned him fame around the world, as hit after hit was produced, almost one a year, throughout the 1960s and 1970s (including *The Real Inspector Hound* in 1968, *The Real Thing* in 1982, *Arcadia* in 1993 – not to mention the films *Brazil* in 1985, with Terry Gilliam, and *Shakespeare in Love* in 1998).

Stoppard and his generation of sparky writers with mainstream appeal (including Michael Frayn, Christopher Hampton, Peter Shaffer and Simon Grey) dominated the rep stages and the West End. But outside the mainstream, something else was afoot. The 1950s generation had reacted against their parents' certainties – by fighting against everything. By the 1960s this reaction had played itself out. It was a boom time – there was economic prosperity, civil rights were on the table, and the world felt as if it was changing. But then there was a new war: Vietnam. It gave a new impetus, a new desire to fight *for* something. This became the era of protest for racial, class and gender equality. All the established order was under scrutiny, and artists were trying to find new forms to reflect the changing social and political times. There was a desire, as the playwright and critic Micheline Wandor expresses it, 'to represent unheard voices', and also to question 'received ideas about conventional work processes'.[16]

A number of companies were formed to work in new, more egalitarian ways to make theatre, often borrowing from socialist models. In New York Joseph Papp's Public Theatre was founded in 1967; and Papp also established the inspirational Shakespeare in the Park, where he was one of the first exponents of 'colour blind' classical casting. In 1962 Ellen Steward founded La

[15] In a conversation with the author.

[16] Wandor, Micheline, *Drama Today, a Critical Guide to British Drama 1970–90* (Essex: Longman, 1993), p. 13.

Mama Experimental Theatre Club for avant-garde work, and Joseph Chaikin's Open Theatre opened its doors in 1963.

Several of the new theatres were founded by or intimately linked to specific writers, such as the Circle Rep, co-founded by Lanford Wilson in 1969, and the Actors Theatre in Louisville, which staged an annual new play festival, and premiered the plays of both Marsha Norman and Beth Henley. The Goodman Theatre in Chicago premiered the works of both David Mamet and John Guare; the Yale Rep (founded in 1966) is where many of August Wilson's plays were first developed.

Chicago started to become the most significant US theatre city outside New York during the 1970s, after Paul Sills, co-founder of The Second City (with its reputation for improvised theatre) invited Stuart Gordon and his Organic Theatre to the city. The Victory Gardens Theatre was known as a writers' theatre, while Steppenwolf, founded in 1974 by Terry Kinney, Jeff Perry and Gary Sinise, premiered the plays of Sam Shepard, Dusty Hughes, John Guare, Lanford Wilson and many more. Tracy Letts and Bruce Norris began work there as actors, and became writers.

In the UK Red Ladder was one of the earliest of the new political theatre groups. The Women's Theatre Group was formed to perform feminist agit prop; Belt and Braces, The Ovalhouse, The Brighton Combination and Portable Theatre (founded by Howard Brenton, David Hare and Tony Bicat) all strove to experiment with form and process, producing political plays and putting the voices of the counterculture centre stage.

Monstrous Regiment was a company born out of the frustrations of a group of talented actresses offered only limited and stereotyped roles. Gillian Hanna, Mary McCusker, Chris Bowler, Linda Broughton and Helen Glavin formed the company and began to seek out and commission plays with substantial and complex roles for women. Among the playwrights whose early work was produced by them were Bryony Lavery, Claire Luckham (*Scum*, with Chris Bond), Susan Todd (*Teendreams*, with David Edgar) and Caryl Churchill. Monstrous Regiment's influence was far-reaching, helping to educate and inform both practitioners and audiences for two decades, and beginning the slow and incomplete process of redressing theatre's gender imbalance.

In the US the same process was going on, but in super-size scale: by some accounts in the 1970s there were over 100 feminist theatre companies producing work and championing women's writing. The sheer number of women writers of that generation – among them Paula Vogel, Beth Henley, Marsha Norman, Ntozake Shange, Wendy Wasserstein – is testament to the positive effects such encouragement can achieve.

In London in 1974 William Gaskill was instrumental in founding the Joint Stock Company, together with playwright David Hare and directors Max Stafford-Clark and David Aukin. Hare described the co-founders as all 'freelance members of the awkward squad … all our experience had been with presentation of new work, usually of a modestly controversial kind'.[17] Joint Stock set about producing new work which adopted a collective approach, but modified it to give the writer ultimate authority – the actors and director were fully involved with the writer during the preparatory research period for a new play, but the writer then went off and produced a definitive script.

As Micheline Wandor points out, Joint Stock's 'links with the Royal Court meant that their work had a far higher profile and greater financial security than many other companies'.[18] The company and its method attracted many of the greatest writers of the age, including David Hare, Caryl Churchill, Howard Brenton, David Edgar, Timberlake Wertenbaker, Trevor Griffiths. These writers all had a more or less explicitly political agenda, which emerges in their plays in intriguingly different ways. They were also unusual in that they collaborated with each other to write plays – something which hadn't happened in British or American playwriting since Middleton, Rowley, Dekker and Ford. Hare and Brenton together wrote *Pravda* (1990) and *Brassneck* (1973), and Brenton joined up with Tariq Ali for *Iranian Nights* (1989) and *Moscow Gold* (1990).

Caryl Churchill had already made a name for herself writing for radio, when in 1972 she was commissioned by Monstrous Regiment to write *Vinegar Tom*, about witchcraft in the seventeenth century. She was then invited to work with Joint Stock, whose method suited her admirably. She developed a successful working relationship with director Max Stafford-Clark (later artistic

[17] David Hare, *Writing Left-Handed* (London: Faber and Faber 1991), p. 65.

[18] Wandor, *Drama Today*, p. 13.

director of the Royal Court from 1979 to 1993), which allowed her the security and continuity to develop her formal invention over several decades. Her plays always take an oblique or unusual angle on her subject matter, from *Cloud Nine* about British colonialism (in which the same characters are seen in both Victorian times and the 1970s, played by different actors) to her comedy of financial shenanigans, *Serious Money*. Her most recent plays have taken formal experiment to an extreme, defining a uniquely British take on postdramatic theatre (see below), while always retaining a human heart.

The combination of a refusal to pontificate about her work in public (like Beckett she remains adamant that the work speaks for itself) and a constant creative self-reinvention mean that Churchill has become something of a legend in her own lifetime. Successive Royal Court artistic directors have described how she will not take a commission, but from time to time sends a new script, unannounced – always the occasion for celebration. Her startling talent continues to command the greatest respect.

At the same time that the Joint Stock writers were migrating from counterculture to the theatre establishment, Alan Ayckbourn was steadily rising to prominence from the regional mainstream. The author of over seventy-eight full-length plays (at the time of writing) Ayckbourn is the most produced playwright after Shakespeare. His carefully honed methodology has been outlined in his own book, *The Crafty Art of Playmaking*, and some have dubbed him 'the Chekhov of the suburbs'. But the craftiest of all Ayckbourn's moves was to establish his own theatre in Scarborough, a seaside town in the north of England, and dedicate it to producing his own plays. This ensured both the certainty of production, and a captive audience. As Ayckbourn's reputation grew he used it to boost the reputation of his own theatre, by insisting that all his plays premiered there instead of in London.

The Traverse Theatre in Edinburgh was founded in 1963 by three legendary avant-garde artists: Jim Haynes (countercultural icon), John Calder (who published Beckett, Ionesco and Arrabal, among others) and Richard Demarco (artist and gallery owner, who introduced Joseph Beuys and Tadeusz Kantor to each other). In its first three years it produced 110 productions, including twenty-eight British premieres and thirty-three world premieres. This extraordinary reputation for promoting new and avant-garde work has continued. The work of many

Scottish writers was launched and nurtured at The Traverse, including John Byrne, Liz Lockhead, Sue Glover, Tom McGrath, Gregory Burke, Zinnie Harris, Rona Munro, Chris Hannan, David Harrower and David Greig.

The seventies and eighties

The 1970s had proved that it was possible to establish new orthodoxies, and companies that had been radical in terms of their politics and working methods now began to appear monocultural and dominated by white, male, university-educated heterosexuals. It was time for the gay community, the black community and women to further their emancipation.

Gay theatre

Gay Sweatshop came into being in 1975 to expose homophobia and redress the skewed representation of gay people in culture. Radically, it was founded to involve equal numbers of men and women, thus giving a platform to gay women. Noel Greig and Philip Osment joined the company in 1977, and both produced lasting and memorable works, including Greig's *Poppies*. Over the following two decades the company worked with some of the key names in the gay theatre world: Nancy Duiguid, Jackie Kaye, Lois Weaver, Martin Sherman, Simon Callow, David Benedict and Bryony Lavery.

Several plays of this era brought mainstream audiences to a new understanding of gay issues. *Bent*, Martin Sherman's 1979 play, exposed for the first time to public consciousness the extent of Nazi persecution of gay people in the death camps, through the complex character of Max. A London production starred Ian McKellan as the gay man who denies his lover and pretends to be Jewish rather than gay. When the play premiered in New York Richard Gere took the part of Max.

The 1980s were dominated by the fear and reality of AIDS, and in 1985 Larry Kramer's partly autobiographical play *The Normal Heart* confronted the issue with sensitivity and complex rigour. In England, Kevin Elyot's *My Night with Reg* managed to disguise itself as a comedy of manners, while delivering a savage tale of love and loss.

In the UK playwright and director Neil Bartlett, with his opulent sets and costumes, and his love of song, music and visual art, laid the ground for a no-less-politicized but less issue-based gay aesthetic, which drew on his background in avant-garde performance art. In the US, Tony Kushner's revelatory *Angels in America* of 1993 tackled the AIDS crisis and the American national psyche under Regan in a bold and almost magic-realist way – an epic sweep encompassing Mormons, Roy Cohn, angels on trapezes, heartbreak, homophobia, Vallium and hallucinations.

Ireland

While all this flowering of opportunity was going on, Northern Ireland was in a state of war. Despite the horrors of that conflict, some of the English language's most inspiring playwrights emerged in Ireland during this time. Brian Friel, who grew up in Derry, speaks of the Troubles in powerfully oblique ways. His *Translations* (1981), for example, set in the nineteenth century, is about the cultural imperialism of the English imposing their language on his countrymen, but takes the form of a love story.

Frank McGuinness was born into a Catholic family in County Donegal, in the Republic of Ireland, but his astonishing third play, *Observe the Sons of Ulster Marching Towards the Somme* (1985) led many to take him for a Northern Irish Protestant. It tells the story of a regiment of Ulstermen in the First World War, focusing on the subversive, cynical figure of Kenneth Pyper, a sculptor who claims to have joined up only to die – but who ends up as the sole survivor. McGuinness's poetic language, his moral and intellectual seriousness, combine with a moving and vivid personal story.

Christina Reid's plays echo some of the concerns of McGuinness. *My Name, Shall I Tell You My Name* is a two-hander about a grandfather who has survived the Somme and is a member of the Orange Order; *Joyriders* looks at the effects of the Troubles on four young people from the notorious Divis Flats area of Belfast. Marie Jones, co-founder of the strictly non-sectarian Charabanc Company in Belfast, has also written a number of plays along similar themes, and is the author of the West End hit *Stones in Their Pockets*, a dark satire about two extras in a Hollywood movie being filmed in their impoverished, no-hope town.

Black and Asian theatre

A number of important companies have been established to ensure that the experience of black and Asian people is represented on British stages. The first, Temba was founded by Alton Kumalo in 1972 to introduce black British and South African writing to the UK, and was later run by Alby James who produced plays by Trish Cooke, Felix Cross, Benjamin Zephiniah among others. Carib Theatre was founded in 1980 by Anton Phillips and Yvonne Brewster. In 1986 Brewster, along with Carmen Munroe, Mona Hammond and Inigo Espejel founded Talawa to produce classic plays with all-black casts (*The Importance of Being Earnest, Antony and Cleopatra*), and to introduce British audiences to plays by African and Caribbean writers, including Dereck Walcott and Wole Soyinka. The company produced some wonderful and important productions, and continues to flourish and expand under the directorship of Michael Buffong.

Jatinder Verma's Tara Arts was established to bring Asian classic texts to British audiences. Much later, Tamasha was formed to bring Asian culture to a wider audience, and commissioned writers including Ayub Khan Din (*East Is East*). It still exists to produce new work which reflects global diversity, with playwright Finn Kennedy as its artistic director – a rare case of a writer running a company. Kali Arts was formed to give voice in particular to Asian women writers.

David Tse Ka-Shing founded Yellow Earth Theatre Company in the UK in 1996 to raise the profile of British East Asian theatre practitioners. While in the US David Henry Hwang's work has made a significant contribution to audiences' awareness of the residual discrimination against Chinese Americans in the theatre (and society).

In the US the latter part of the twentieth century was dominated by **August Wilson**, who died in 2005 leaving as his legacy a cycle of ten plays depicting the experience of black people in America. John Lahr describes the plays as 'a sort of feverchart of the trauma of slavery'.

The descendant of slaves himself, Wilson was born in Pittsburgh in 1945. His white father was largely absent, a frightening, violent figure in early childhood; but his mother finally left his father when Wilson was five and married the man Wilson considered his real father. He was a black community leader, a kind and inspiring man. Wilson only discovered after his death that he had served a twenty-year prison sentence for theft.

Wilson had a disastrous school career and effectively left formal education at the age of sixteen. He began writing poetry at the age of twenty, and in 1968 he co-founded a black arts theatre in Pittsburgh, dedicated to propose 'a separate symbolism, mythology, critique and iconography' for black people. In order not to jeopardize the authenticity of his voice, he chose not to read or watch any classical or contemporary plays.[19] His influences instead were painting, poetry, and above all 'the Blues' ability to transmute suffering into affirmation, seemingly random events into form, the carrier of a culture.'[20]

His early plays were heavily poetic. By his own account, Wilson didn't know how to write dialogue. When he asked his friend Rob Penny, co-founder of the Black Horizons theatre, how to make characters talk, Penny replied: 'You don't. You listen.' Later Wilson described waiting for a voice or an image to come to him as a starting point: seeing Troy Maxon, for instance, the hero of his third play *Fences*, 'standing out on this brilliant starry night with this baby in his arms, talking to this woman. I didn't know who the woman was'.

The first draft of that play was four and a half hours long, and by some accounts unstageable. Lloyd Richards, who had directed Lorraine Hansbury's *A Raisin in the Sun* on Broadway in 1959, helped Wilson reduce *Fences* by an hour and a half, transforming it into a resonant Pulitzer and Tony award-winning play.

Together they worked out an enviable methodology, whereby each new play would go through two or three development phases, each time being further rewritten, and ending up on Broadway. Wilson wrote with a driven intensity all of his life, and died at the age of sixty, between the premiere and the Broadway opening of his final play, *Radio Golf*. He told John Lahr that writing 'is for me like walking down the landscape of the self … you find false trails, roads closed for repairs, impregnable fortresses, scouts, armies of memory, and impossible cartography'.

---

[19] As a poet Wilson regretted having read so widely that he was inhibited in finding his own poetic voice.

[20] Christopher Bigsby (ed.), *The Cambridge Companion to August Wilson* (Cambridge: Cambridge University Press, 2007), p. 11.

Women's theatre

In the UK during this period, women made sure their voices were heard. Sarah Daniels caused palpitations among conservative-minded audiences with her uncompromisingly feminist, lesbian (*Neaptide*), anti-pornography (*Masterpieces*) plays, while *The Madness of Esme and Shaz* in 1994 attracted some breathtakingly chauvinistic reviews from uncomprehending male critics, even though the play was so popular with audiences its run was extended.[21] Pam Gems put women centre stage at the National Theatre and elsewhere with high-profile plays including *Queen Christina, Piaf* and *Camille*. (Dominic Dromgoole dubbed her affectionately 'the greatest living provider of turns for star actors', meaning of course star turns for female actors – still a rarity.)

Bryony Lavery collaborated with many of the women's and gay theatre companies of the time, producing witty, off-beam plays ranging from *Calamity*, a spoof about the Wild West, to *Her Aching Heart*, a lesbian pastiche of romantic fiction. Her reputation was secured by her award-winning 1998 play *Frozen*, about the interconnecting lives over the years of a serial killer, the mother of one of his victims and a psychiatrist, and their gradual process of becoming unfrozen.

The fruit of this widening of opportunity for women, bolstered by the appointment of Max Stafford-Clark as artistic director of the Royal Court from 1979 to 1993, was a cluster of great plays in the late 1980s. These include Sharman Macdonald's *When I Was a Girl I Used to Scream and Shout*, Charlotte Keatley's *My Mother Said I Never Should*, Anne Devlin's *Ourselves Alone*, Winsome Pinnock's *Leave Taking*, April De Angelis's *Ironmistress*, Timberlake Wertenbaker's *Our Country's Good* and Clare McIntyre's *Low Level Panic* – all produced between 1984 and 1989.

Avant-garde, experimental, alternative, performance and live art

The late 1980s and early 1990s saw a flowering of experimental, avant-garde work which was not particularly interested in 'new writing' or employing

[21] David Benedict, *The Independent*, 2 March 1994.

playwrights, but skirted the borders of live art, a hybrid form encompassing theatre experiment, performance art and the avant-garde.

Mark Ravenhill reflected later that there was a period when nobody was interested unless you had an acrobat and a couple of clowns in your play, but the influence can't be ignored: Impact, Station House Opera, IOU, Forced Entertainment, Welfare State, Insomniac, the People Show and Stan's Café were taking theatre on new formal adventures. Tim Etchells, David Gale, Deborah Levy and Claire Macdonald were the writers happy to engage in these new forms, while Abi Morgan worked with Frantic Assembly (*Tiny Dynamite*) and Lloyd Newson's company DV8 have consistently worked with text. The London International Festival of Theatre (LIFT) and Artangel brought international work to the UK (including the Wooster Group and Robert Wilson). The effect has been to widen our sense of what is possible on stage, giving audiences a taste for work which is visually stunning, non-naturalistic, playful with narrative.

In 1991 the French-Canadian theatre maker Robert Lepage brought his seven-hour epic, *The Dragons' Trilogy*, to London. The production had already earned cult status abroad for its mesmerically beautiful, multilingual theatrical storytelling. The interlinking stories played out like a dream, as Chinese paper dragons festooned the stage, shoe-boxes became shops and streets, Japanese screens concealed secrets and shadows.

Lepage's methodology was unusual: the piece began with six actors (including Lepage himself), two set designers and a producer, without a script. They pooled their collective memories and imaginations and found ways to express them theatrically. Lepage's work developed to integrate what was then radical and cutting-edge technology into his stagecraft: screens, projections, computers – all the innovations which have entered the mainstream now.

This was a time of formal experiment and a striving for new approaches to break down the formality of the roles of playwright and director, to develop a more collaborative, workshop-based practice and to incorporate devising work into a finished text. Writers including Carl Grose (who worked with Kneehigh) and the sometimes provocative Tim Crouch (*The Author, England*) came out of this devising practice. The Young Vic Studio under Sue Emmas and Battersea Arts Centre under Tom Morris became homes of these new types of work, and a plethora of new companies sprang up, including Kneehigh, Improbable, Told By An Idiot and Rufus Norris's Wink Theatre.

The fact that Norris is the first director of the National Theatre without either an Oxbridge degree or an acting background has been welcomed by the theatre community. His background is solidly in theatre-making, and his first company, Wink, was highly collaborative in nature. Wink used a devising process which put aesthetics at its heart. Director Norris, designer Katrina Lindsay and lighting designer Natasha Chivers were all integral to the work from its inception, and worked with a writer and a company of actors to produce resonant, visually inventive work. *The Art of Random Whistling* in 1996 presented a gritty tale of a missing child on a South London estate, but brought beauty out of dereliction and was not afraid to be emotional and poetic.

The 1990s

In 1993 23-year-old Bristol drama graduate **Sarah Kane** began an MA in playwriting on David Edgar's Birmingham course. During that year Kane produced the play *Blasted*, which was to become both notorious and celebrated. She was writing in the comfort of suburban Birmingham at a time when the war in Bosnia was at its most horrifying. Images were being broadcast of ordinary-looking European men in tracksuits and jeans breaking into their neighbours' homes with Kalashnikovs, and reports also showed the victims – thousands of ordinary citizens massacred, raped and held in concentration camps.

The play premiered at the Royal Court Upstairs on 12 January 1995. The mainstream critics were horrified by the violence and nihilism they perceived in the writing. The normally measured *Guardian* critic Michael Billington wrote:

> Far from crying, like the man in front of me: 'Bring back the censor', I was simply left wondering how such naive tosh managed to scrape past the Court's normally judicious play-selection committee … the reason that the play falls apart is that there is no sense of external reality – who exactly is meant to be fighting whom out on the streets? … it is so full of horrors that we are reduced to bombed out indifference.[22]

[22] *The Guardian*, 20 January 1995.

The *Daily Mail*'s Jack Tinker declared himself 'utterly disgusted by a play which appears to know no bounds of decency yet has no message to convey by way of excuse ... [*Blasted* is] utterly without artistic merit'.

Billington later recanted and regretted his 'dismissive tone', but in the furore that followed eminent writers including Pinter and Churchill came swiftly to Kane's defence. Kane – and *Blasted* – became a cause célèbre. She was a trailblazer, and part of a generation of writers working with a similar sensibility (Joe Penhall, Dennis Kelly, Anthony Nielson, Martin McDonagh), which the academic Aleks Sierz dubbed 'In Yer Face' theatre. The old ideals of socialism, equality and political correctness seemed sullied, ineffectual and outmoded, now representative of the old guard and needing to be overturned. As Robbie says in Mark Ravenhill's *Shopping and Fucking*:

> And I think a long time ago there were big stories. Stories so big you could live your whole life in them. The Powerful Hands of the Gods and Fate. The Journey to Enlightenment. The March of Socialism. But they all died or the world grew up or grew senile or forgot them, so now we're all making up our own stories. Little stories. But we've each got one.[23]

Sarah Kane continued to write challenging and formally groundbreaking plays, working closely with Vicky Featherstone, then artistic director at Paines Plough. Kane's fame was such, and her instinctive bullshit detector so strong, that she submitted a new play (*Crave*) under a false name to make sure she was not getting her work waved through merely because of who she was. (She wasn't – *Crave* was immediately recognized and lauded.) Her devastating insights into human suffering combined with her brutal yet lyrical expression and instinct for dramatic form ensured her continuing success; but tragically that was not enough to keep her own demons at bay, and she committed suicide in 1999.

Simultaneously, other quieter but no-less-important writing was also happening at new writing venues around the country. At the Bush Theatre, writers of exquisite naturalism were thriving, among them Billy Roche (his

[23] Mark Ravenhill, *Shopping and Fucking* (London: Methuen Drama, 1996), p. 63.

Wexford Trilogy was first produced at the Bush) and other writers including Catherine Johnson, Sebastian Barry, Jonathan Harvey, Helen Edmundson, Lucinda Coxon, Simon Bent, Naomi Wallace, David Harrower, David Eldridge, Amelia Bullmore, Samuel Adamson and Conor McPherson.

Verbatim

Nicolas Kent, artistic director of the Tricycle Theatre, established a reputation for staging 'tribunal plays', beginning with *Half the Picture* by Richard Norton-Taylor and John McGrath, about the arms to Iraq scandal. After the murder of the black South London teenager Stephen Lawrence, and public outrage at the police's handling of the case, Kent felt compelled to take action. He collaborated with the *Guardian* journalist Norton-Taylor to edit and condense hours of testimony which had been given to the Macpherson Inquiry. TV cameras were not allowed into the proceedings, but Kent's theatre production recreated the hearing word for word. Despite their best intentions, officers and suspects alike revealed themselves, and their real attitudes, even while attempting to conceal themselves.

A month before Sir William Macpherson was due to deliver his report, in January 1999 *The Colour of Justice* had been running for two weeks, and the box office was overwhelmed by the response. The play transferred to the West End and won numerous awards.

Theatre's place as a form of public debate, education and engagement with society had been restored, and the plays sparked a wider passion for verbatim theatre.

In 2002 playwright Alecky Blythe was prevented from reaching her Hackney flat by a police cordon. An armed man had barricaded himself into his flat with a hostage. The ensuing siege lasted for fifteen days, during which Blythe recorded the reactions and conversations of the bystanders, editing her recordings into a script, *Come Down Eli*. The startling innovation she employed when staging the play (a technique pioneered by Mark Wing Davey) was to play the audio of the real voice to the actor as they performed on stage, so that they could reproduce the words exactly as they were originally spoken.

Blythe continued to adapt this verbatim approach with other plays, adding a new and dazzling innovation with *London Road*. Having interviewed the residents of the streets in Ipswich where five women were murdered in 2006, she then collaborated with Adam Cork to set their words to music. The resulting production was a groundbreaking success.

As a result of these developments, there has been a proliferation of verbatim theatre. James Graham's 2013 play *Privacy* was fashioned from interviews with journalists, politicians and analysts about how our personal data is digitally collected; Nadia Fall's *Home* interviewed the residents and workers in a Hackney hostel for homeless young people. Truth has proved itself to be not just stranger than fiction, but box office gold for the theatres producing it.[24]

Faction

'You can also argue that interview-based, verbatim drama represents a kind of abdication of the political writer's previous mission – not just to present, but to explain',[25] wrote David Edgar in 2010. He advocates presenting the facts in a fictional form with the benefit of the organizing principle of an author's moral viewpoint. He points to a hybrid form which he terms 'faction', which includes Edgar's own plays, including *The Shape of the Table* and *The Prisoner's Dilemma*, and he includes Laura Wade's *Posh* as another example.

The genre has flourished, and not just in the theatre: TV and film are equally enthralled by reality in drama, for example by Peter Morgan's play *The Deal*, a fictionalized account of a meeting between Tony Blair and Gordon Brown which arguably was partly responsible for Brown's huge popularity before he became prime minister.

Postdramatic theatre

The term *postdramatic theatre* derives from Hans-Thies Lehmann's book *Postdramatic Theatre*, published in Germany in 1999 and translated into

[24] See also Dennis Kelly's ingenious spoof verbatim play, *Taking Care of Baby*, which beautifully illustrates all the moral pitfalls of the form.

[25] *The Guardian*, 21 July 2010.

English in 2006. In it he questions theatre's representation of the external world, and its structuring of time. Once theatre is freed from the constraints of character and plot, the stage, as David Barnett describes it, 'becomes a generator of shared experience rather than knowledge, and spectators are confronted with the question of how they deal with such phenomenon'.[26]

Effectively, all of Aristotle's supposed unities – time, place and action – as well as character are under scrutiny. The Austrian playwright Peter Handke's *Offending the Audience* (1966) featured four unnamed speakers who tease the audience with talk of what the performance might be. Martin Crimp's 1997 *Attempts on her Life* offers seventeen scenes in which somebody – it's not specified who – talks about the central character, who never appears, offering contradictory versions of who and what she is (or was). In a similar way, Kane's *4:48 Psychosis* eschews named characters for a number of voices speaking to the audience. Tim Etchells works almost exclusively with his own company, Forced Entertainment, producing fascinating performances which may be durational, promenade, dialogue free; and whose characters may carry placards to tell us who they are.

Site-specific, immersive and durational

Site-specific theatre has been happening in the experimental fringes of theatre since the 1960s. But the current more mainstream desire for theatre to be anywhere but in a theatre was arguably kicked off in 1995, with Deborah Warner's *St Pancras Project* and Robert Wilson and Hans Peter Kuhn's *HG* in the Clink Vaults. Site-specific, durational and immersive theatre (some bundle them together to market them as 'event theatre') are now all the rage. Dreamthinkspeak create site-responsive works which integrate installation, live performance and film. Punchdrunk have founded their reputation on immersive theatrical experiences based on classic texts or films and performed in empty buildings, and there are many other companies taking audiences on similar adventures. Non-building-based companies such as the National theatres of Wales and of Scotland – which make a virtue of

[26] Drama Online: http://www.dramaonlinelibrary.com/genres/post-dramatic-theatre-iid-2516 (accessed: 5 September 2014).

necessity in commandeering non-conventional spaces for their work, have also encouraged this popular tendency. (See also *Reflections on Space*.)

The role of the audience is a key area of experimentation for contemporary theatre-makers, and the influence of gaming is clear to see in the work of companies including Blast Theory. The use of apps, voice recordings, texts and tweets to guide audiences, or to influence the outcome of the performance, is all part of a hunger among practitioners to borrow from and respond to the digital age.

Contemporary

Theatre at the moment is experiencing a golden age of playwriting, which proves the relevance of theatre in our time. Among the writers whose work is finding resonance with audiences are all those mentioned or featured in this book – plus, of course, many others. Their preoccupations include technology, ecology and economics, and they are testing the versatility of dramatic forms to comment on them. Politics is again unashamedly resurgent in contemporary plays, while a new generation of women writers is considered on equal terms with male contemporaries. Writers of all ethnicities, sexualities and cultural heritages are starting to get the audiences and the exposure they should. There is a pleasing cross-pollination of talent passing both ways across the Atlantic.

Even though we are seeing a rebalancing of the number of women playwrights being produced in the UK and the US, the question has to be asked why so few women have managed to break through until so recently; and why have the ones who broke through in earlier times so often been neglected and left unperformed?

Victoria Benedictsson and Shelagh Delaney both had a hit, and were then viciously panned by influential critics, which stopped them writing for the theatre. In a culture which doesn't want women to succeed and tells women they are inferior, it's hard for writers (already an insecure breed) not to believe the criticism. Jeanette Winterson writing about Delaney observes: 'She can't be one of the boys. Harold Pinter and Peter Hall could go out drinking with Kenneth Tynan – the most influential theatre critic in the world in the 50s and

60s. Sam Beckett befriended Pinter …. Joan Littlewood … did her best to help, but she couldn't give Shelagh what gender and class made impossible: a community of equals'.[27]

Again and again we see writers who are about to founder, but who are saved by attracting the attention of powerful supporters: Chekhov had Stanislavski, August Wilson had Lloyd Richards, Tennessee Williams had Elia Kazan. The gatekeepers and those with influence need to be as diverse as the writers, so that many 'communities of equals' can be established.

What then does history tell us about what it takes for playwrights of all genders, ethnicities and sexualities to flourish? Talent, supported by confidence to believe in your own work. Formal inventiveness, and the good fortune to be telling the stories that audiences and theatre managers want to hear. But above all else, supporters and collaborators who are loyal and influential, who want to hear your stories and stage your plays.

[27] Programme for Royal National Theatre production of *A Taste of Honey*, 2014.

Reflections on source

Clare Bayley

The original play

Theatre is where you can be experimental, political, uncommercial. This is a freedom you won't have in film, TV or radio, where you have to watch what you say – no swearing on the radio, nothing to frighten the ratings on TV or alarm the producers in film. Make the most of that freedom.

If you close your eyes, and sit in a dark theatre, what would you most like to watch when you open your eyes? If you can dream up your play – something of what it looks like, or sounds like, an atmosphere or tone that you want to capture, that can be a useful way to begin.

What is your play about? Sometimes you won't know fully until you've completed it; sometimes you discover what a play's really about when you're in the rehearsal room and you overhear the director or the actors talking about it in a way you hadn't foreseen. But in order to start you do need to have an idea.

Every writer is different. You might start with a central dilemma for your character to solve; or it might be that you know your character before you understand what their story is. Pirandello is strongly in this camp:

> A play doesn't create people, people create a play. So first of all one must have people – free, living, active people. With them and through them the idea of the play will be born. [1]

You might instead start with a snatch of dialogue, a visual image, a place, a theme, an injustice or a mystery. By the end of the process, you will have to realize all of these things. But first things first…

---

[1] 'Spoken action', tr. Fabrizio Melano in Bentley, E. (ed.), *The Theory of the Modern Stage* (London: Penguin, 1968), p. 155.

You also have to consider that whatever you write will have to be performed with real performers and a live audience. Actors have human rights too, so consider what you're putting them through. And there are practicalities to address. While directors and designers enjoy a challenge, if you show no thought whatsoever for how your vision could be achieved theatrically, you may lose respect from your colleagues. In *Epsom Downs*, for example, Howard Brenton, with characteristic chutzpah, specifies in the stage directions:

> The Downs, still. Primrose sunbathing. Above, the kite flutters. Superintendent Blue and Charles Pearce appear on the skyline, on horseback.

But he then helpfully elucidates: 'The horses are played by naked actors.'

The moment of beginning an original stage play is a moment of extreme freedom. An important question to ask yourself before you start is: why do you want to write it? And why now? These are the questions commissioners always want a play to answer. You may reasonably feel that you won't know why or why now until you've written the play. But it is essential to consider the question. And while you're about it, think about other plays on a similar theme or subject that already exist. If you're planning to write a play about the rivalry between young Mozart and the older composer Salieri, for example, you'd better be very sure that your take on the subject offers something that Peter Shaffer's *Amadeus* doesn't.

The 'why now' question doesn't mean that all plays have to be about the state of the nation or confront a hot topic from current affairs. But theatre is a public art form, and it works best when it succeeds in reflecting our world back to us, with new insights. This can be achieved by the most intimate or specific type of drama, so long as it resonates with audiences, not just with you and your mates. Theatre is a metaphorical medium. The world of the play stands in for the real world, and you don't have to set your play now to write about now. This is why there are so many plays in which play-making is the main action – from Timberlake Wertenbaker's *Our Country's Good* to Anne Washburn's *Mr Burns*.

Where do you get your ideas from?

Freedom can be the most inhibiting thing, creatively. The blank page, the permission to write about whatever and however you desire is enough to stop you ever starting. Willem de Kooning apparently overcame this problem by taking a wide brush loaded up with paint and scrawling an obscenity on the canvas, just to get himself started.

You need to devise your own method to trick your unconscious mind into revealing its plans to you. David Hare has said the beginning of his seminal play *Plenty* was the image of a woman sitting in an overcoat on a packing case, rolling herself a cigarette, with her husband lying naked at her feet.[2] Others start with a dramatic scenario, a 'what if' question which plays out through the course of the play (for example, what if Prince Charles came to the throne and decided that he wanted to have a say in how things are run, as in Mike Bartlett's *King Charles III*).

There is no foolproof way of getting to the starting point of a play. But you do know when you are there – it's when you suddenly wake up in the night or drop your fork in the middle of lunch and realize that you know what you're going to write about, and how. It's when you can no longer stop yourself from writing – on scraps of paper or in your notebook, little sequences of dialogue or whole pages, unbidden.

In Part 3 of this book there are sections on all the things you need to get to grips with – character, dialogue, plot, action, image and symbol, time, place and situation. But the only way to get there is to start. And once you have started, carry on. And keep carrying on. Even when this play that you are writing is the very last thing in the world that you ever want to see, or think about, or work on – don't stop until you get to the end of your first draft. And then, however ragged it is, it exists. That's not the end, of course, there's a lot of hard graft ahead. You may have written out the story, but not yet found the structure. What you think was one character's play may turn out to be better served from another character's point of view. There is certainly a lot of cutting and redrafting ahead. But don't think about that yet. As the novelist Colm Toibin said:

---

[2] David Hare, *Plays One*, Introduction (London: Faber and Faber, 1996).

Finish everything you start. Often, you don't know where you're going for a while; then halfway though, something comes and you know. If you abandon things, you never find that out.[3]

Adaptations

When adapting another piece of writing, whether it's a novel, a short story or a film – much of this difficult work has already been done for you. The characters exist, the plot has been worked out. But don't be fooled. Is the plot one that will work on stage? Do the settings translate theatrically? How do you convey the voice and tone of the novel? For example, DBC Pierre's *Vernon God Little* is written in the first person from the point of view of a hapless teenage boy, which is challenging to convey on stage, as Tanya Ronder explains:

> We are in Vernon's head on the page, with him every step of the way, so the appalling horror and loss which underpins it all is never far from us. Trying to reduce the to-audience stuff (another note to self) but upping the emotional stakes was the key challenge.[4]

When adapting work, you have to be loyal to the original, but not slavishly faithful. To fully honour the work, you may have to do things which initially seem disrespectful: lose or conflate characters, rearrange plots, swap locations, rationalize events.

As for dialogue – don't be deceived by what you have in the original. Novelists aren't well known for their skills in this department, and even when they are, the dialogue in a novel serves a different function to that in a script. Even if there are some sections of dialogue that can be kept from the original, there will certainly be much more that you will have to write, since your dialogue will be replacing pages of prose, and there will be scenes in your play which don't exist in the original.

---

[3] *The Guardian*, 20 February 2013.

[4] http://nickhernbooksblog.com/tag/tanya-ronder/ (accessed: 31 July 2014).

One of the challenges facing the playwright adapting a novel is the discrepancy between the length of the novel (often 500 pages or more) and the length of a stage play (three hours is already a long evening in the theatre). David Edgar, an early exponent, set a new high watermark with his eight and a half hour epic adaptation of *Nicholas Nickelby* for the RSC in 1980. It had a cast of thirty-nine playing 132 characters and played in two parts over two nights, with both parts playing together at weekends. Later versions whittled it down to more manageable lengths, but the full-length version was such a hit for the RSC on both sides of the Atlantic that it led to Ken Campbell's wonderful prank press release, declaring that the company would thereafter be renamed the Royal Dickens Company.

A decade later Polly Teale and Helen Edmundson, working with Shared Experience, perfected this highly theatrical type of adaptation for ensemble companies, though on a smaller scale, from Tolstoy's *Anna Karenina* and *War and Peace* to Charlotte Brontë's *Jane Eyre* and Jamila Gavin's 2005 *Coram Boy* for the National Theatre. (Edmundson was the first living female playwright to be produced on the Olivier stage, even before Rebecca Lenkiewicz with her original play, *Her Naked Skin*.)

'I begin by trying… to identify the theme which I would like to focus on', Edmundson writes.

> This doesn't mean that the other ideas within the novel are lost or that I am reducing it completely, but it gives me a through-line, a touchstone for the way I will tell the story… It is also essential that my chosen central theme has dramatic potential – in other words it needs to have some tension or conflict within it…. I then try to find a dramatic, theatrical way of expressing it, and when I feel I have found that, I begin to write.[5]

With *The Mill on the Floss*, a Victorian epic spanning its central character Maggie's life from early childhood to her death, Edmundson decided that

[5] Shared Experience education pack for *The Mill on the Floss*. http://www.sharedexperience.org.uk/media/education/mill-on-the-floss_edpack.pdf.

the central theme of her play would be 'a woman being forced to change her behaviour, because her true nature is at odds with what society expects of a woman'. To express this inner conflict, she represented Maggie with a different actor for each stage of Maggie's life. This way her adaptation for an ensemble of eight portraying fifteen different characters was able to clearly demarcate the phases of Maggie's life.

It may not be a novel or a story you are being asked to adapt, but a film (David Eldridge memorably adapted Thomas Vinterberg's Dogma film, *Festen*; and Roberto Aguirre-Sacasa and Duncan Sheile transformed Bret Easton Ellis's *American Psycho* into a musical stage version, for example). With a great deal of luck you may even, like Tom Stoppard, be asked to adapt your own hit screenplay (*Shakespeare in Love*) into a stage version.

Conversely, some adaptations end up attracting more attention than their original progenitor did. Michael Morpurgo's story *War Horse* was not his most famous children's book until Tom Morris and Marianne Elliot adapted it for the stage, using Handspring puppets to portray the horses; £11 million and counting later, plus a Stephen Spielberg movie of the same name, and Morpurgo's story is cemented into the cultural consciousness.[6] Rather than feeling apologetic about adapting another writer's work, consider Walter Benjamin's description of translation as 'rescuing a text'. You will be giving the original a new lease of life, often for a new generation.

Translations and versions

Fortunately, you don't have to be a fluent Norwegian or Russian scholar in order to translate Ibsen or Chekhov, although some of the most celebrated theatrical translators are also linguists (Michael Frayn, for example, Gregory Motton and Christopher Hampton). Writing to defend his version of

[6] *War Horse* cost the National Theatre £50,000 in development and £500,000 to produce, and made the theatre £11 million (according to Nicholas Hytner in an interview in *The Daily Telegraph*, 24 April 2013), of which £7.5 million of these profits have been reinvested into NT Future.

Chekhov's *Cherry Orchard* for Katie Mitchell, Simon Stephens wrote in the *Guardian*:

> It seems especially odd to suggest that a play text, out of any literary form, should be carved out of an attempt to accurately translate the original language of an author writing a century ago. Playwriting, for me, is not a literary or linguistic pursuit and plays are not literary artefacts. I think of them instead as being starting points for a night in the theatre.[7]

Stephens wrote his version with the help of a literal translation, which is the usual method for dramatic translations. Written by native speakers or academics, their job is to convey the precise meaning of the words, with all their connotations, cultural references and double meanings. If a character takes his or her leave of someone else, the literal translation must indicate whether it is a casual 'see you later' or a formal 'good bye'. Is it final, 'adieu', or provisional, 'until we meet again', an archaic 'fare-thee-well' or a contemporary 'laters'? The formulation may be unique to the culture of the playwright, or imply the relative social status of the protagonists. Once you understand the implications in the original writer's choice of word, you can set about choosing your own equivalent.

Translations can be more faithful to the original by allowing them a resonance with the culture and society they are going to be translated into – as Steiner said, translation is 'not a science but an exact art'.[8] In the same way that a good adapter has to take liberties with the original text, translators have to allow themselves a freedom to deviate from what is a literal equivalent. For example, working on Victoria Benedictsson's *The Enchantment* for the National Theatre, I was struck by the timeless quality of the friendship between the two women, Louise and Erna. As the play opens they are drinking tea and enjoying some kind of pastry. I changed it to biscuits – completely inauthentic for two Swedes in late nineteenth-century Paris – because I thought that

[7] http://www.theguardian.com/stage/2014/oct/16/the-cherry-orchard-chekhov-simon-stephens-katie-mitchell (accessed: 20 November 2014).

[8] George Steiner, quoted in *Theory & Practise of Translation* (Department of Italian, Trinity College Dublin), www.tcd.ie/Itlaian/0111.COC.TPT.html (accessed: 15 January 2015).

audiences would immediately recognize the nature of the moment, and the friendship, once tea and biscuits were involved.

Brian Friel's translations of Chekhov retain the samovars and the birch trees of Russia, but find powerful echoes with rural Ireland through the use of language and idiom. His translation of *Three Sisters* for Field Day in 1981 keeps closely to Chekhov's original, but allows the audience to see the yearning that the sisters have for urban Moscow as a parallel for the feeling of exile experienced by an Anglo-Irish family in Northern Ireland. Friel reputedly referred to six existing English translations of the play when working on his own version. [9]

Another Irish writer, Thomas Kilroy, took a bolder approach to translating Chekhov with his 1981 version of *The Seagull*, which substituted rural Russia for the west of Ireland at the time of the Irish National Land League. Similar acts of cultural appropriation were also cleverly performed by translators such as Ranjit Bolt, who successfully transposed *Cyrano de Bergerac* to 1930s India and *The Marriage of Figaro* to eighteenth-century India for Tara Arts. Bolt's work shed new light on old texts, gave opportunities for Asian actors to get their hands on classical roles, and allowed audiences to engage with cultures which until then were rarely seen on main stages.

More recently, Roy Williams has written a new version of Sophocles' *Antigone*, which switches Ancient Greece for contemporary Britain. King Creon, aka Creo, is now a gang leader; his assertion of his own power and authority, his tendency to enforce his will through violence, his obsession with his family's reputation and with revenge all fit perfectly with the original.

There is also a need for acts of rediscovery as much as reinvention. The foreign language plays which have made it into the canon are a fraction of the plays which might be performed in English. Tanya Ronder has made a name for herself producing English versions of lesser known foreign texts, including Pirandello's *Liola*, Ionesco's *Macbett*, De Fillippo's *Filumena* and Lope de Vega's *Peribanez*.

[9] His version was much acclaimed, and in 1990 Dublin's Gate Theatre mounted a new production starring all three Cusack sisters, Sorcha, Sinead and Niamh, alongside their father Cyril.

Verbatim, documentary and faction

There's a great thirst for 'reality', or versions of it, for entertainment in our culture. It started as a way to talk about serious or difficult issues, from the tribunal plays at the Tricycle, to plays about suspicious deaths of young recruits at an army barracks (Phillip Ralph's *Deep Cut*) or the radicalization of young people who commit terrorist acts (Robin Soans' *Talking to Terrorists*). But increasingly more domestic or personal issues are being addressed using interviews, testimony, vox pop, transcripts and formal documentation as the basis for the script. As I write (in 2014) there are verbatim plays being performed about gender identity, alcoholism, trams, poverty and debt, victims of the Bradford City fire, human rights issues and the Sochi Winter Olympics, everyday sexism experienced by women, homelessness, young people and coming out stories – all these at the Edinburgh Fringe Festival alone.

Max Stafford-Clark has called verbatim 'the last great pulse in theatre' (*The Guardian*). It's unlikely to be the last of anything, but it is a vibrant pulse, which documents real, lived experience and reaction to events of national or international importance. Some may argue that since theatre is an empathic medium you don't need it to be 'real' to get the insight. At worst, verbatim can seem like a lazy cobbling together of random voices on a subject. But at its best, verbatim can shed light on a culture and a time in a new and revealing way.

In any case, the 'reality' or 'verbatim' we are showing is never unmediated; it's always a carefully edited and crafted piece of work bearing the imprimatur of the playwright. As it must: a verbatim work has to observe the basic requirements of any other play. It's just as artful a form as fictional writing – even if the basic material appears to be wholly authentic. Increasingly, writers are experimenting with combinations of fictionalized elements and fact-based material.

There are two main approaches to verbatim plays based on interviews: in the first the subjects are interviewed and recorded, the recordings are transcribed verbatim and edited into a script which the actors learn. The other, pioneered by Alecky Blythe, is that the actors hear the actual voices of the people they are portraying via a live feed in their ear as they are performing; their performances mimic as accurately as possible the manner of speaking, as well as the words.

Given the journalistic nature of the enterprise, certain skills need to be brought to bear to obtain the material:

- If you're using people's real names, you must have their permission to use their words, and you must spell their names correctly. It's a small thing, but important (and easy to get wrong).
- When interviewing, you must be scrupulous about recording accurately, which you can't do without a good recording device. It's advisable to make extensive notes as well, as a backup – though if the device doesn't work, you will have to go back and redo the interview.
- It's good practice to transcribe the recording soon after the interview, while it's fresh in your memory, in case there are parts which are hard to hear.
- When you're working on the script you can edit what the interviewees say, but you cannot paraphrase and you cannot alter or adapt their words to fit your agenda. You're not a hack journalist, after all.
- Nor should you use that old journalist's trick of getting a quote by asking the leading question (You want Mrs X to say, 'That man is a monster who should be locked up for life,' by asking sweetly, 'Do you think that this man is a monster who should be locked up for life, Mrs X?')

The great pleasure of verbatim theatre lies in the surprising and unexpected things people say, the unique and eloquent way they say them. You will destroy that if you wade in with your own agenda.

When transcribing your recordings, pay attention to the throat clearings, the sips of water, the moments when people speak very quietly, or very loudly. These not only add colour to the text, but also reveal truths. It's amazing how often people will drop their voice, swallow before they speak, or unexpectedly ask for a cup of tea when they are saying something that isn't quite true. This also provides a masterclass in writing authentic-sounding fictional dialogue.

When you've written your play, you need to consider whether you are going to show it to the interested parties, to make sure they are happy with what you've written (and don't become litigious). Journalists are always reluctant to give their subjects the right to edit, because people tend to want to change what they've said, to make themselves look better, or to back down from offending somebody. In strictly journalistic terms, once they've said it to you, and provided you can prove that (hence the importance of the recording), it's too late. But depending on the type of play you're writing, it may be counterproductive to upset your subjects, and thus politic to bring them into the process at this point. Before you show them anything, it's wise to have somebody (possibly a lawyer) read it for you, to spot any potential trouble. If you decide to show it to your subjects, make sure you are clear about the terms on which you're prepared to change things. If they think it's a free-for-all, you will have your work cut out for you.

Devising

Devised theatre has produced some of the most memorable and compelling theatrical experiences – from Mike Leigh to Complicité, Lumière & Son, Shared Experience, Forced Entertainment – even *War Horse* began from a devising process. There are many pleasures to be found in devising new work – but many pitfalls for a writer as well. By definition each writer and company will make up their own rules and conventions about their process. But looking at some of the ways people have worked in the past can give you a clue about to go about it – what to expect, and what to ask for.

When many imaginations and intellects are brought to bear on a subject, the result is almost bound to be richer than it otherwise would be. The fact of tapping into a greater breadth of experience and a larger set of skills can be hugely rewarding for a writer. It goes without saying that you have to go into the process with an open heart and an open mind, and that is only possible if everyone in the room is in a similar state of generosity. There's no place for defensiveness or rigidity – and only a little room for competitiveness, so long as it serves the joint enterprise.

Having a designer and director as well as actors in the process can be inspiring for the writer, as each collaborator can offer new solutions and practical possibilities which will stimulate untapped parts of your creative process.

Before you start you need to establish who – ultimately – controls the work that results. Sometimes the writer will be asked to go away at the end of the process and produce a script, over which they have artistic control, and which the company will then perform (this is broadly the Joint Stock method). Everyone in the room needs to be clear about this, and understand that their contribution is serving the script, and the writer has the ultimate say in shaping that.

It may, though, be that the director sees the whole process as a way of authoring their own new work, and that the writer, actors and designers are all equal, and all subordinate to his or her vision (this is roughly speaking the Mike Leigh approach). This is a perfectly reasonable way of working, provided it's clear from the start. But as the writer you need to understand the extent of your power, autonomy and responsibilities.

If the writer has initiated the devising process to work on a script, it can be useful to delegate the job of running the room to somebody else (usually the director) so that you can focus on watching and documenting the work going on. But that doesn't mean the writer relinquishes authority. If the balance starts to go awry, you may have to delicately intervene to redress it – it will be to everyone's benefit.

The question of authorship can be problematic, so to avoid bad feeling later on, it's important to clarify this before you start. If the writer is copying down the exact words of the actors as they improvise, and using them in the script, the actors will rightly feel a sense of ownership. Many plays have been written in this way, and as long as the contribution of all involved is properly acknowledged, nobody should feel exploited. If the writer has gone away to shape and structure the work and to decide on the characters' stories, then that contribution should be recognized. If the writer has been brought in to generate text which the director is then going to fashion without consulting the writer, you need to decide whether that's a role you are willing to accept. There are various formulas available, from a sole credit for the writer (Shared Experience always gives the writer sole credit), to 'devised by the company and scripted by the writer', or to Robert Lepage, who credits all the performers for the text, even though he is the auteur.

Reflections on writing by scale

Fraser Grace

Which is more useful – to base your thinking about a play on the scale of acting forces required, or on the scale of venue? The link between the two is not as simple as you might think. In this section we consider the following:

- The solo play
- The epic
- The small-scale play
- The main stage play

The solo play

The adventure of writing a play for just one actor has a lot to offer the playwright; like the short story, it is fearsomely difficult to excel with so spare and concentrated a form. Maintain dramatic urgency and compel a reader/audience's interest with a solo play, and you are clearly getting to grips with your craft. It's also a great place to practise developing a complex character – and an opportunity to gift an actor a great role.

For the actor it's a kind of high-wire act, with no safety net, while for audiences, a solo play offers an intimate and intriguing encounter.

Commercially, the advantages are equally sharp – many festival directors programme solo plays as a way of spreading funds across the maximum number of commissions. Solo plays are also ideal for a festival's shorter playing slots, since there's a limit to how long the intensity of a play with only one actor can be sustained.

Finally, the solo play is, as we'll see, the shoestring route to the epic; if you can't have a cast of thousands, but have a sweeping story to tell, the solo play might just be the solution.

Making the most of a little

As the Ancients knew, one actor does not have to equal one character; using one actor to double several roles allows the scope of any drama to be expanded in terms of historical reach, array of characters and multiplicity of perspectives. The only limits are the audience's toleration, or their ability to comprehend what's going on.

At the same time, one of the great draws of the solo play is the intensity it can generate. There is huge power in committing ourselves as writer and audience into the hands of one principal character for the duration of the play, following every nuance of their shifting fortunes.

These two objectives are easily reconciled, thanks to the power of a character in a solo play to mediate their world to us.

In fact in writing this kind of play, it's worth considering the job in terms of a (large) handful of activities that you will need to persuade your main character to attempt:

- winning over the audience
- mediating the world
- handling the meeting
- reporting events
- finding action
- revealing truth

Some of these activities apply only to the solo play, but others are considerations in writing any kind of play.

Winning over an audience

With a solo play, the excitement lies to a large extent in the fact that this is a direct encounter, one-on-one, between the audience on one side and a single actor on the other. The fourth wall between stage and auditorium – that invisible, protective shield sealing off the action from the audience – is almost always pierced in a solo play. Who else can the actor talk to, if not to us? What this fall-of-the-wall initiates is a face-to-face encounter – with all the intensity, delicacy of construction and risk of open conflict that any encounter between wary strangers implies. An actor, working through a character, must first win the indulgence of the audience by intriguing, charming and entertaining us, initiating a conversation and drawing us into the events of the drama. This does not mean the character has to be 'nice', or like us in any way – far from it. As long as they strike us as surprising and unique, any edginess, any hint of danger, even downright hostility towards us will prove equally gripping; they will have earned an audience with us, and we will be glad to spend time in their company.

This requires a character to become, however grudgingly, garrulous. If the character is not naturally talkative, the tongue must be loosened by some combination of driving motive, pressure of events, strong emotion, or by some instrumental means like getting the character drunk (a much-used device) or placing them in a format that leaves no option – a suicide note 'to camera', for instance.

'Why is this person talking to me?' is a good first question to ask of any character in a solo play.

Mediating the world

As noted above, in a solo play we meet the world of the play through the principal character. This means crucially that we will meet all other, secondary characters not objectively, but subjectively, coloured by our main character's attitude towards them. This is where much of the fun can be had in a solo play, as we are treated to the principal character's jaundiced take on those around them. Given this, it's not just the writer of a solo drama that needs to deliver a multiplicity of distinct and consistent voices, but also the character (and the actor). In a good solo piece, we meet a number of memorable characters, all with their own mode of expression, their own physicality, their own views on the world, their own place in it – and their own part in the drama. Victims, perpetrators, witnesses – we meet all the players in the drama through this one main character.

And it is not just the other characters in the drama that we are introduced to in this way, but all the realities of their world. Again, all is subjectively filtered through the central character's sensibility.

Handling the meeting

Viewed like this, the solo play is not only an encounter between actor and audience, but a meeting between the main character and the audience.

With this in mind, here are some useful questions to ask about this dramatic meeting:

- Who called the meeting? Is the main character relieved to meet us? Have they actively engineered the meeting, or have they been dreading it, dragged here by circumstance? What are those circumstances?
- What is at stake in this meeting? Are there consequences if the central character does not succeed in changing the course of events they are telling us about?
- Is the character hoping to get something specific out of the meeting with us? What pressure can they put on us to elicit this response? How does our empathy help their cause? Does it help them muster courage to act in a certain way, or is it forgiveness they are looking for? Or do they simply want someone, anyone (us) to know the truth as they see it, however much they are ignored in their own world?

Once we begin to get a sense of what is being demanded of us, the battle for our complicity in the drama now unfolding will have been joined.

Reporting events

The solo play's epic reach – that is, its ability to cast its gaze over a sweep of history and across multiple geographical locations – lies in its storytelling capability. Through the chief character, we not only meet other characters, we also learn about their shared or various worlds. In addition we are also filled in on *events* – what's been going on in the past, what is going on now but elsewhere, what may be about to happen here (or there) – all reported by the character before us.

This means that any solo play is almost bound to contain a lot of plot information, relating to several spheres of action, in addition to the sphere we are sharing with the storyteller – our meeting place. (For a useful exercise exploring a play's 'reach' across these spheres, see Part 3 'Onstage and Offstage Worlds'.)

Two points are worth making here. First, all this 'reporting' of information would be very, *very* dull if not coloured by the character's unique mode of expression and attitude – another reason we need to be enjoying the character's idiosyncratic 'take' on the world.

Second, it's important not to get carried away with all this storytelling. Drama is essentially about things happening before our eyes. The writer of the solo play has to ensure that everything that is described by this now-talkative principal character is somehow relevant and contingent on the present. Only when something is enacted, here and now, before us, does all the plot taking place in other spheres have its pay-off. A solo play, like any other, depends for its success on action we can see.

Finding action

The Greek word for 'drama' (*dran)* means 'to do'.

In order for a play to encompass the moment when something pivotal takes place, any play has to be set at the critical time. If a gang of street kids habitually gets money through various kinds of robbing, a play about them will focus on the time when the category of crime attempted goes up a notch, or when violence becomes unexpectedly involved, or on the occasion when they discover that the case they've stolen contains not a phone and a few credit cards but a nuclear button, or a human hand or a single ticket to the World Cup.

In a solo play too, we must meet a character at the critical moment. This may be the moment when our character's hope is finally dashed, or is sprung again after a long period of despair, or when our character is finally able to exact a terrible revenge, or when at last the truth dawns. The central character in a solo piece is, then, either a witness of remarkable events, or a victim of them or their instigator. A witness, if purely passive, untouched by the experience, is rarely dramatically satisfying. The event must have implications for *them*. Victimhood is not much better. The really exciting character is one who, through witnessing events, is compelled to act in a decisive way – however futile the act might turn out to be.

This shifts what we need to be observing on stage far beyond bits of business, or any activity the character might engage in while talking to us – e,g.

making a meal or sealing envelopes. In the best dramas, and the best solo plays especially, even the licking of envelopes carries some freight in terms of meaning. It contributes to and develops our understanding of what is happening, and in turn it makes other things happen – and thus becomes genuine action. In the theatre, we want to see people being made by the world or crushed by it, or better still, to see people push back and attempt to change the world around them. A solo play, like any other, succeeds best when we realize that the sealing of an envelope is actually destroying a civilization, or creating a family or marking the beginning of forgiveness.

Revealing truth

As we've seen, the main character in a solo play has a limited number of people to talk to. To be fair, they have access to more than we might initially think. There may be offstage characters to whom a character might shout. Or these 'others' might be addressed on the phone or via some other technological link. They might even include historical characters, like those that haunt Becket's character in *Krapp's Last Tape* – notably his former, younger, tape-making self, whose recorded voice Krapp is able to listen to, over and over, and sneer at. A character might also talk to themselves, or to the universe, as when Hamlet works his way towards a path of action via his soliloquies.

Failing all these – or in addition to them – a character in a solo play can talk directly to us, to the audience. There is often a confessional aspect to this, casting the audience in the kind of role naturalistically enjoyed by a therapist, a priest, a confidante – someone to whom the character can safely offload. Opening up to us is a kind of reporting, not of events pure and simple but of truths, a confession from the heart, a baring of the soul.

As ever for the dramatist, this presents opportunities, but also a vice that can seriously defuse the dramatic power of the encounter.

When a character in a regular play is honest about their thoughts and motives and feelings, it generally comes at the crux of the play. Pretence has been stripped away by the preceding drama and now the truth is laid bare. In a solo play too, it is likely to be the most private, most intimate of exchanges – after all there is no one in the room to hear it but us. Faced with this kind of intimacy any audience is likely to feel privileged (if perhaps a little terrified); for some reason of the character's own (which hopefully we will at some point understand), we are being admitted to an extraordinary level of confidence. But it is an inviolable rule of drama that what is revealed without cost is worthless. This is why revelation in a regular play occurs only after the operation of the drama. If someone spills the beans without sweat, we become suspicious; either we are being played for some ulterior motive, or these secrets are not, after all, so important. Worse, we are apt to decide the character is shallow, or stupid.

In sum, as with any other drama, secrets in a good solo play only surface under pressure. This may be the pressure of despair, desperation, fear, triumph, or some other strong emotion, created by events.

Now it's worth asking a further question or two:

- What makes the story a difficult one for my character to tell?
- As well as making it possible, how can I, the dramatist, make it costly?

External obstacles will do here: an airport announcement cutting in every thirty seconds, a telephone ringing at critical moments, a language barrier – these can make the revelation physically difficult to complete. But internal obstacles or inhibitions are better, since they take us deeper into our understanding of the character's fears and hopes.

Is it fear, or shame, or pride or distrust of others that makes the words stick in our character's throat?

What is going to make the journey to this disclosure a circuitous one, one that will fill the next forty minutes with anticipation and keep those minutes gripping?

It's worth noting here that, because of the confessional nature of the encounter, it's easy to assume that a character making such a revelation – particularly if they seem to be overcoming significant inhibitions to do so – is in fact telling us the truth. But just as in other plays, characters in solo plays often have ulterior motives, hidden agendas; they can tell lies and deceive. They can do this to other characters; they can also do it to us. The unreliable narrator is never more powerful than when we have been lulled into trusting and identifying with them – and in the solo play, that was secured in the first few moments.

Even if a character in a solo play deceives us at first, the deception must be revealed by the process of the play. What's more, the character will almost certainly believe their actions are justified, and will try to persuade us so. The character in a solo play usually has a contention to make – about their world, about the tragedy of their plight, about human nature – and this again lifts the play away from a mere descriptive account of past events. It puts the audience in the dock: something is demanded of us in the present; whose side are we on? If we were inside the world of the play, what would we be prepared to do about it?

Finally, the solo play, like any other play, can exploit the gap between what the character intends or is able to reveal, and the truth that is communicated by the play itself. The unreliable narrator is one game; the deluded or incompetent narrator is another. A once-great footballer who has finally been sacked by a non-league team for his drinking is full of bluster. But a play can undermine his protestations of confidence in the future through simple subtext or counterpointed action. This trick – of allowing us to 'read between the lines', to see more than the character can see or will admit to knowing – is one in which Alan Bennett's *Talking Heads* excels.

If the writer of a solo play has considered all the above, they will be well on the way to creating a powerful pocket drama. But one last thought: one attraction of the form is that a monologue is not so far distant from the first person narrative of a novel or short story. We are seeing the world through a character's eyes, described in their words. But a solo play is different from a novel or story in two ways. First, as noted above, in a genuine drama something of consequence must happen to the character *here*, in the present. Second, in drama, as with any other kind of fiction, events have no choice but to unfold as dictated by the writer. But just as vital to a play is the *illusion* that things in the present could easily go the other way; that fate might take a hand that has not been anticipated, or the character might simply make a different choice and the whole thing spiral out of control. The real excitement in a play lies in the pivotal moment, the moment when all control is in the balance. We hold our breath, trying to prepare ourselves for devastation.

The epic play

The subject of the epic – as someone has surely said before – is history itself.

Whether it is Homer's epic poems about his returning hero Odysseus, or Shakespeare's plays about the fall of kings or a modern play like Peter Shaffer's *The Royal Hunt of the Sun*, the epic's principal characteristic is not length – as we might assume from the name – but scope. The epic is about massively significant events: the rise and fall of civilizations or of dynasties, colossal journeys as the world itself changes, the shedding of old ideas and the formulation of new ones; all of which take time, measured not in seconds but in decades, if not generations and centuries.

As outlined above, this can be encompassed by a single actor and a bare stage. There's also a case for saying that all powerful drama involves an element of the epic, since the fall of a character like Miller's eponymous salesman, or the crumbling of the patriarchy in Pinter's *The Homecoming*, is intended to feel like the end of an era, a loss of whatever-has-always-been; the fixed-and-known giving way to the terrifying, unknowable, less-certain future. The axe itself may fall swiftly, but the blow has been coming forever, and will have repercussions far beyond the present.

But epic theatre is worth considering as a discrete form, where the term also has implications of scale in terms of cast size and staging, and in the size of ideas. We are all a product not only of our parents but of a vast and complex history, and our actions too may create ripples far beyond us. Sometimes a bigger canvas is needed to establish that. This epic form of theatre also has something of a unique character when it comes to scene structure.

In a naturalistic drama, the scenes are always related to one another in terms of time. At one extreme, in a play set entirely in real time, where a minute of stage time equals a minute of real time, the seconds simply follow one after the other. This in fact is very rare in the theatre – we dramatists simply have too much to say, too many points of view to present, too many interesting places to go to allow it. But a play does not have to be so literally tied in time to follow the time-link pattern. A play which sees a group of office workers at their annual office party three years running is still sequenced by time.

In the truly epic play, the link between these chunks of action needs follow no such time sequence; the links are instead dictated by narrative. The move to the next act or scene in the epic play is not purely a case of what happens next; it can be what happens elsewhere, in a different time or place – so long as it is in some thematic way related to what we have just seen. This relationship is often far from transparent; and in fact, the assertion that one piece of action *is* related to the last becomes part of the play's argument or thesis. In Howard Brenton's play *The Romans in Britain,* the first act takes place in ancient Britain, the second in Northern Ireland. Go figure the connection, is the challenge Brenton is giving us, and he ends the first act with the noise of helicopters to drive home that challenge. In Caryl Churchill's *Top Girls,* the play argues a connection between the dinner party to celebrate Marlene's promotion (attended fantastically by famous women, real and mythical) and the scenes which follow, first in the employment agency where Marlene is now the manager, and then in Marlene's sister's home. The scenes are connected hardly at all in terms of time (though one can with a bit of work, place them in sequence). They certainly don't connect in a straightforward way, since the first act's dinner party might even be happening inside Marlene's head. The bits of action we see are instead connected in terms of narrative – the meaning lies in the connection between them.

Although epic in intent and structure, *Top Girls* cleverly fits itself into a more modest cast size and staging by doubling the parts, so that all the grand historical figures in the first act are played by actors who turn up later in the contemporary scenes. This points to one of the great (and obvious) challenges with the play that is epic in scale as well as intent and form: the commercial problems of requiring a cast of thirty.

A further, more subtle challenge lies in the difficulty of delivering the enormity of history's impact on an individual when the form is all about the aggregate. In demonstrating patterns of history, we risk losing that direct, sustained contact with any one individual. The epic makes us stand back and consider connections, but is less concerned, or able, to make us *feel* – and that clearly has risks with an audience accustomed to following an emotional journey.

The small-scale play

This is where most writers begin; a handful of actors, a simple stage, minimal lighting/costumes, a story to tell and a relatively short playing time in which to do it. Increasingly, that means a maximum of ninety minutes stage time without a break, or two and a half hours with a break. Most of these parameters are determined by practical economic considerations – what is the theatre company prepared or able to commission and stage? How powerful is the bar manager at the venue? (Bar managers do like an interval.)

It's a relief to learn that these considerations are as powerful a force in many starrily cast commercial productions as in a touring or festival show. The commercial producer often wants to put the cash into casting a small number of big names, and to keep a tight control on the other overheads. It follows that new plays that succeed commercially are often not dissimilar in terms of cast size, or the extravagance of the staging, to those available to the struggling touring company, though perhaps the sets are a bit less wobbly.

The good news is that in some respects this is exactly how the ancient Greek dramatists began. As we saw in 'Reflections on the History of Playwriting 1', strip away spectacle and chorus, and the Ancients were working with essentially a small-scale cast. In the very first plays, there was no dialogue, just proclamation by a single actor, examined by the chorus. Aeschylus introduced a second actor, and dialogue was possible – a simple debate between two opposed parties. Plays were judged according to the eloquence with which the playwright articulated these arguments. The conflict at the heart of many a modern two-hander – David Harrower's *Blackbird* or David Mamet's *Oleanna* for instance, or even Katori Hall's *The Mountaintop* – illustrates how powerful this binary model still is; and two-handers remain a popular subspecies of the small-scale play.

It is Sophocles who is credited with introducing the third character, which introduces to the dramatic scene a new level of complexity. The third character introduces, among other things, the possibility of an interruption in an ongoing confrontation. In fact, all three of the plays above use the constant *threat* of interruption to heighten tension on stage. All the encounters they depict are in some way illicit (and 'illicit' is always delicious for an audience). Characters are fearful that they might be discovered, their deeds exposed. In David Harrower's play, an actual interruption eventually does occur, with devastating effect.

Although we've cited it as a two-hander, strictly speaking *Blackbird* requires a third actor, a child. The introduction of this innocent in the closing moments of the play radically ups the stakes; the play is no longer a forensically observed struggle between adults over the interpretation of past events and their current choices. We are now forced to consider the implications of those choices on a vulnerable child in the present (and by implication, every child in the real world). Since the subject of the play is a man's sexual predation of a minor, the introduction of the third character, a child, albeit in an almost symbolic way, is vital in pressing home the play's urgency.

In a fully fledged three-hander – that is, a play with a third fully rounded 'someone' with their own motives and volition – the newcomer often provides an allegiance which can be fought over; someone who the drama demands must make a decision between already established forces or interests. Joe Penhall's *Blue/Orange* features a psychiatric patient whose fate is fought over by his psychiatrist and a consultant. Still in therapeutic country, Bryony Lavery's *Frozen* – where a grieving mother is trapped between the man who murdered her daughter and the psychologist treating him – likewise shows how powerful this three-way power struggle can be.

These plays offer plenty of evidence that for the contemporary playwright, even working with only two or three or four characters provides immense opportunities, sufficient for many of the fundamentals of theatre writing to be explored. True, in a four-hander in the West End a revolving stage or other scenic or lighting effects may help mask awkward scene changes, but for the most part the playwright working on this scale is still seeking to be practical and economic in all things; the construction of the play must reflect this, skilfully juggling entrances and exits, monologues and dialogue, time and place, to fully explore character and shift plot forward. If each actor plays one character, then each character can – and usually must – be explored in depth. An incidental character in a naturalistic small-scale play is a rare luxury. As with the solo play, the focus is intense on every role.

Although a play like *Blackbird* can disprove the common argument, the fact remains that being allowed only a small number of actors – if married to too naturalistic a form – *can* conspire to trap new writing in the domestic or commonplace. Here the number and type of characters makes effortless sense, easily matching the scale of the setting. The kitchen at a party, a suburban lounge, a dingy bedsit, a deserted office – all are conveniently about the same size as many studio playing spaces. The isolation of two or three characters in such a space does not need to be explained or tortuously engineered (unlike, say, two or three soldiers in the middle of a pitched battle, or a single couple at a Moonie wedding).

A play on this domestic scale might also offer an easy fit for the composition of the acting company involved. The cautionary tale often cited is of a play about four impoverished twenty-somethings in a shabby flat in Neasden performed by a company of four twenty-something, profit-sharing actors on a shabby set in … you get the picture. Too easily, the scale of the themes tackled can be equally diminished: Terry Johnson's advice to new writers, 'Write about people you know, what they want and why they can't have it', makes a useful point, but can also be reductive.

Ambitious new writers attempting to break out of these confines to write big plays in small spaces may need to break out of slavish naturalism, if the dangers of overstretched characterization, mundane worlds and an over-contrived plot are to be avoided.

Formal conventions of the kind deployed by Bryony Lavery in *Frozen*, or by Abi Morgan in her play *Splendour* – where not just one but all four characters directly address the audience while also functioning 'within the scene' – can be powerful aids in this. Alternatively, a much broader poor/rough theatre aesthetic can be adopted, such as those deployed in sizzling epics such as *Woza Albert*. A play that wants to treat big themes with a tiny cast has to recognize that a dogged naturalism may not be the way to go.

Which is good news too. After all, a play is called a play for a reason …

Mid-scale/main stage

What makes the difference between a small-scale studio or touring play and one fit for the main stage is quite difficult to identify. As we've seen, it's not just a matter of cast size, since many commercially successful main stage plays have casts only a little larger, if at all, than those being performed in a studio's black box.

A skilfully crafted play like David Lindsay Abaire's *Good People* can cross the gap. It has a cast of six, so in terms of acting forces it bridges the distinction between small-scale and main stage or mid-scale. It shares with many small-scale plays an acute ability to deliver fully developed characters and to shift the action forward via scenes featuring encounters between two or three or at most four characters at a time. (It also makes great use of the offstage character – a staple of the small-scale play – in two of its acts.) But its concerns are immense – it is one of the few American plays to deal with social class and to critique the blame culture that underpins notions of class (im)mobility. It also features a barnstorming role for a star actor in Margie, the woman from the projects who first tracks down, then faces down, her childhood sweetheart-who-made-good. In a West End production in 2014 the play proved it has the chops as a main stage work, despite and also perhaps because of its economy.

Of course, a play like *Good People* is eminently producible as a small-scale production, though the artistic team would have to be inventive about its transition between scenes. *Blue/Orange*, Joe Penhall's three-hander mentioned earlier, also enjoys numerous productions in both small-scale and main stage theatres. What is certain is that a play will only bear the extra commercial pressure of a main stage production if it has a certain broadness of appeal, offers sufficiently meaty roles for accomplished actors and has something significant to say, with a particularity and power about the way it says it.

In addition – and this may be the defining aspect of a main stage play – it has to be projected. This means the writing itself must have a certain scale of its own, a power and substance that a play can sometimes survive without in the intimate space of a studio. In the studio we enter the environment of the character, and can eavesdrop; on a main stage, the character's world must be projected to envelop us. The force of the language and the power of the images in a drama play a huge part in that. Cast size apart, a small-scale or studio play *can* have amplitude (to revisit Aristotle's word); a play for the main stage *must*.

Reflections on space

Clare Bayley

You never know for certain where the play you are writing will eventually be staged. Even if it's been commissioned by a building-based company, and the whole process goes according to plan, one day another company in quite another space may want to produce it. So there's no point being proscriptive in your script about how or where it's staged (unless it's intended to be site-specific – see below). Write the play you want to write. But there are general principles you can usefully consider, which apply to the type of stage and the scale of your project.

If the theatre that's commissioned you is building-based, you will have a space in mind, which can be a creative spur. You can sit in the empty theatre to inform your writing: notice its shape, its acoustics and atmosphere, its offstage areas and the possibilities for entrances and exits. The open-air, historic Globe, for example, with its standing groundlings in the pit and its seated audiences in the balconies, demands a very different type of play from an intimate in-the-round theatre or small studio.

Even if you have a commission from a building, however, you should take it all with a pinch of salt. You might write your play for the 750-seat main stage, only to find that when finished it is considered more suitable for the 350-seat studio. You might have been commissioned to write for the National Theatre's smallest space, the completely flexible Dorfman, only to find that your play has been promoted to the proscenium arch Lyttleton. Equally, if you've written intending to fill the vast expanses of the Olivier, but the play is ultimately rejected, you may struggle to find a home for it with a similar-sized space.

If it's a commission for a touring company, your only certainty will be the scale to which you're writing. Small scale means a minimum of set and stage furniture, which has to be put up and taken down nightly, and fit into the back of a van. Middle and large scale will give you bigger vans and possibly longer residencies, but the principle is the same – nobody will thank you for specifying a grand piano on stage.

On the other hand if you have written your play on spec, and are looking for a suitable venue to approach, here are some of the things you might want to consider.

Cast size

It's obvious, but a tiny space will quickly appear crowded with a large cast. A wide expanse of playing space cries out to be peopled with characters. It often seems a surprising waste of resources when you see a one- or two-hander being performed on a big main stage; but if it's a star vehicle, the star will pull in the punters, and no theatre will compromise their ability to sell tickets.

Scene structure

Lots of short scenes can give rise to a very inventive and theatrical aesthetic. This works best in a flexible space. Traditional theatres lend themselves to conventionally structured plays, punctuated by actors entering from the wings and curtains falling. In a studio space you won't have a curtain to bring down between scenes or acts; the most you'll have at your disposal is a blackout, or partial blackout.

Entrances and exits

If you have lots of short scenes, the mechanics of the exits and entrances become significant. In the theatre you're approaching, how easy is it for actors to get on and off stage? Are there wings and ample backstage areas, or is the space limited, with actors crouching behind curtains or hiding behind flats when not in a scene? If it's really hard to get characters on and off, can you make this into a virtue, and keep them all onstage even when not in a scene? Find ways to keep the amount of on- and offstage traffic to a minimum.

One setting or many

A naturalistic play can work beautifully with a realistic set in either a small or a large space. If there is more than one setting, it's useful for the crew to have the interval to change it around. But if you choose to set your play in multiple locations, they will have to be suggested in a non-naturalistic way, otherwise the effort of the scene changes will be cumbersome. If you are writing naturalistically but are intending the playing to be of a more impressionistic style, it's worth stating this at the start of the play.

These caveats aside, these are the spaces to consider, and some examples of how they have been put to good use in the production of plays.

Proscenium arch theatre

It all began with the Greeks building amphitheatres for their dramas. These remain in various stages of ruination throughout the Mediterranean, some with wild flowers blowing through them and goats clambering up the stone seating, others almost intact. Even in the ruined ones you can still stand in the middle of the stage and talk in a normal voice, and be heard at the very top of the seating. In these amphitheatres, the proscenium referred to the area in front of the stage.

In Britain and large parts of the US, however, the rain, the cold and the darkness rule out this type of theatre. Buildings had to be built. When this happened the architecture very often mimicked the places where plays had taken place informally, before theatre building began. So in England, theatre architecture reproduced the conditions of inn courtyards, while in France they reflected the fact that right up to the time of Molière many theatres were adapted tennis courts – long and narrow with galleries at the side.

In Renaissance Italy, the rediscovery of Vetruvius's writings describing the Ancients' theatre practices led to a new craze for an arch in the proscenium, which was used to hang curtains and drapes to frame the stage picture. The English architect Inigo Jones saw these Italian proscenium arches, and introduced them to England for court masques in the mid-1600s.

From then on the 'pros arch' became a standard feature of theatre architecture, a permanent wall dividing the stage from the auditorium, which can still be seen in many of London's West End theatres, and in old regional playhouses that date from the late seventeenth and early eighteenth centuries.

Today the pros arch is no longer in vogue. It creates an unhelpful distance between the stage and the audience, which may have been appropriate for the formal acting styles of David Garrick or Mrs Patrick Campbell, but doesn't suit our times. Gradually old theatres which manage to raise sufficient cash to revamp themselves – like the Royal Court or the Liverpool Everyman – are opting for more flexible spaces.

There remains the problem of the old West End theatres, many of which are literally crumbling (viz. the collapse of part of the roof during a performance of *The Curious Incident of the Dog in the Night-Time* in 2013). Plays that do brilliantly at the Traverse or the Royal Court, and see the chance for a commercial life in the West End, still have to cram themselves into the old pros arch theatres. Designers are cunning at adapting to space and some productions work brilliantly in their new homes. Mostly audiences are unaware of any design compromises which have to be made, or any change in dynamic and mood. But there is often something lost in the translation. It's fair to say that nobody building a new theatre today would choose to include a proscenium arch.

Thrust staging

With slightly more intimacy than a pros arch theatre, a thrust stage projects out into the audience on three sides, while the back of the stage connects with the offstage area. Shakespeare's Globe had – and still has – a thrust stage around which the groundlings cluster to get closer to the action. In a nod to this fact, the Stratford Shakespeare Festival of Canada introduced a thrust stage for its productions.

Flexible spaces: The black box, the studio theatre

The flexible playing space was developed in the US in theatres attached to universities from the 1950s onwards. Conventional theatres wanting to stage more experimental or smaller-scale work took up the idea, and began to build additional studio theatres alongside their main stages. Theatre-makers soon realized that any room can be blacked out and used as a studio theatre. As the fringe in London and off-Broadway in New York began to develop organically in the 1960s, every pub room (e.g. The King's Head), loft (the Circle Rep) or basement (La Mama) became a potential new venue.

Configuration

In a flexible space the playing area and the audience can be configured in a number of different ways. Most closely mimicking the old pros-arch style is the end-on, open style of playing, where the stage is at one end and the audience faces it.

In small spaces designers often seat the audience on two or three sides of a rectangular playing space, so that everyone gets a closer view of the action.

A traverse production seats the audience on either side of a long 'runway' type of playing area, making the action very close and immediate – but challenging for the direction, to avoid backs being turned to the audience for too long. A play like Lope de Vega's *Fuenteovejuna*, for example, memorably directed by Declan Donnellan in traverse at the Cottesloe in 1989, took us right into that rousing rebellion in a sixteenth-century Spanish pueblo. The dynamic staging perfectly fitted the spirit of the play.

In-the-round

In-the-round was a breakthrough in theatre staging, flying in the face of everything that previous generations had held dear, and later generations hated – the fourth wall, and that peculiarly artificial manner of constraining actors always to face the front. In-the-round – with the audience seated on all sides of the action – leaves nowhere to hide. Revealing all, integrating scene changes and offstage areas into the playing space, allowing the audience to see, as in real life, the back of someone's head from time to time – the effect of all this is energizing, and increases the sense of immediacy.

The first theatre purpose-built for in-the-round productions was the Circle in the Square in New York, for Joe Quintero and the Loft Players, which opened in 1951. The inspirational Margo Jones also popularized and developed this kind of stage configuration. In 1947 she opened her Theatre '47 in Dallas, Texas, to champion new work and provide a new prototype for the regional theatre movement.

In the UK Stephen Joseph was an early adopter of in-the-round staging, opening theatres in Newcastle-under-Lyme and then Scarborough for the purpose. The theatre which now bears his name in Scarborough is an in-the-round theatre, run by Alan Ayckbourn, Joseph's pupil and successor. Consequently, most of Ayckbourn's plays have been written for in-the-round staging. In 1983 the Stephen Joseph Theatre undertook an exchange with the Alley Theatre, Houston, which was founded in 1948 by Nina Vance, inspired by Margo Jones, and consistently produces new work.

Site-specific

Site-specific performance was first practised by visual artists in the 1960s, with companies like Lumière & Son performing in shopping centres, ferryboats, botanical gardens, castles and swimming pools. But site-specific theatre joined the mainstream in the UK thanks to Deborah Warner's captivating *St Pancras Project* in London in 1995. Each audience member had a timed slot and had to walk alone into the huge decaying belly of the semi-derelict St Pancras Hotel (now a luxury destination). Behind the dust and rubble were the vestiges of Gilbert Scott's Victorian gothic grandeur: sweeping staircases, mosaic flooring, elaborate plasterwork. Just as you began to relax a little into the old building, you were startled by a sudden movement out of the corner of your eye – a glimpse of a Victorian maid in bonnet and apron scurrying up the staircase and disappearing behind a green baize door; a pianola quietly playing to itself in an empty room, its ivories moved by unseen hands; a lawn smelling of summer growing incongruously in a bedroom with crumbling plaster and rain-smeared windows. The drama here was entirely elliptical, with no coherent narrative, and the only really solid character was the building itself. Not a word was spoken. But the drama and mystery of it inspired everyone who saw it.

Academics and practitioners are keen to point out the differences among different types of site-specific theatre. The Exeter-based company Wrights and Sites have offered the categories of site-specific, site-sympathetic and site-generic work. In the former the play is wholly inspired by the place in which it is going to be performed; in the others, as we'll see, the staging of an existing play in an unusual location sheds new light on its meaning and contemporary relevance. In site-generic work a production is created for a type of space, such as a hotel (so, for example, The Other Way Works set their 2008 production *Black Tonic* in a hotel, conceiving it to be performed in hotels generally, rather than in a specific hotel).

The Welsh company Brith Gof specializes in this kind of work. Their *Gododdin* (1998) was based on an early sixth-century Welsh epic poem, and first performed in a disused Rover car factory. The first production was designed for this space, revelling in the dissonance between the ancient text and the contemporary commentary which the setting suggested (the glory of ancient Wales now sadly fallen into industrial decline and economic deprivation). Its success was such that it went on to tour internationally, in 'site-sympathetic' locations. Where it wasn't possible to find disused factories, other industrial relics were discovered – a former quarry in Italy, an abandoned crane factory in Germany and a disused tram shed (the Tramway) in Glasgow. Each setting offered a new slant on or interpretation of the work.

Theatres themselves can become the setting for site-specific work. Intriguingly, Fire Exit turned a real theatre – the Glasgow Citizens – into a site-specific location by staging *Sub Rosa* not on the stage, but in the backstage areas, including a bar, a room beneath the stage and an old dressing room, to reveal the ghosts of the old building.

Alan Ayckbourn's experiments with staging reached their peak with his paired plays *House* and *Garden*, designed with minute attention to timing and continuity to tell the same story with the same cast in two adjacent theatres simultaneously. The plays were first produced at the Stephen Joseph Theatre, but subsequently at the National, in the Lyttleton and the Olivier theatres. The backstage areas at the National Theatre are famously confusing, but the *House* and *Garden* cast survived to tell the tale – albeit often one of sheer terror, running full tilt down the labyrinthine corridors praying that they would arrive at the correct theatre in time for their next entrance.

As the Edinburgh Fringe Festival grew and competition for the official spaces grew fiercer, companies began to seek out more and more unlikely buildings to perform in. The former University of Edinburgh Officers Training Drill Hall was the perfect setting for Gregory Burke's harrowing play *Black Watch*, based on interviews with soldiers from the Black Watch regiment serving in Iraq. Even the official festival offered challenges to celebrated directors with unlikely venues. In 1993 the revered German director Peter Stein brought his epic five-hour production of Shakespeare's *Julius Caesar* (in German) to the official Edinburgh Festival, where it was performed in the Highland Exhibition Hall – a rattling, draughty metal hangar on the outskirts of the city. It seemed a very unprepossessing setting for the play, until the entrance of the 200 extras Stein had hired to play the Roman populace. Their arrival was heard before it was seen: the sound of 400 boots stampeding along the metal walkways echoed terrifyingly around the space, before the mob streamed into the auditorium from every corner of the building. It was a chilling and unforgettable moment, which wouldn't have had the same impact in any other building.

Audiences love to be taken out of their comfort zone and into hidden or normally inaccessible spaces. Spectators of my play *The Container* always chat merrily as they take their seats inside the container unit, then fall into alarmed hush as the huge rear metal doors bang shut, plunging them into darkness. If you're going to give audiences a surprise of this sort, it's worth issuing warnings on the publicity, so that they know what to expect – as well as clear instructions to the nervous about what to do if they need to leave.

As a writer, if you can find an evocative enough site, half of your work is already done – the imagination is easily stimulated by the ghosts of past occupants and the stories they hint at. The practical difficulties are myriad – fire exits, toilet facilities, box office, ensuring the safety of the audience, heating, lighting, etc., etc. Leave all that to the producers to resolve.

One word of warning: it's every writer's hope that their play will have many productions in theatres of all shapes and sizes, so you have to be aware of anything that will limit that. A play designed to be performed inside a small space, such as a taxi, a container or a public toilet, will never be able to play to a big audience, and so will not make any playwright's fortune.

Promenade theatre

Promenade productions are nothing new – the medieval mystery plays blazed a trail for the concept of audiences moving from place to place between scenes. In those days there were sound and practical reasons for the promenading. Now too it's important that moving an audience can be rigorously justified – they will quickly get grumpy if it feels like a gimmick.

Jim Cartwright's *Road* is a play which lends itself to the form, as the audience can follow the narrator Scullery as he leads us to meet the play's other characters. Max Stafford-Clark's production of *Macbeth* at the Arcola in 2005 set the action in a war-torn African country with suggestions of the Lord's Resistance Army in Uganda. Gun-toting soldiers in pink women's wigs and no formal uniform took the tickets as the audience entered, and continued to keep a threatening eye on us throughout Act One. For the banquet scene, they herded us at gunpoint into a different room – the sense of threat was palpable and greatly heightened our sense of the terrifying murderousness of Macbeth's regime.

In both these cases, there was a narratively justified solution to the question of how to move the audience from one scene or setting to the next. In *Road*, the audience follows the narrator; in *Macbeth*, they are moved by cast members in character, without breaking away from the fictional world of the play.

Immersive theatre

Macbeth seems to be a favourite text for promenade and immersive companies to play with, fear being one of the easiest emotions to evoke in audiences. Companies like the much-lauded Punchdrunk have taken the concept of promenade theatre a step further, making the audience immerse themselves totally in the world of the production, letting them wander at will in a building which becomes an enormous stage set. The audience can choose where to go and what to see, so what is lost in terms of narrative complexity is replaced with a heightened sensory experience. Their version of *Macbeth* seen in New York and London – *Sleep No More* – took place over three floors of an office block. As the audience stumbled upon another jigsaw piece of the action taking place inside an elaborately styled location, they created their own bespoke version of the Scottish play.

Another company, Rift, told the story of *Macbeth* over the course of one whole night in 2014 in an empty tower block in East London, taking the audience creepily into an underground car park to meet the witches. In this case the play retained its narrative order, using three sets of actors to keep the action flowing while addressing the logistical challenges of doing this over a vast space.

Kate Bond and Morgan Lloyd's *You Me Bum Bum Train* gained a cult following by taking the audience on a similarly tailor-made theatrical voyage of discovery into the unknown. Their website advises would-be audiences not to read any press about the show or to do any research, as the less you know what to expect, the greater your experience will be. Suffice it to say that in one of their shows, each audience member was individually wheeled around the venue in a chair.

In all of these immersive theatre companies writers are notable by their absence, with companies relying on classic and well-known texts to hang their stagecraft on. This is an area ripe for exploitation by writers.

Outdoor theatre

In Shakespeare's plays, woods and the outdoors generally unlock a kind of licence, mischief and enchantment in the protagonists. Outdoor productions can be similarly magical, in spite or because of the many natural and man-made distractions and surprises that can crop up. Rain and wind, helicopters, sirens, birds, dogs, drunks and intruders are all a part of the action. In London the Regent's Park Open Air Theatre used to stage an annual *Midsummer Night's Dream* to make the most of its bosky setting; imaginative programming has seen the potential to expand, to include *Into the Woods, To Kill a Mockingbird, Lord of the Flies* and others.

More and more cities are staging festivals of outdoor or site-specific theatre, so companies are always alert to inspired ideas about work in unusual spaces.

Reflections on genre

Fraser Grace

'Tragi-comic' is the tonal register almost every modern dramatist works in.

The original genres of comedy and tragedy – as identified by Aristotle – were arguably obsolete even when they were conceived. By that time, Euripides had already ditched the seemless austerity of Aeschylus and Sophocles to introduce lighter moments into the drama.

The old binary distinction lost its grip further in the Elizabethan age. It continued in the publishing and marketing of plays – though this too was problematic. While it was convenient for a publisher to label *King Lear* as a tragedy, it was less clear which kind of play Shakespeare intended *The Merchant of Venice* to be (and its classification has consequently changed over time). *The Tempest* is likewise trickier to box. *Hamlet*, the archetypal tragedy of the age, is still the one we turn to most as an exemplar – but within that play there is more tonal variation than anything Aeschylus would recognize, let alone approve of.

Another important truth about genre can be gleaned from the above: the notion of genre is less exciting to playwrights themselves than to those who make their living from describing the playwright's work. This includes critics (like Aristotle), academics, theatre managers, marketing executives and publishers. Put simply, analysing or marketing a play is a much simpler affair once a shorthand has been found to describe it. The shortest shorthand is to assign a play to a genre; immediately an audience or readership has a broad idea of what the play is like.

By contrast, many playwrights actively and instinctively resist any pigeonholing of their work. Simply fitting the work into a box is inevitably reductive of a play's vision and complexity; you have to ignore some aspects of the play to make the fit seem good. The cautionary tale is told of the Miami Playhouse's US premiere of *Waiting for Godot* in 1956, in which the play was promoted as 'the laugh hit of two continents'. Not surprisingly, early audiences went away baffled. This 'easy reference' might be bearable if it helps get a play off the ground (that production of *Godot* did eventually transfer to Broadway, with much greater success). But when a classification is used to dismiss or criticize a play, the playwright is likely to contest this kind of genre assignment.

Primarily then, genre is a reactive, descriptive and analytical tool, not necessarily one a playwright has or should have in mind when planning or beginning a play.

All the same, playwrights are inescapably involved with helping to develop genre identities, because the currency of every genre is reassessed by each generation. Dramatists try to address the concerns of their age in forms that work for their audience and appeal to producers, as well as simply 'making sense' to the playwright. For this reason writers find themselves working within established formal constraints, bending and extending them as necessary. In other cases, perhaps at exceptional times, tired forms seem redolent of a past world; the playwright is forced to think outside the box, to forge a new path. As noted in 'Reflections on the History of Playwriting 1', writers in the early part of the seventeenth century began producing a kind of play that became known much later as the Revenge Tragedy: playwrights instinctively or consciously dramatized power and violence inspired by current events, in a way that chimed with the appetites of their audience. This appetite, like the playwrights' interests, was schooled by the real-life machinations of the powerful at the time. The new genre fitted the bloody age.

In more recent times, genres have likewise come and gone. The whodunit and the melodrama have all but disappeared from the output of contemporary playwrights, while 'kitchen-sink drama' – originally a disparaging label – put working-class domestic life on the stage, allegedly for the first time, in the post-war British theatre.[1] At the turn of the twenty-first century, an attempt to quantify and explain plays that seemed to share an explicit approach to the depiction of violence, sex and drug-taking led to the coining of the term 'In yer face drama'.[2] More recently still, a subclass of the political thriller has

[1] The relocation of tragedy and comedy to a domestic setting does have a precedent as far back as the mid-eighteenth century, though the themes then were far more sentimental.

[2] Aleks Sierz, *In-Yer-Face Theatre: British Drama Today* (London: Faber and Faber, 2001).

appeared, which puts real-life, still-living public figures on stage (unthinkable in some more deferential ages) though no one seems to have made a genre title stick as yet.

In fact, genre considerations in general play a less-dominant role in contemporary theatre than in any other kind of dramatic writing. At the theatre box office, or in its publicity, it may be sufficient to describe the show simply as 'a new play' – the public will know to expect anything.

By contrast, the film industry famously depends on genre distinctions. This is due in part to even greater commercial imperatives. The movie 'thriller' has a dozen subspecies (chase, crime, spy, heist, psychological and so on) which also have to jostle at the box office with the war movie, the romance, the rom-com, the biopic, the western, the coming of agemovie, the spaghetti western, the sword and sandals epic, science fiction, period drama.... There is even a genre for directors and publicists who despise the genre movie: arthouse.

If genre helps people select the film they want to watch (or produce), once inside the cinema it becomes important in a way that has much more in common with the theatre. This is the most important aspect for the playwright to consider: genre is primarily a way of establishing expectations.

Genre as expectation

In a movie marketed as a rom-com, we expect the central couple to initially get off to a bad start with each other. The pleasure of the film is to watch as the warring couple are, via a series of complications, inexorably drawn together, so that the end of the film reverses its beginning. A good rom-com pushes these complications to an extreme (Shakespeare's original, *As You Like it* is still the best) so that an audience is almost unable to work out *how* the couple are going to come together in the end. But rest assured, they will: a rom-com in which the final scene is not a wedding or the symbolic equivalent is either exceptionally brave, or tragically flawed.

While theatre is less invested in genre – perhaps because less is invested in marketing – critics do sometimes refer to *types* of play – the family drama, the black comedy, the literary play, the epic, the farce (domestic) and farce (political), the suburban comedy, the whodunit – and an audience will have some idea of what to expect. What's more, some writers manage to establish a 'house style' that becomes virtually a genre in itself: 'Pinteresque', 'Stoppardian' or 'Beckettian' are terms that work in this way, and many of us will likewise have a good idea what to expect from 'an Ayckbourn', 'a Bennett' or 'a Mike Leigh'.

For a playwright, genre means expectations, and in this respect, considering a play's genre identity may help in a number of ways.

- As an aid to problem-solving: if a draft feels unsatisfactory, it may be because certain expectations have been set up in the opening scenes but remain unsatisfied in the denouement. Identify what genre your play is closest to, and you may be able to work out what 'set-ups' need to be 'paid-off' (or expunged).
- As a means of describing the not-yet-written play: when talking to a literary manager or a director, or attempting to secure a commission, it may be necessary for a playwright to describe the play, even if it is only at the conceptual stage. In an effort to be both succinct and understood, reaching for a genre label may prove irresistible.
- As a way of deciding which producer or theatre to approach with your play. (See Part 3 'Finding a suitable theatre'.)
- As something to have fun with.

So what are the most current genres in today's theatre?

Below, in the spirit of a parlour game, we offer a stab at nailing a few of modern theatre's genres, followed by a few of their variants, and the likely sources of material.

A few things to note:

The list is far from exhaustive, and by the time this book has been on the shelf a few years, there will be new genres as yet undreamed of.

Second, we've restricted ourselves to the most common genres of the last fifty years. The theatre industry programmes plays from many more genres than are mentioned here, but playwrights reading this book – unless attempting a parody – are working within genres that are current, or else striving to explode them.

Third, as we've seen above, genres are both imprecise categorizations and constantly shifting ones – shifting in their nature, their titles, and in their currency; art is a slippery thing, and a subjective one too. What strikes you as a political play may well seem more like a history play to me, or even a family drama with historical tendencies (!?). Nor do plays always stay where they are put. Think of a work like Terrance Rattigan's *The Winslow Boy*. A play from 1946 that took issue with the notions of respectability and honour in Edwardian England some thirty years before, it has often been criticized as being far too decorous in both construction and 'attack'. When revived in 2013, however, it appeared to *New York Times* critic Charles Isherwood as a 'stirring drama about the rights of the individual in conflict with the imperatives of the government (a topic that could hardly seem more pertinent, in the post-Edward J Snowden era), and a moving, surprisingly ambiguous tale of the price to be paid for the relentless pursuit of even an honorable goal'.[3]

Fourth, beware terminology. It's almost impossible to imagine a contemporary play that does not make any political or social comment whatsoever – but that does not make every play a political drama, and many playwrights are very happy about that. Similarly, as noted above, 'tragi-comic' might apply to almost all modern plays; a play no longer has to be called a comedy in order to deliver laughs, and even the Greeks expected a comedy to land a punch or two.

Fifth, if the play you're planning doesn't seem to fit any of these genres, maybe you're helping to create a new one. What would you call it? Which plays can you think of that would also belong to it?

Finally, in order to set up expectations, a genre has to gain some currency beyond our own thinking, to become a commonly used label. And that, as we've seen, is in the hands of critics and academics – if not of the gods themselves.

Family drama

Characteristics: multiple generations, forensically observed; contested history and long-held secrets explored; domestic settings predominant. Often presented naturalistically, approaching real time – although 'rites of passage' that bring members together (funeral, wedding, reading of the will, etc.) are

[3] *New York Times*, 17 October 2013 www.nytimes.com/2013,10/18/theatre/reviews/the-winslow-boy-is-revived-at-american-arilines-theatre.html, (accessed: 26 August /2013).

often employed. The long-lost returning family member is another trope. Some family dramas use more intricate time schemes, in order to offer comparisons of experience across history, and to reflect changing family structures.

Subspecies: kitchen-sink drama.

Single-issue drama

Characteristics: 'importance' of the subject is the reason for the drama: debate more important than character; character dominated by position or view on issue being explored. Includes many Theatre in Education plays; plays on current affairs and moral panics.

Political drama

Characteristics: public and/or private settings; sometimes epic reach, but private secrets, relationships, loyalties, dilemmas and choices are significant insofar as they impact upon the public realm. Historical, contemporary or even futuristic subject, but in any case intended to offer strong commentary on contemporary events and concerns, or to challenge existing order and orthodoxy, sometimes via iconoclasm.

Subspecies: contemporary tragedies of those in power; state of the nation play; political thriller; plays about real-life public figures and political scandals; issue plays where characterization/complexity of the drama raises interest beyond the immediate subject matter.

Sources: historical accounts of events/characters, contemporary affairs, journalism.

History play

Characteristics: known events or personalities explored for hidden motives, or established truth exposed as falsehood; character development puts flesh on the bones of facts, humanizing history. Contemporary social/political comment inescapable, but not the driving force.

Subspecies: colonial history; kings and queens.

Likely sources: biographies, historical accounts.

Social comedy-drama

The most prevalent contemporary genre, comprising the following important subgenres. All involve some element of social comment.

Attritional or black comedy: struggle for power between a handful of people tied to each other by bonds of blood (some family dramas qualify) or other association; confinement often reinforced by single set. At one extreme, lack of specifics helps create tension, comedy. Doesn't preclude satiric comment, but this is not driving force. Threat comes from other people in the room, expressed in physical and psychological violence, verbal aggression.

Contemporary nostalgia play: near past revisited with relish for character; incident and character valued for ability to evoke values of a particular time, place or social milieu. Often affectionate, frequently comic or bitter-sweet, but can also offer eulogy for era/class lost or threatened; some overlap with family drama, history play or attritional comedy, but likely to go beyond blood ties, and more affectionate than critical. Social comment may be trenchant, but less driven by focused political intent.

Likely source: personal recollection, memoir, social history.

Strangers in a flat (or other shared space – bar, hospital ward, prison cell, old people's home, workplace): contemporary work or domestic setting. Disparate characters thrown together by circumstance rather than choice or family ties; working out or reversing of pecking order; stakes likely to come from threat to whatever institution holds the disparate group together. Frequently an outsider group of some kind, themes of alienation and dependency.

Likely source: personal experience, memoir.

Comedy of manners: every age arguably produces plays which satirize contemporary mores. Criticism is intended, but this is about observation of a particular class or social mileu, rather than savage condemnation or demand for change. Some overlap with other plays in the social comedy category, as each generation dissects the foibles of its elders.

Likely source: personal experience, historical accounts, memoir.

The 'post-dramatic' text

Characteristics: this most recent of genres seeks to challenge many of the accepted conventions of the play script, allowing directors/theatre makers authorial decisions over choices previously made by the playwright. These include physical location of the action, size and make-up (gender, age, ethnicity) of the cast, the order in which scenes are presented, attribution of lines to specific characters. Likely (on current evidence) to be concerned with dystopias.

Likely source: Caryl Churchill, Martin Crimp.

Part 2

Tips and tales – guest contributors

April de Angelis

April De Angelis' plays include *Jumpy* (Royal Court/West End), *Wild East* (Royal Court), *A Laughing Matter* (Out of Joint/National Theatre/tour), *The Warwickshire Testimony* (RSC), *The Positive Hour* (Out of Joint/Hampstead/ Old Vic/Sphinx Theatre Company), *Headstrong* (National Theatre Shell Connections), *Playhouse Creatures* (Sphinx Theatre Company), *Hush* (Royal Court), *Soft Vengeance* (Graeae Theatre Company), *Amongst Friends* (Hampstead), *The Life and Times of Fanny Hill* (adapted from the James Cleland novel for the Red Shift Theatre Company), *Ironmistress* (ReSisters Theatre Company) and *Wuthering Heights* (adapted from Emily Brontë's novel for Birmingham Rep).

Advice I wish I'd been given

Work incredibly hard. Much harder than you think you can or ever imagined possible. Go to the theatre. Study theatre. Read plays all the time. Read theory. Have an opinion on Artaud, Brecht and Beckett; all artists who understood that form speaks as powerfully as content, and that without inventing new forms you are only imitating, not creating. Develop your own aesthetic. Read the greatest writers of our time: Caryl Churchill and Sarah Kane. Keep an eye on who's writing on great form at the moment, for example Mike Bartlett, Lucy Kirkwood, Moira Buffini. Read the plays of Shakespeare. If you can't see a new play then read it. Don't waste time. Keep notebooks for ideas. Keep writing. If you are stuck it is because you haven't worked hard enough on the research. Be inventive with your research; in the past I have interviewed futurologists, ornithologists and ex-IRA paramilitaries. I have sat in Dr Johnson's house and wondered about him. I've recorded my dreams, listened to music. Be bold enough to think about what will truly inspire you. Take yourself seriously and take theatre seriously. Talk to writers. Read about writers. Read great poetry and novels. See great movies. Be political. Travel or go to different places. Read history. Read Freud. Read Max Stafford-Clark – note his ideas on actioning.[1] Be curious about people. Live your

[1] Actioning is the practice of assigning an active verb or intention to each line of dialogue. For an exercise in actioning, see Part 3 'Dialogue'.

life to the full so you have stuff to write about. Don't be afraid to write about that stuff! Be emotionally connected. Don't make easy judgements about the people you are writing about. If you're in a rehearsal room get the actors to improvise. Actors are brilliant. Find someone who can ask you the right questions about your work. Questions unlock answers. There is a kind of alchemy that happens if you keep trying forever. Finally, enjoy your vocation!

Howard Brenton

Howard Brenton's plays include *The Arrest of Ai Weiwei* and *55 Days* (Hampstead Theatre), *Anne Boleyn* and *In Extremis* (Shakespeare's Globe), *The Ragged Trousered Philanthropists* (Liverpool Everyman/ Chichester Festival Theatre), *Paul* and *Pravda* (with David Hare; National Theatre), *The Romans in Britain* (National Theatre), *Moscow Gold* (with Tariq Ali; RSC), *Iranian Nights* (with Tariq Ali; Royal Court) and *Greenland* and *Bloody Poetry* (Royal Court).

How to succeed in playwriting

Alas, you have to treat playwriting as a job. You have to be disciplined, whether you're a Dionysian ecstatic, getting a play out in a few non-stop days and nights, or an Apollonian labouring on a line or two a day. And, if you're lucky enough to begin to make a living, you have to have professional support: an agent to steer your way through the treacherous shallows of contracts, particularly for films and TV, and an accountant, because a playwright's tax affairs can be very messy. And you find yourself saying 'I'm going to work now' to cover up what you're actually doing … BECAUSE OF COURSE it's not a job at all. It's a calling. And the Arts are NOT an industry, they are a way of imagining what we are living and how to change the world. They are more important than religion – and a lot more fun!

So writing plays is not 'work', it's a compulsion, a gift and a curse, at times a joy and at times a burden. And you're never quite in control of it, it's in control of you.

There are odd psychological effects. You can write in your sleep. Some early mornings a scene will just go straight onto the page, you have no idea 'where it came from' – it's the subconscious, it set up a night-time theatre.

And this sounds nuts: you feel you are a servant of a kind of force which some call a 'muse' or 'the goddess'. Really nuts ...! But if you're a writer you'll know exactly what I mean. We rationalize this by saying we are servants of a view of the world – in my case a socialist one.

You also sense that a play exists before you write it. Think of the language writers use: we say 'I've not got that scene right', or 'I've messed up that line', or 'I can't see or hear them today', as if you are trying to retrieve the play from somewhere... like a Michelangelo sculpture from inside a rock... It's a strong sensation but nonsense, of course. A play only really exists when it is performed.

One of the best pieces of advice I ever had was from Bill Gaskill, when he was running the Royal Court in the late 1960s/early 1970s. He commissioned my first full-length play. Naïvely I said that I wanted to learn everything about the theatre – lighting, staging, all the techniques. 'Don't bother, we look after that,' he said. 'You're a writer, stay out of the theatre, bring news of the world into us. Tell us things.'

Behind Bill's remark is a profound insight: theatre isn't a job, it isn't just a 'mirror up to nature', it's a human laboratory where we entertain ourselves with possible ways of living.

Lin Coghlan

Lin Coghlan is from Dublin. She has written widely for theatre, film, TV and radio including *The Miracle* (National Theatre), *Apache Tears* (winner of the Peggy Ramsey Award) and *First Communion Day* (winner of the Dennis Potter Play of the Year Award). Her film *Some Dogs Bite* won the Audience Prize at the Nantes Film Festival. She has recently adapted Elizabeth Jane Howard's *The Cazalets* for BBC Radio 4.

A vital link in my story

I came to writing via devising. Like many of us who trained and then joined theatre companies in the 1980s, we discovered our stories together and learned how to write them down in an act of communal authorship. The process at its best was electric; at its worst it produced a mishmash of unfocussed scenes and unshaped dramatic arcs.

After ten years working as an actor I started to write full-time. Commissioned to write my third play for Theatre Centre, I was teamed up with Philip Osment as my director and dramaturg. What was about to unfold would ultimately turn my process right around.

While supporting me to develop the early drafts of the play Philip asked me forensic questions about the characters' objectives – in the play, in their lives and in specific scenes. I was certainly familiar with the whole concept of character objectives and felt sure I knew all about them. But as we moved deeper into creating the play I became more and more aware that my understanding of my characters and their hopes and dreams was erratic and confused. For years I had worked on plays as an actor simply 'making up' the objectives, and 'going with' ideas which were not based on evidence in the play. Philip was all about the text. The characters must be true to their deepest wants and needs, even those desires of which they were not consciously aware. I realized, with both a sinking feeling in my stomach and a sense of thrilling revelation, that up to that moment I had never really understood how to use a deep knowledge of character. I had instead relied on my 'voice', on plotting, and on luck to produce stories which at times succeeded in spite of me.

So what was the key to the puzzle that Philip had helped me, finally, to grasp? I can only put it in my own words, in the way it has impacted upon me.

I had thought that creating character was all about the detail, and lots of it – I would do acres of research, write their dream diary, figure out their shoe size, know what was hanging in their wardrobe. All of this was useful, and fun too, it got your imagination going, it helped you get alongside the character for the journey, but it might never give you a story. A dramatic story with psychological depth. For that you needed to know just a handful of essential elements on a deep level. The character is driven by a 'want' in the play – what is it? It must be a real thing, a practical objective, something solid. Perhaps they want to win a race, or find a friend, or be a hero or swim the channel. This is their Play Objective. But this is inextricably connected to their Life Objective, a need for growth on a deeper level – to be respected or valued, to be empowered or redeemed. This yearning is buried deep in the character's subconscious and is brought to the surface via the drama.

Two such simple ingredients, yet they instantly provide the writing with complexity and depth.

Over the years I have built on the ideas Philip introduced me to, adding layers of my own, but I will always remain grateful for having had that one brilliant insightful mentor at exactly the right moment.

E. V. Crowe

E. V. Crowe is a graduate of the Royal Court Young Writers Programme Super Group. Her first play *Kin* was nominated for Most Promising Playwright at the Evening Standard Awards. Her second Royal Court play, *Hero,* was part of the Olivier Award-winning Season in the Theatre Upstairs. She has also written plays for Nabokov and the RSC. She was part of the writing team for the eight-part series *Glue* (E4/ Eleven Films).

How to succeed in playwriting

Any advice I have is offered with the precursor that writing a play when you've had plays on before is really similar to writing a play when you haven't. In a sense, we all know as much or as little as each other.

However, here are three bits of advice that might help. The first is that I still like reading plays by writers who set something alight inside me. I also like seeing plays (mostly) and I like talking to writers about plays too, because it makes you feel that theatre is alive, and that there is a purpose to writing something – a play – that seems to be a living organism itself, a living breathing thing. Knowing that theatre is alive, and that therefore your play has to be too, is really helpful. I still go back to Albee, Miller, Ionesco, because I like them. They just fit with me, they make me feel good, and most importantly they make me want to write a play.

The second thing is to cultivate your obsessions. It feels useful and important not only to be interested in theatre, but to cultivate the particular and instinctive in yourself. You need to value the things that you are interested in, simply because you find them interesting – you don't really have to understand why. Craft is maybe the thing that will help you communicate your perspective on the world, but having a perspective at all comes from nurturing your instincts and ideas. Interestingly, when you're starting out, these things often get flagged up to you as criticisms. But even criticism can be productive, if you can find a way to use it. Value the pressure points in yourself, and the massive question marks that you carry around with you – they will sustain you in the journey ahead. The sense that regardless of a commission/production/support there are things you HAVE to find out, gives you a sense of mission that can be answered only by writing a play. There's no other way to get answers or to feel okay, or to exist.

Third (there has to be a third, narratively speaking!) if you are reading this and you are a woman, ignore the fact that the majority of plays are by men. You are more likely to end up in a low-paid admin job than most men and you are more likely to have responsibility for childcare; you are less likely to be commissioned, your play is far less likely to be produced, and the run is likely to be shorter than the plays of your male counterparts. Know this: I DON'T CARE. I want to SEE YOUR STORIES on STAGE. Do not self-censor, do not be afraid, write fearlessly.

Dennis Kelly

Dennis Kelly wrote his first play *Debris* when he was thirty, then *Osama the Hero* (Hampstead), *After the End* (Paines Plough), *Love and Money* (Manchester Royal Exchange/Young Vic), *Taking Care of Baby* (a fake verbatim play; Hampstead), *DNA* (National Theatre Connections) and *Orphans* (Birmingham Rep/Traverse). He co-wrote BBC Three's sitcom *Pulling* with actress Sharon Horgan, and co-wrote *Matilda the Musical* with comedian Tim Minchin. Dennis also wrote and produced Channel 4's conspiracy thriller *Utopia*.

Writing courses? Save your money

I've always had a sneaking suspicion that not only are writing courses a waste of money, but they might actually be doing more harm than good. I've been cautious about saying this as I know some really very good people who teach on courses and I feel guilty about shitting on them. And I suppose I'm not at all sure that I'm right – I mean I've never actually been on a course, so what do I know? But in the ten or twelve years I've been writing I've watched these things multiply like a virus in a warm, wet place – nearly every theatre now has a young writers' course, MA courses lurk in every town centre, even fringe theatres are running attachments packed with people teaching how to write. So I think it's probably time to speak out, even if I am completely wrong.

My view is simple: we should not be teaching 22- and 23-year-old playwrights – they should be teaching us. This country has a long tradition of young writers coming along and telling everyone to go fuck themselves. They destroy things, reinvent things and show us all a new direction in which to head. My great fear is that writing courses are spelling the end of this. It's long been argued that the creative writing industry is having a homogenizing effect in the world of prose and novel writing – we need to start having that debate in theatre.

It's not that you can't learn as a writer, of course you can and you must; and there's nothing wrong with the odd workshop, or with writers getting together in groups and learning from each other. But when it becomes a writing course things get dangerous. People are shown stuff they really will just pick up anyway; only they would've found it out in their own, unusual, singular and idiosyncratic way. You see, the problem with opening a door for someone is that they tend to go through it, meaning that all those thousands of other completely mental and unexpected paths that they might have taken are now closed and forgotten. And by the way, I just want to make clear that this is not anti-education – education is life-enhancing and is something I believe everyone should have the right to. It's specifically writing courses I have a problem with, and the writing industry that has grown up around them.

You may well be reading this and thinking of names of very good writers who have recently emerged from courses. And you're right – I have my own list running around my head (I won't mention names as that would be indiscreet). But my contention is that these people would have come through anyway – they're all smart and brilliant, why do we think they wouldn't manage where others have? In fact I would say that given the sheer proliferation of courses it's beginning to be almost impossible for a young writer *not* to come through one, so the writing course hit rate should be much, *much* higher. And for every writer who has come through a writing course, how about all the others who didn't – let's start with Shakespeare, Wilde, Pinter, Churchill and Beckett, and work our way down, shall we? Why do we think we have no Churchills or Shakespeares today? If you're still in doubt make two lists – your favourite writers who were on courses and your favourite writers who weren't. See which list is the longest.

If I ever had any power in a theatre (which, thank God, I probably never will have) I would run a young writers' programme. But it would employ just one person, whose job it would be to look after the cash. The writers could do what the hell they wanted, they could put on plays, they could hire theatres, they could even use the money for workshops, but it would be their choice. And as long as they didn't spend it on dog racing or cocaine and it was generally about theatre everything would be fine. I would hand it over to them. It would probably be a fucked-up mess. But it would be a glorious fucked-up mess.

One last thing. I don't see this as some kind of conspiracy. I mean, it's not as if there's anyone making shedloads of cash out of this industry. It's just something that hasn't been questioned. And as for those writers who do end up making their living teaching, often it doesn't do them any good either. I've seen many talented writers get lost this way – they start as a means to pay their bills and five years later they don't write. There are exceptions, but I've seen enough fall by the wayside to advise people against it. There is nothing wrong with teaching; it's a fantastic, noble and creative profession and if it's what you want to do you will have a very fulfilling (if stressful) life. But the creative energy it requires can leave nothing left for writing. And writers who don't write aren't writers.

David Greig

David Greig graduated from Bristol University in 1990 and formed Suspect Culture with Graham Eatough and Nick Powell. Over two years he wrote and directed five shows and was twice nominated for The Guardian Student Drama Award. He won a Scotsman Fringe First for *Stalinland* (Citizen's Theatre). Since then he has written many plays, including *The Architect* (made into a film of the same title), *Outlying Islands* and *The Cosmonaut's Last Message to the Woman He Once Loved in the Former Soviet Union* (Paines Plough); *Victoria, The American Pilate* and *Dunsinane* (a sequel to *Macbeth*; RSC). From 2005 to 2007 he was the first dramaturg of the National Theatre of Scotland.

Welcome to the gym

Theatre, at its most basic, is a ritual act: the gathering together of people in one place, for the purposes of an enactment. The enactment itself might have many purposes – to elicit laughter, shock, delight, to conjure sadness or anger – but the fuel of the ritual is always empathy. My friend, the playwright Jo Clifford, once said, 'Empathy is a muscle and theatre is the gym.' I think that's right. Everyone who participates in the theatrical event – audience, actor or writer – is driven by the question 'What would I do if I were in this situation?' Farce derives its laughter from the sense that, as the man hides the vicar in the cupboard, the audience thinks with him, 'Yes! I would do that too!' and laughs at the ridiculousness of it.

In tragedy we think 'Could I do that?' And, of course the empathy is reflected the other way. When the play is good the audience find themselves reflected in the characters and their actions. Chekhov is the master at this. Watching his plays, there are a thousand moments when you find yourself thinking, 'That's exactly how it feels to be me.'

Through the ritualized formation of empathy the theatrical enactment becomes a kind of shamanic exorcism, a healing of the community's spirits. In the dark of the theatre we play out our fears and desires, we explore the limits of our selfhood, we become, imaginatively, other. Empathy enlarges the space of ourselves. So, for me, a play can only begin to form when I find myself drawn to another soul ... first in glimpses, then in scenes and a plot: when I find myself wondering, 'What would it be like to be him? Or her? Or them?'

Thereafter the writer's job is relatively simple to articulate but extremely difficult to do. You imagine, really, really hard. You imagine so hard that you burst away from the realm of thinking and enter into a different realm – feeling? being? – and when you're in that realm, you let the play be written. In essence, you must transcend yourself. Of course, there are acres of craft involved in writing a play. There are tricks and rules and ways of shaping material. There is also re-writing. It takes a very great deal of thought, words, work and logic to turn the chaos of life into theatrical order. But unless at its core there is a transcendent ritual empathic act – there is no play at all.

Tanika Gupta

Born in London the year after her parents arrived from Calcutta, Tanika graduated from Oxford University and worked as a community worker and in an Asian women's refuge for several years. She became a full-time dramatist in 1996. Her stage plays include *Meet the Mukherjees* (Octagon Theatre, Bolton), *Great Expectations* (Watford Palace) and *Wah! Wah! Girls* (musical for Sadler's Wells; Peacock Theatre/Theatre Royal Stratford East). Tanika has been writer in residence at the National Theatre and at Soho Theatre. She has won numerous awards for her work, which also includes regular forays into film, TV and radio.

Why I write for theatre

I grew up listening to my father telling me endless stories of the *Mahabharata* and *Ramayana*, of his childhood in India, of our distant relatives and ancestors, and even the plot lines of his favourite films – both tragedies and comedies. The thing that he did was to act it all out for me and my brother, recreating (often hilariously) all the expressions and actions of his protagonists. That's where my love of drama comes from.

I write to entertain, move and inspire audiences. I don't like to say I 'educate' people through my plays because that sounds very worthy and dry, but I feel strongly that theatre has a certain power through its live action which can reveal a world in a very visceral way. I write all kinds of plays from verbatim, devising musicals, hard-hitting dramas and performance art with actors. I always try and work with different directors so that I vary my style.

My play *Gladiator Games* was about the murder of Zahid Mubarek in Feltham Young Offenders Institute in 2000. He was clubbed to death by his cellmate in a racist attack, and there were questions raised at a public inquiry as to the culpability of the prison officers who had placed those mismatched young men in a cell together. The play was an in-depth look at the events leading up to the tragic attack and even showed the murder on stage. That was a tough decision. Why show violence on stage? Is it gratuitous and tasteless? The director, actors and I decided it was important to show the reality of what happened to Zahid, and the effect on the audience was electric. It certainly moved them and made them think about the society we live in today, where young people are locked up in cells in overcrowded prisons for twenty-four hours a day.

On the other hand, I enjoy writing plays which give the audience a fun night out. I remember watching a preview of my adaptation of *Hobson's Choice* at the Young Vic. An audience member laughed so loudly and so hard that he fell off his chair. Everyone turned to laugh at him and the laughter rippled almost contagiously through the auditorium for a long time afterwards. It was a colourful and humorous play in which, in the third act, the director Richard Jones and designer Ultz made the entire audience leave the comfort of their theatre seats and traipse across the Cut to another venue (a church hall) to attend the wedding of two of the main characters. Indian sweets were handed to the audience and the evening suddenly felt like a big Hindu wedding with hundreds of guests.

It's a privilege to be able to write a variety of plays with contrasting subjects and thereby enter very diverse worlds. Each theatre has its own personality and audiences. My play *The Empress*, produced at the RSC in the Swan Theatre, was a big historical, political drama about nineteenth-century British Asians and even had Queen Victoria in it. Most of the audience were

English and extremely knowledgeable about theatre. My play *Love N Stuff* produced the following year at Theatre Royal Stratford East was a slapstick comedy set in East London – written specifically for two actors who played over twenty parts in front of an incredibly racially mixed London audience.

Ultimately, even though each play is different, it's still the same thing – which is telling a story through characters, action and a good plot. I don't worry so much about the demographics of my audience but more – is there a universal truth in each play? And most importantly: is it a good story that I can tell on stage with actors?

Zinnie Harris

Zinnie Harris is a playwright and screenwriter. Her early play *Further Than the Furthest Thing* (National Theatre/Tron Theatre) won the Peggy Ramsay Award, the John Whiting Award and a Fringe First award and is now performed in translation all over the world. Her recent work includes *How to Hold Your Breath* (Royal Court) and *The Wheel* (National Theatre of Scotland/Steppenwolf Theatre, Chicago). She has also written extensively for television, including *Spooks* (BBC One) and *Partners in Crime* (BBC One).

Watching a script become a play

Rehearsal rooms can be the most wonderful places, and they can also be miserable. Over the years I've had brilliant and awful experiences in equal measure, and oddly it doesn't always follow that a good production will come from a good rehearsal process, although it should.

At its best the rehearsal process should be a playful and creative space where things can be tried, discarded, built on, incorporated, thrown up in the air and loved, and where alchemy takes place between the script, the story, the characters and the actors. Sometimes this can be a straightforward journey of discovery; sometimes it can involve a series of blind alleys that can be uncomfortable for the playwright, but nevertheless are completely necessary to finding the right way forward; sometimes the script itself may dissolve under scrutiny, and you need to get out your pen and write your way out of a hole; sometimes the play may only really appear and make sense as late as during the previews. One thing is always true – it's tense and exciting, with a new thing being forged in front of you. Your job is to remain cool in all this, to have a calm hand on the tiller, and keep watching for the story. That is all that matters now: the story and if it is being told. If you are working with a good director and a dramaturg, then you're lucky because they'll be watching out for this too. But you need to play your part in letting the necessary experimentation happen, and for that you need to lose a bit of the detail and control you have had over the piece until this point. Of course you have imagined every nuance, emphasis and line, but what good is that to people who need to find the meaning themselves? So let them find it. Stand back a bit, enjoy it if you can, and with any luck they'll bring out things you never dreamed of. Keep your eye on the story and it can't go wrong.

Repeat it like a mantra, is the story being told? You may find in the majority of cases it is. If it isn't, and you feel the production is being blown off course, certainly you should intervene. But if you can frame your thinking and apply that question to every scene, every moment, then your notes and thoughts will be really useful, and you'll become one of those writers welcome in the rehearsal room. If you can't, you'll find yourself being sent over the road to get the sandwiches.

David Henry Hwang

David Henry Hwang's work includes *M. Butterfly, Chinglish, Yellow Face, Golden Child* and *The Dance and the Railroad,* as well as the Broadway musicals *Aida, Tarzan* and *Flower Drum Song* (revival). He is a Tony Award winner and three-time nominee, a three-time OBIE Award winner, and has twice been a finalist for the Pulitzer Prize in Drama.

Boom or bust?

We are in a 'Best of Times, Worst of Times' moment for theatre. On the plus side, the commercial theatre is healthier than I can remember in my lifetime. Just a few decades ago, Broadway theatres routinely sat empty. Today producers fight to fill these houses with their shows. As recently as the mid-1990s, there were years when Broadway couldn't even find four shows to nominate for the Best Musical Tony Award. Today, musicals are arguably closer to the heart of popular culture than at any point since the 1950s. Though plays are considerably less popular, I believe we will look back on this period as a golden age of playwriting.

The digital age, contrary to some earlier predictions, has proven to be good for the theatre. Live entertainment in general has grown more valuable. At least for the moment, the live experience cannot be duplicated digitally. As a result, the proportion of income that pop musicians receive from touring, for instance, has grown. Theatre has also benefited from this cultural shift.

So much for the good news. However, the increased viability of commercial theatre means that Broadway now pulls the cart of the entire field in a way it did not previously. The not-for-profit (or subsidized) theatre movement began in the States in the 1950s and 1960s as a reaction to commercial theatre. Subsidized theatres were founded to produce more risky and groundbreaking work, which would not be dependent upon box office for survival. Today, however, subsidized theatres generally serve as feeders for the commercial theatre, providing a relatively inexpensive means of 'trying out' shows for a possible future on Broadway. I value Broadway, but it needs to be part of a larger theatrical ecology. Shows which are never meant to make money should once again be accorded as much value, if not more than those capable of racking up financial profits.

Furthermore, the theatre today risks growing obsolete, due not to technology, but to its inability to face changing demographics. In America, for instance, Caucasians will become a plurality rather than a majority of the population in roughly twenty years. Yet on Broadway and the major NYC subsidized theatres, about 80 per cent of roles are still cast with Caucasian actors, according to data provided by the Asian American Performers Action Coalition. This would be a poor diversity figure in any field, and means that the theatre continues to draw its audience and talent from a shrinking proportion of the population. In an age when most industries recognize this fact and are taking steps to engage a multicultural future, the theatre lags behind, which amounts to a poor business decision. As theatre artists, we face both great opportunities and great challenges as we look to the future of our field.

Bryony Lavery

Bryony Lavery is the author of many plays for theatre, including *Queen Coal* (Sheffield Theatres), *Last Easter* (premiered at The Lucille Lortel Theater in New York City, and produced at Birmingham Rep directed by Douglas Hodge), *Stockholm* (Frantic Assembly/Sydney Theatre, Australia/ Hampstead Theatre), *Beautiful Burnout* (Frantic Assembly/St Anne's Warehouse, New York City) and *Kursk* (Sound&Fury/The Young Vic). *Frozen* (Birmingham Rep) won the TMA Best Play Award and the Eileen Anderson Central Television Award, and was produced on Broadway where it was nominated for four Tony awards. Bryony has also written many plays for BBC Radio, and works in TV and film. She is a former Assistant Director of Gay Sweatshop, and of her own company, Les Oeufs Malades.

Teaching a craft

There's recently been a deliciously crosspatch, sabre-rattling debate raging over that dullest of questions:

> 'Can Playwriting Be Taught?'
> Here's my experience.

Hundreds of years ago, I was asked to be a playwright-in-residence at The Unicorn Theatre. On the plus side, I got some regular money and an office in town, which seemed very *cool*; on the minus side, I was expected to *teach* a playwriting course. I didn't want to do it *at all*. I was nervous, arrogant, reluctant and *grand* about it. I was afraid that (a) I'd give up all my power and secrets and (b) everybody would copy my *majestic brilliance* and write like *me*. (Hey, I was very *young*!)

Here's what I discovered.

Pride often comes before a fall.

Especially in my case.

I was wrong about *everything*.

Fasten your seat belts, we're heading into The Sea of Metaphor …

Writing is *robust*.

We are play *wrights*.

We are trying to make stout, workable, moveable structures.

It is a very, very good thing to take the machine out, put it up on the blocks and look at all its working parts.

Assistants and technicians and specialists are helpful.

Sometimes, somebody saying 'Have you tried switching it off and on?' is the right question.

Writing is about inhabiting that weird, tipping, bucking spectrum between complete *confidence* up one end of the dial and utter black encompassing *doubt* down the other end.

Sometimes you are incredibly talented and inspired and you don't need *anybody*.

Sometimes you are hopeless, idea-less and you need *everybody*.

In my long stumble through all the attempts I've made to teach others while I've been desperately trying to learn to fucking write plays myself, I realize what I've *always* been really doing is – trying to teach *myself* how to write …

If you want to learn to write better …

Try this.

Try thinking up some devices to reveal how to others.

Try finding those keys that fit those locked doors into something glorious.

Personally, I've assembled a very capacious belt of useful tools.

You should see the workbench inside my head!

The chisels, hammers, saws, the allen keys, the power drill ….

The talented bit, the inspiration, the idea… is floating around *anyway*… So… mostly we're hanging around in the workshop, waiting for it to fly down off the rafters…

Trying to *teach* playwriting has always got me teaching *myself* at least.

It often hones my plethora of unsharp cutting edges, it empties my old used screws and nails and wooden bits…

It makes me throw out those unused gadgets that don't help a bit.

It's not foolproof.

Look. I'm *still* overusing metaphors.

Now, where do I return the money?

Frank McGuinness

Frank McGuinness is a playwright, poet and novelist who works in the School of English, University College Dublin. His plays include, among others, *The Factory Girls, Baglady, Observe the Sons of Ulster Marching Towards the Somme, Carthaginians, Someone Who'll Watch Over Me, Mutabilitie* and *Dolly West's Kitchen.* He has written English versions of Ibsen, Chekhov, Lorca, Brecht, Sophocles, Strindberg, Euripides, Racine, Ostrovsky and Tirso De Molina.

Playwriting – a joy unconfined

In so far as I'm sure of anything, I know where I'm going when I write a play, but I never know how I'll get there. A timid traveller in life, I am always laden down with far more than I need, conceiving all that could or could not happen on the journey, remembering and inventing panic and pandemonium, ready to abandon every attempt, reading luckless premonition in the most ludicrous of signs. Yet when I write the first draft, I am reckless, agile, ready for all comers, careless of convenience, jumping on trains, hijacking liners, ignoring the emergency exit, not giving a curse if I spend all I possess or, preferably, do not possess – more will be provided. Who by? I'll tell you.

Today I'll say I imagine them as a couple, Diamond Jim and Diamond Jemima Brady. They are absolutely loaded, the pair of them. Since they have money, and brains, to burn, they are in the business of causing chaos, ensuring you never know where you stand with them and that they are as likely to lead you into quicksand or quarantine as into harbour, if the humour strikes them. First of all, though, they seem perfect, like fairy godparents, out to humour my every whim. Banish all Catholic guilt. Gift me for being gay. Silence every censor. Grant the biggest wish of all. Get me past page twenty of the play that's emerging.

Still, as I say, Jim and Jemima can turn. If I keep doing nothing, looking out my window, they whisper they will hurl a brick through it. This is not an idle threat – they let it be known they prefer the house they visit to be empty, easier to pick a fight in – and in return for their gifts of collisions and crises, of grief, they make sure I have to slog to get past that magic number of writing twenty pages. I will not then dare abandon this brute of our making, after all that effort, the blood, the sweat and the stewed tea. What is the reward for going on, for finishing?

Doubt, fear, cowardice, self-pity, kicks to the face from theatres you've packed before but now have lost faith. To top all that, a pleasure beyond compare, a high like no other, a drug more beautifully exquisite than my long-abandoned Irish delicacy, Red Silk Cut (just after I stopped smoking, one night I sang Whitney Houston's 'I Will Always Love You' to a friend's packet of twenty, and I meant it). Look, it's the play, complete, born, smelling of strangest, sweetest blood, straining at the bit to take on the world, already in heat, a joy unconfined, for a day, at least.

Lynn Nottage

Lynn Nottage is a Pulitzer Prize-winning playwright and a screenwriter. Her plays have been produced widely in the USA, England and throughout the world. They include *By the Way, Meet Vera Stark, Ruined* (Short List: Southbank Sky Arts Award), *Intimate Apparel* (Short List: Evening Standard Award) and *Fabulation, or the Re-Education of Undine*. Nottage is the recipient of numerous honours including a MacArthur Genius Grant and the Steinberg 'Mimi' Distinguished Playwright Award.

In praise of procrastination

Anxiety has always been my principal adversary when it has come to confronting the blank page, an annoying by-product of doing battle with persistent writer's block. Festering and growing, my anxiety would take on an unfortunate life of its own, and completely consume all aspects of my life. It would beat up on me, and wreak havoc on everything from my fragile digestive system to my emotional stability. When I couldn't write, I felt as if I was betraying and abandoning a lover at a time of greatest need. Subsequently, my guilt became a pall of terror that overshadowed my life and paralysed me.

Then several years ago, I heard a stark unadorned piece of advice that changed my approach to writing. I was sitting in an acoustically challenging auditorium at Princeton University straining to hear Nobel Laureate Toni Morrison discuss her latest novel. In the middle of the talkback someone in the audience asked her for advice on how to deal with writer's block, and she stated in a grand clarion voice, 'I HONOUR THE BLOCK!' In her simple declaration, I found a strange liberation. I realized that my overpowering anxiety came from resisting the block, doing battle with it, rather than allowing myself to push back and explore the reasons for the block.

Over the years, I've come to embrace that writer's block as the mind's assertive way of saying 'You're not yet ready to commit to writing. STOP FIGHTING.' Indeed, the mind needs ample room for reflection, space to read and roam, stretch and exercise. Now, I view my writer's block as an excellent adventure, time for me to slow down my process and investigate the nooks and crannies of my resistance. I've surrendered to the fact that procrastination is an essential part of my creative process. On days when I feel my resistance to writing building and I struggle with my character's reticence despite persistent coaxing, I push back from my computer and go on urban safaris around my Brooklyn neighbourhood, or take welcome sojourns in the 42nd Street branch of the New York Public Library. I've allowed research and reflection to become an important part of the writing process, as important as putting words on the page. I forgive myself for not physically writing every single day, and in the forgiveness I've found greater productivity.

Honouring the block is like the long inhale/exhale at the start of a yoga class, and it's allowed me to be more disciplined, patient and mindful in how I develop and approach new work.

Christina Reid

Christina Reid's play *Did You Hear the One About the Irishman?* won the Ulster Television Drama Award in 1980, while her breakthrough work *Tea in a China Cup* was a runner-up in the 1982 IT/DTF competition for plays by women. Other plays include *Joyriders, Reid's Clowns, The Belle of Belfast City* (which won the George Devine Award) and *The Last of a Dyin' Race* (which won the Giles Cooper Award). She has been writer in residence at both the Lyric Theatre, Belfast, and the Young Vic, London.

A vote for the playwright

I have never had it in me to write a rough, fast, first draft of a play. I rewrite and rewrite each scene as I go along. When I submit a play, it is way beyond being a first draft – which is not to say it is writ in stone. From page to stage involves many people whose talents I don't have – directors, actors, designers, musicians, technicians. More rewrites will follow, but before it gets to the collaborative/rehearsal process, I need to get the play from my head to the page without taking in ideas that haven't originated with me.

If need be, I can talk about the idea in my head, but not in great detail. Too much talking in advance of the writing of a play and you can lose the plot. The detail of the story (all my plays are stories) happens during the writing of it, when it's just the characters and me. We inhabit another world together. (Tell us about it, I hear my nearest and dearest say!) Seeing the characters becomes hearing them in my head. We get to know each other and the writing happens – and not always as I intended. For example, in one early play I knew right from the beginning which one of the characters would be dead by the end. I was so wrong. I had intended to kill off a boy (I didn't like him much) but as the dialogue between the characters took hold, he emerged as a born survivor. A girl (I liked her very much) emerged as the victim. That she would die instead of him was as much a dramatic shock to me during the writing of it as it was to the audience when the play was staged. I doubt that that big dramatic change would have happened if I'd got locked into my original idea by talking too much about it in advance.

Those were the days, my friend, when the voice of the individual writer was encouraged and supported in the theatre. Increasingly, these days, the emerging voice of the new young writer is in constant danger of being adulterated and fragmented by the notion that new plays are best written from the very beginning in conjunction with a committee of theatre 'experts' – mostly non-writers. I'm not saying that the end result of that collaborative process in advance of the writing is always bad. It can work and some writers choose it. But they shouldn't have to choose it because of the increasing pressure that 'writing by committee' is the best way/the only way to realize/get funding for a new play.

I believe passionately in the voice of the individual writer, flaws and all. All I am saying is give it a chance.

Polly Stenham

Polly Stenham's plays include *Hotel* (National Theatre), *That Face* (Royal Court/Duke of York's) for which she was awarded the 2008 Critics' Circle Award for Most Promising Playwright, the Evening Standard Award for Most Promising Playwright 2007 and TMA Best New Play 2007, and *Tusk Tusk* and *No Quarter* (Royal Court).

Watching a script become a play

I remember the first time I had a reading. It was of *That Face*, the first play I had written. I was nineteen; nervous, and completely unprepared for the effect it would have on me. I had only ever watched a finished play. I had never been at the beginning of the process, so I'd never witnessed the alchemy that happens when work goes from two- to three-dimensional. A script exists on a flat page, inked symbols on paper, cool to the touch. Yet there's such heat in a play. It moves, breathes, sweats.

It's that difference in texture, that transformation from script to play, from cold to hot, that never fails to blow my mind. When the shapes on a page become sounds in mouths of moving faces. It feels like conjuring. It's the closest I've come to experiencing something like magic, watching what didn't exist before begin to live.

Tom Stoppard

Tom Stoppard was born in Czechoslovakia and began his career in England in 1954 as a journalist, moving to London in 1960 to start work as a playwright. His second play, *Rosencrantz and Guildenstern Are Dead*, began at the 1966 Edinburgh Festival and was subsequently produced at the National Theatre and on Broadway. Other plays include *Every Good Boy Deserves Favour, The Real Thing, Rock 'n' Roll* and *The Hard Problem (2015)*. Over the course of his career he has written for radio, television, film and stage. In 1998 he co-wrote the Academy Award-winning screenplay for the film *Shakespeare in Love*.

What's in a play?

Considered as a text, a play is odder than simply another literary form, another way to tell a story. A play is the transcription of an event which has not yet taken place.

This assertion can be unpacked.

Is a play a literary form? For me it is, but I should acknowledge that there are plays in which movement, sights, sounds and silences stretch the term all the way to self-contradiction; but they are still theatre.

Is theatre a storytelling art form? Almost always, but not necessarily. Theatre can be an immersion into an experience with no narrative.

Is the event being transcribed by the playwright necessarily – in the event – imagined completely? No.

Finally, is it right to privilege the event over the text? Yes.

The first time I spoke in public as a playwright, to a thousand undergraduates studying English and drama, I remarked that I had never written anything for study, and I caused a ripple of disturbance across an audience who spent half their time 'studying drama' but seldom saw a play. But from that day to this my mantra has been 'Theatre is an event, not a text.'

The story so far, then: for me, a play is a storytelling 'literary' form in the service, ultimately, of an event happening on a stage.

Typically, I am sparked by a preoccupation with something so abstract that I consider myself to be 'working on a play' before I have any notion of a story, a setting or characters.

During the whole of my play-writing life, I've come up against the conundrum that I can't start writing until I know where the play is going, and don't know where it's going until I'm writing. This can go on for years, during which I'm 'working on a play' by reading stuff, and often it's only a deadline which calls a halt to my procrastination.

From this, I offer my solitary piece of wisdom (by no means only mine). Don't tell the play where it has to go. Let the play tell you where it has to go, from moment to moment. I hope that doesn't sound mystical or pretentious. I've come to believe in it as a literal truth. If you work out the narrative in advance you're making yourself (and the audience) hostage to a structure which is likely to creak under the strain of false motivations and false behaviour.

Finally, the privileging of the event over the text is simply an empirical fact about theatre. While you're writing, you're as self-sufficient as if you're writing a sonnet. From the moment you get into rehearsal – and more so when you're in technical rehearsal involving light, sound, scene changes, etc. – you're confronted by the fact that your precious text will deflate, rip apart or just sit there unconvincingly until the whole mechanism comes together as close to perfection as possible. That's why – when you think back – many of the best moments you experience in the theatre are not on the page. The transcription is never complete in advance of the event. That's why the second edition of my published play is almost always a little different from the first edition: the transcription has been brought into line with the event. That seems the right way round to me.

Jack Thorne

Jack Thorne's many plays for the stage include, among others, *Hope* (Royal Court), adaptations of *Let the Right One In* (National Theatre of Scotland at Dundee Rep/Royal Court and Apollo Theatre, London) and *Stuart: A Life Backwards* (Underbelly, Edinburgh/tour), *Mydidae* (Soho/ Trafalgar Studios), an adaptation of Friedrich Dürrenmatt's *The Physicists* (Donmar Warehouse), *Bunny* (Underbelly, Edinburgh Fringe/ Soho), and *2nd May 1997* and *When You Cure Me* (Bush and Radio 3's Drama on Three). He has written extensively for TV including *Skins, This Is England '86, '88* and *'90* (with Shane Meadows), and *Glue*.

The importance of moo

The great Mike Bradwell was my first professional director – he directed a play I wrote called *When You Cure Me*. An extraordinary man, he ran the Bush in his own image, which is to say a cross between bullish and slightly dangerous. Before I went into rehearsals he said there were three answers to every question – 'yes', 'no' and 'moo'. 'Moo' means (and I hope he feels I'm quoting him correctly) 'I know the answer, I'm just not going to tell you the answer because it won't be useful for you to hear it.'

I'm not really a rehearsal playwright, I don't like giving answers to questions, in fact if I had a preference I'd be treated like a dead playwright. These characters lived in my head and I'm now happy for them to live in another head. In fact, I mostly think I'm quite a negative presence in the room – because I inhibit discovery. And so the older I've got, the more I believe in 'moo'.

Anne Washburn

Anne Washburn's plays include *Mr. Burns, The Internationalist, A Devil at Noon, Apparition, The Communist Dracula Pageant, I Have Loved Strangers, The Ladies, The Small* and a version of Euripides' *Orestes*. Awards include a Guggenheim, an NYFA Fellowship, a Time Warner Fellowship, Susan Smith Blackburn finalist, residencies at MacDowell

and Yaddo, and an Artslink travel grant to Hungary to work with the playwright Peter Karpati. She is an associated artist with The Civilians, Clubbed Thumb and New Georges, and is an alumna of New Dramatists and 13P.

On the difficulty of being an alive playwright

I saw a panel a few years ago in which directors talked about the particular challenges of new work, and the advantages and disadvantages of having a playwright in the room. One director described an experience of working on an Arthur Miller play in which there was a punctuation mark he was convinced was just wrong. 'I went "It doesn't work, it just doesn't work. I can't get him on the phone, I can't take it out..." – and three days later, the actors and I discovered that it actually *did* work. And I know, in my heart of hearts, that if a new writer had been in the room I'd have been convinced, I'd have said "It just doesn't work, what else can you possibly do?" '

This speaks to a continual perplexity of the living playwright participating in a rehearsal process. On the one hand, it's really best for everyone to approach the play as if it is canonical, isn't it? On the other hand – it's not, and you're in the room.

This is not to say that playwrights should sit magisterially to the side and insist on the rigid perfection of their work. But it's a trick to make sure that the text is given its deepest due, as written, and at the same time plunge in and make whatever changes seem right and amusing and necessary.

Because the truth is, the text can be almost as perplexing to the playwright as to everyone else in the room. The part of your brain that writes the play is not the same part that shows up to rehearse it, and I know I'm not the only playwright to not fully understand her play until long after it was first produced. So when you're in the room you have a dual responsibility, both to the new understanding you are gaining of the play as it unfurls in front of you, embodied by actual humans, and to the vision of the very different part of you which originated it.

You're protecting the play not just from the interloping impulses of directors and maybe actors or producers, but also from yourself, and from the common inclination to make changes to please others, to create a feeling of purpose, or to stem boredom and to feel like you're actually working in the room alongside everyone else. I have on more than one occasion been willing, in the spirit of fierce camaraderie, to sell some part of my own play down the river when it was mysterious to me in the cold light of the room, and have on more than one occasion been rescued by a director more clear-headed than myself.

Of course there's no graceful solution. Being alive is awkward on all fronts.

Steve Waters

Steve Waters' plays include *After the Gods* (Hampstead Theatre), *Fast Labour* (Hampstead/West Yorkshire Playhouse), *World Music* (Sheffield Crucible/Donmar Wharehouse), *The Contingency Plan* and *Little Platoons* (Bush Theatre) and *Temple* (Donmar Warehouse). He has also written *The Secret Life of Plays* and several plays for radio. He is published by Nick Hern books and is a senior lecturer in Creative Writing at the University of East Anglia.

Why I write for the stage

I don't come from a theatre background. I don't spend a great deal of time amongst theatre people. I say all that to prompt myself to answer the question as to why I write for the stage.

For those near to me, it's not an easy question to answer. 'Why don't you write *Dr Who?*' my kids ask. 'When are things going to really take off for you?' my family ask.

Also, aren't I a political writer? When a performance finishes everyone's very clear: this should be a film, this should be on the radio, then you can really reach people. Why don't you put it on YouTube? Aren't you keen to reach AS MANY PEOPLE AS POSSIBLE?

And sometimes, I feel an incredibly long way from the theatre and begin to doubt its virtues myself. I see it as those around me see it: as something happening miles away, a diversion, a preamble to real success, a mystery.

Yet I have been writing for the stage for over a decade now.

I happen to think theatre is good for us. I think it's good to go out and go to see a play. It feels a very much more active thing to do than to slump in front a television screen, or worse, hunch over a laptop. OK, I sometimes resent the fact that it needs to be planned; I am not good at thinking ahead. But then, as it does need to be planned it offers the first gratification – anticipation. The surveying of news, the scanning of reviews, the emergent noise about this imminent experience.

Then there is the journey. Like sometimes on a train to a city you barely know. I once went on the hottest day of the year to Chichester; I had to change trains twice; I had to walk in the heat through a town I hadn't visited since childhood. So many stations in every sense to pass through before the event began. It almost makes sense to speak of pilgrimage.

Similarly, I am most excited when I have a play on in a town I don't know so well. I once had a play on in Leeds; I stepped from the train and there was a poster for the play – at the train station! As if somehow I had entered the town with an occupying army. I walked to the theatre feeling like I was going to explode.

So why might this be good for us? Is it simply that theatre takes place in places? That in real rooms real people (the actors) shape themselves to the shared project of the play. Then real people buy tickets, eat a meal, meet with friends and go to sit and watch the play. Real people leave, perhaps disappointed, maybe confused, sometimes elated, and go out into the night in a quickened conversation this event in their lives has made possible.

(All too often people with disposable income and surplus time, I admit that.) But not sitting on a sofa surrounded by coffee cups, entertained or comforted, but still alone.

That's why I write for the theatre.

Timberlake Wertenbaker

Timberlake grew up in the Basque country. A multi-award-winning playwright, she has been Arts Council Writer in Residence with Shared Experience and at the Royal Court. She was the Royden B. Davis Visiting

Professor of Drama at Georgetown University, Washington D.C., 2005–2006, the Leverhulme Artist in Residence at the Freud Museum in 2011 and is currently Chair in Playwriting at the University of East Anglia. Plays include *Our Country's Good, Three Birds Alighting on a Field, The Love of the Nightingale* and, more recently, *The Ant and the Cicada* (RSC), *Our Ajax* (Southwark Playhouse), *The Line* (Arcola) and *Galileo's Daughter* (Bath Theatre Royal). Translations include *Britannicus* (Wilton's Music Hall), *Phèdre* (Stratford Shakespeare Festival, Ontario), *Antigone* (Southwark Playhouse), *Elektra* and *Hecuba* (ACT, The Getty), *Wild Orchids* (Chichester Festival Theatre), *Filumena* (Peter Hall Company at the Picadilly) and *Jenufa* (Arcola).

How to succeed in playwriting

For me, there's only one thing to remember when you're writing a play and that's to have courage. A lot of it. I'm probably speaking as a natural coward and this may be no more than a personal reminder, but too often, I see a play and I think: a little more courage would have made that play so much more interesting. Maybe not better in a conventional sense but more interesting: the writer's heart, however costumed behind characters, beating, bold.

I'm not saying never feel fear. It's rather the opposite: feel fear and try to overcome fear. It's about mental ambition, like being an adventurer and having the guts to wander into unknown, maybe even unmapped territory. I worry about that famous dictum given to beginner playwrights: write about what you know. A writer doesn't know anything, a writer discovers while writing. You don't have to be a fully fledged murderer to write about a criminal. It may not be as far from you as you think and you can discover the impulses with a little self-knowledge and some imagination. Can you not imagine circumstances in which you might become a terrorist? Or a saint? You may not be religious yourself but does that mean you can't understand why someone might be so? Or mad? Or silent? It's always a question of the imagination. And imagination requires daring. Climbing over the fence and entering the area that says Keep Out.

I say this particularly for women. There's always the danger that women will leave the adventures to the men. I mean not only the imaginative, intellectual adventures but the real ones as well.

Ambition is often slapped down, discouraged, considered unseemly. But the word ambition comes from the Latin *ambire*: to go around (usually, it seems, looking for votes – but listen, a playwright needs an audience). Courage comes from the Latin *cor*: heart. To go around with a heart seems a good definition of the playwright.

Researching plays is fun because it takes you into unknown territory. But you can also go deep into yourself and find unknown territory there. Plays are at this cross-section of the writer's heart and the event, so to speak. The private and public spheres. If a poem is usually private and a speech public, then the dialogue of a play is somewhere between the two.

Adaptation or translation means you can go off on your adventure with a companion. It's lovely. But you have to hold your own and help find the route. You're responsible for the communication and the language. No travelling works well when someone is too passive.

Ask yourself this question: do I have the courage to leave the safe island I've inhabited? If you do, sail on. Winds will be good or contrary, rough and dangerous. Depressing maybe. And sometimes exhilarating. Boats sink, people drown, people also swim, wave, get rescued or end up on an interesting and unknown island. However, as soon as you feel comfortable on that island, move on: writing plays cannot and should not be a safe option.

Roy Williams

Roy Williams is a multi-award-winning playwright, whose plays for stage include *Lift Off* (National Theatre Studio/Royal Court), *Sing Yer Heart Out for the Lads* (National Theatre Studio), *The Gift* (Birmingham Rep/ Tricycle), *Fall Out* and *Sucker Punch* (Royal Court), *The Loneliness of the Long Distance Runner* (Pilot Theatre/tour), *Category B* (Tricycle Theatre), *Angel House* (Eclipse Theatre/tour), *Days of Significance* (RSC), *Joe Guy* (Tiata Fahodzi), *There's Only One Wayne Mathews* (Polka Theatre),

***Baby Girl* (National Theatre Connections) and *Absolute Beginners* (Lyric Hammersmith). He also writes for television and radio.**

Why I write for theatre

One of my earliest memories is of being at primary school. Every Friday afternoon, thirty minutes before we were allowed to leave to enjoy our weekend, Miss Graham would sit us all down in the corner of the classroom and read another chapter from a children's book.

I was allowed to listen, take in, and daydream. I was a hopeless academic at school. Anything that required me to use my imagination like English, Art, I was good at, but practical subjects like Maths, Geography, the important stuff, I was bloody terrible. I agreed to be taught by a private tutor, every Saturday morning, from 10 am until 1 pm. My tutor was a guy named Don Kinch, who as well as being a teacher, was an actor, writer and director with a black theatre company at the time called Staunch Poets and Players. Every now and then, instead of our usual Saturday lesson, Don would go and work with his actors on their latest production, and I would tag along. Seeing live actors perform had a real effect on me. At the time, I knew very little about theatre, except that it was a place that a lot of white people went to, to watch a lot of other white people running about in tights, talking in a funny language that was written by this other white man called Shakespeare who was a long time dead.

Like most teenagers, I just drifted around for a few years. I worked in McDonalds, Safeways, warehouses, offices. I never stayed longer than a couple of months in any of those jobs. My life as a playwright had begun. And I had learned my first lesson about being one: the key to writing is to write.

Years had passed since I had left school, I had decided to take myself and my writing seriously. I came across an ad for a writers' course at Rose Bruford College. I decided to apply and then I was offered a place. Three years later, I came out with my first play, *The No-Boys Cricket Club*, loosely based on my mother's experiences growing up in Jamaica and living here. The reviews were good, but I still held onto my job as a theatre usher and stage door keeper.

Another lesson in writing: never believe your own hype.

No-Boys Cricket Club came about because in about ten to fifteen years the Windrush generation, including my mother, won't be here any more. When that happens, we will have a lot of questions to ask ourselves. Which brings me to three more lessons of playwriting.

> Everybody has a story to tell.
> Question everything!
> Always know that you want to know more.

In my writing at the moment, you could say I am asking questions myself. Who am I? Where we do I go from here?

Next lesson: everything begins with the written word.

People often ask me, how do I churn scripts out so fast, which I find is a crude way of describing my work. Writing any script is bloody tough. I do not feel that I am churning them out. I love writing. I have been often asked if I mind being called a 'black playwright', or do I address myself as one. The fact is, I am a playwright. Full stop. I don't write because I am black, I write because I don't know how not to.

Part 3

Write on: Writing a play

Fraser Grace and Clare Bayley

Research and planning

Fraser Grace

> **IMAGINING THE TRUTH**
>
> Once, in a post-show Q&A, I was asked how old I was when I left the country in which my play was set, and what did I miss most. I had to admit I'd never been there. Thankfully, this was greeted with some amazement rather than cries of 'No kidding'. In all modesty, and on behalf of playwrights everywhere, I then confessed that my next play was set in the sixteenth century, and I'd never been there either; imagining our way into other places, different times – this is what writers do.

They also research.

Most writers recognize research as a reasonable, often unavoidable, usually advisable, and reasonably discrete activity. It is used to substantiate our guesses and hide our ignorance, or merely to provide a wider context for the first-hand experience we do have. For the curious minded, it can also be an immensely enjoyable activity, and not only because it might put off the moment when the blank page must be faced. So how does a playwright research a play?

Beginning with a blank

There's an old joke, attributed to the sculptor Jacob Epstein, which aims to debunk the mystery of artistic genius.

> Question: How did Michelangelo produce the miracle that is his 'David'?
> Answer: He got a lump of marble and hacked away everything that didn't look like David.

This, in one model of the playwright in research, is the beginning of writing a play. Carving out your blank/choosing your lump of marble – for which read 'choosing your subject' – is the first act of making a play.

Two kinds of research might follow this simple choice of subject:

Dragnet (or open) research

- You decide to write about slavery and so read everything you can on the subject.

  Or

- You wish to set your play in a village in Somerset between the wars, so you rush to just such a village and interview as many people as you can find who might remember how it was.

For many writers, myself included, the dragnet model doesn't work well. There are just too many interesting stories; deciding where one finishes and the next starts is tricky. It's easy to get lost and end up with disparate interests, a collection of scenes or incidents, or a bunch of themes, with no centre and no drive.

Pole and line research

A useful question for any playwright is, What does my play need to be clued-up about? This might include anything from aspects of the highly specialized chemistry that the scientist in my new play is studying for her PhD thesis, to the kind of boots she wears and the vagaries of the Wiltshire accent sported by the colleague who has been so friendly and helpful.

How do you find out all the things you need to research in order to complete the play? Again, you have a choice of two paths.

TOP TIP

- Design the play in detail.

Mapping, plotting, dry running: a kind of cerebral improvisation. Probably most playwrights employ a degree of this; working everything out in detail *in advance of writing* is an extreme version. Plan out the play, perfect your design, realize where the play takes you and where your pockets of ignorance lie, and then go research. Once the info is collected, you can at last begin to write.

Or

- Write the play, and then do the research.

The last strategy presupposes that you know *something* – enough to get you going. This 'something' may be an idea about a character – the scientist's voice or the way she hangs her head – or a particular scene; the one in which she murders her Wiltshire colleague for reasons as yet unknown.

Taking this last approach, you will very likely have to break off from writing at some point – in order to find out what you now realize you don't know, but need to be sure of. Alternatively, you skim over sections of, for instance, detailed scientific analysis and keep on writing. You'll have to come back to these sections later and let the facts fill them out, but you can move on with the flow of the drama for now.

Although untidy, the positives of approaching research this way are:

- Play, design and research feed each other, offering a variety of activities rather than having to work in disciplined, discrete blocks.
- Time spent in hardcore research is finite, and well spent, because it almost certainly returns answers to questions the play is actually asking.
- A live play will be developing from very early in the process; all you have to do is feed it.
- As a playwright you are forced to begin with what you intuit about characters, about connections between characters and themes and so on.

The above makes for an exciting writing experience, and promises a more potent play than anything you might lift from a book of bald facts.

Types of research

- **Factual-historical data gathering**

This is the first kind of material we think about when the word 'research' arises. Some plays are more fact-reliant than others, for example, writing a documentary drama may mean there are things that have to be checked against the public record, or credibility will evaporate. But even in a play like this, factual research – dates, records, nomenclature – is only one kind of research required.

- **Cultural research**

The way people speak or greet each other, the relative popularity of a brand of washing powder or beer used in a particular time or part of the world, typical 'ways of seeing', local idioms, or (as in the example above) the *type* of person who ends up as a research chemist – such anthropological concerns provide pegs establishing the 'authenticity' of the world you're creating. These are often the things – more than dates or statistics, etc. – which convince an audience that the play/playwright knows the world being presented.

Other methods of establishing cultural information include:

- *Secondary research* – talking to people who *do* have first-hand knowledge.

  Useful because: you will also be learning about the *kind of person who knows this stuff.*

  Beware: the perceptions of your 'source' may be coloured by cultural or political factors you are not aware of.

- *Direct experience* – visit the country or work in the laboratory.

  Useful because: an hour of experience is worth a lot of research.

  Beware: Does 'parachuting' into another country, or another social world for a couple of weeks, or even a year, really tell you any more than what it is like to be tourist in these places? As is often said, until you swap your passport, you're always passing through.

- *Diaries, journalism and memoir* – probably more reliable than short-term 'postings', and readily available.

  Useful because: first-hand accounts of life in the appropriate place can offer a wealth of social detail.

  Beware: times change, and so do 'facts' when worked on by memory or subtle prejudice.

- **Imaginative research**

This the one form of research that applies to all plays, including the historical. Conditioned by what you've read/heard, within the factual/cultural parameters you've established, you *imagine* what people do, the choices they make and why – based on what you understand about humanity in general and their (imagined) character in particular.

AUTHENTICITY

In the famous quotation often attributed to Laurence Olivier, but believed to be originally by George Burns, 'The one thing the public must have is authenticity; and if you can fake that, you're made'.

TOP TIP

- **All worlds on stage are imagined** – and symbolically constructed. Hamlet believes something is rotten in the state of Denmark, and so it transpires. Yorick's skull is a token of this (and of Hamlet's own mortality); Ophelia's madness is both sign and product. Find the potent detail – whether that is object, vocabulary, or action – that conjures the essence of a particular world.
- **All characters are fictional**. This is true even of characters representing 'real' people, those currently living as well as dead. Once a character in a play, Napoleon Bonaparte will always be your 'Boney'; Robert Mugabe, my 'President Bob'. There's a lot about even well-documented figures that can't be known – the smell of their breath, the state of their fingernails.[1] This you make up, along with motive and, in many cases, action. The gaps in the record are as valuable to the playwright-in-research as the facts – if not more so, for here the imagination can roam freely.
- **All characters are also functional**. Characters are forged not only by 'facts', but by the needs of the drama. In other words, the things you need to get right are not just 'facts' but the things that make your play work. The tic by which President Nixon always checks himself in the mirror before leaving may help the play, whether or not this actually was the case.
- **Don't be intimidated by your ignorance**. Your job is not to know every inch of the ship, but to convince me that you do. As an audience, we have come prepared to believe. You job is to do what the disciple Thomas asked of Jesus: 'Help our unbelief'.
- **It doesn't have to be historically 'proven'** – but it does have to be within the realms of credibility and possibility. Unless the aim is purely to have

[1] This may be useful for the dramatist, but not necessarily for the play.

fun, a play will get little mileage out of suggesting that Tony Blair designed the Forth Road Bridge.

- **Keep notes**. If a play is any good, by the time you get to the Q&A after the first Wednesday of the production, you won't be able to remember whether what you 'learned' actually happened, or is an invention.
- **Theatre is about experience, not information**. Everything known on the stage is known *by someone* – partially, secretly, accidentally, boastfully, mistakenly. It is warped by a character's mode of expression, and its revelation is loaded with motive.

Question: When does 'well-informed' become the 'dead-hand of research'?

Answer: When information reaches the stage in an unfiltered state.

EXERCISE

- Think of someone you know only by sight – a celebrity, someone in your street or workplace, someone you've seen in a photograph or painting.
- Write down five things you can say for sure about them.
- Write down five things you think are true, but can't say for sure. How could you establish this beyond doubt, without asking them?
- Write down two things you want or suspect to be true about them.
- How might someone else – another character – discover this truth (a) by accident, (b) by seeking it out?

Character

Clare Bayley

All writers have a complex relationship to their characters, which Gustave Flaubert concisely encapsulated when he said: '*Madame Bovary, c'est moi.*' The characters are us, yet not us; we have to love them, even if we hate what they do; and sometimes we feel we can't even control their actions, and wish they wouldn't do the things they do.

The key thing is to have that passionate relationship with them. If you don't care about your characters, why should anyone else? – and there's nothing more deadly in a script than a boring, ill-defined, caricatured or 'typical' character.

Where they come from

Different writers claim all sorts of provenance for their creations. Some are inspired by newspaper cuttings or conversations overheard on buses; others draw shamelessly on their own relatives and friends; others start with a central concept or dilemma and devise the people who will illustrate it best. But however observant writers are, however much research is conducted, ultimately all characters come from somewhere within us, whether we're prepared to admit it or not.

Gore Vidal described Tennessee Williams' family as 'his basic repertory company' on which he drew to create his characters. Inevitably, we exploit our own emotional intelligence to make those characters live, though we don't always realize it at the time. In *Timebends*, Arthur Miller writes:

> 'I still feel – kind of temporary about myself,' Willy Loman says to his brother Ben. I smiled as I wrote the line in the spring of 1948, when it had not yet occurred to me that it summed up my own condition then and throughout my life.

Whatever their provenance, the greatest dramatic characters (Willy Loman, Uncle Vanya, King Lear, Hedda Gabler, Medea, Johnny Rooster ... and on and on) have entered our collective imaginations, not as archetypes but as individuals. They are as vivid to us as if they were old friends. Not that any of the above would make a wise choice of friend. But this is the point – these are not goody two-shoes conformists, but complex, difficult souls whose stories we find ourselves wanting to watch over and over again. We recognize their weaknesses and their mistakes. Their actions are open to interpretation. With luck, each time we will come out of the theatre with a slightly different view of them.

This ambiguity makes watching their stories active, not passive, and opens up debate amongst audience members. What is undisputed are the facts of the case: what the character actually does.

Character as action

'Tell me what they want, and I'll tell you who they are', wrote Chekhov, paraphrasing Aristotle. Every great character, as well as every minor character, has a great desire, goal, quest or need which compels them forward. The play begins when that desire meets impediments. David Mamet believes so strongly that character is action that he never gives characters a backstory. Everything we need to know happens on stage.

As it was once explained to me, put a character on stage eating an ice cream, and you have an image. Put a second character on the stage, who wants to get that ice cream off them, and you have the start of a play. How will they manage to get the ice cream? By trickery? Cajoling? Theft? Aggression? Charm? Sympathy? What will they do if all that fails? How far will they go to get what they want?

Usually it would be good advice to say that you need to choose a substantial desire for your central character, one big enough to sustain the drama through the play. But sometimes, the major character's desire can be quite a mild thing. In Jez Butterworth's *Jerusalem*, Johnny 'Rooster' Byron really only wants to be allowed to get on with his life undisturbed: to live in his caravan in the woods, hang out with the kids, have a few parties. It's his refusal to bow to his enemies from the council, and the increasingly epic nature of his battle to live his life as he wants to, that transforms his struggle into something fundamental, a quest for freedom, self-definition, identity.

The journey of that character pursuing their desire forms the substance and plot of the play, and its completion – or not – leaves them a changed person. They may start off naïve, and by the end of the play have acquired wisdom. They may begin the play good, and become corrupted. The obstacles they face may be beyond their control, as in the Greek tragedies, or they may be brought about by their own feckless nature or reckless behaviour.

The role of the antagonist

To create strong characters on stage, then, you need to pit them against powerful antagonists. You need to push your protagonist to the limit and beyond, out of their comfort zone, to make them show their true mettle. You constantly need to up the ante, raise the stakes – and then see what they do about it.

Four tools to create character:

- what they say,
- what they do,
- what others say about them,
- the interplay and inconsistencies between the previous three.

If there is no contradiction between what someone says about themselves and what others say, or between what they say and what they do, the character is less interesting to us. There's less work for us as an audience to do.

But when a character tells us, insistently, something about themselves we know to be untrue, it can be funny, sinister or deeply moving. This is starkly true in Lucy Kirkwood's searing portrait of the trafficked sex-worker Dijana in *it felt empty when the heart went at first but it is alright now*. Throughout the play she is cheerful, irrepressibly optimistic. We first see her matter-of-factly counting up the used condoms in her bin to tot up her total earnings, and calculate how soon she can buy back her freedom. In the final scenes, when the truth of how much she has been duped by her boyfriend is dawning on us, Dijana is still telling her unborn child a rose-tinted version of her life story:

> And I come here. And I am scared but also I hope. And I meet a man. And I fall in love. And I make you! And I learn the language better and better. And now the man who sell Turkish sweet on Kingsland Road know my name. And I work. And I have Oyster card. And I have iPhone! With Apps! And I make my life. And I am so
>
> so
>
> *happy.*

… and how they say it

This little extract shows us another important thing about creating characters: it's not just what they say, but how they say it. Dijana's frequent use of exclamation marks, her pride in her iPhone, her reference to the Kingsland Road and her partial grasp of the English language tell us much about her.

Minor characters

All of the above – that they need a strong desire, that they are defined by their actions, that how they say it is as important as what they say – applies equally to your minor characters as to your heroes and heroines. Purists would say you must apply it equally to the offstage characters whom we never even get to meet (Dijuna's boyfriend, for example). There should be no insignificant character in a play – if there is, you need to cut them.

To come alive, even a minor character needs to have their own powerful drive and motivation for their actions; their own ambiguities; their own voice. We may not see much of it, but the writer has to know and understand it.

A masterclass in the creation of minor characters is provided by Chekhov's character Soliony in *Three Sisters*. Here is a man who desperately wants to be admired, especially by the eponymous sisters. But the more he tries to impress them, the more dismally he fails, to the point that they physically recoil from him. On one level this makes for amusing and poignant drama. But Soliony's function in the play is important, so Chekhov needs us to notice him even while dismissing him as insignificant. He does this by creating him as an oddity, even a grotesque. He has the unusual and unattractive condition of excessively sweaty hands, and consequently always carries with him a bottle of perfume to sprinkle on his palms. This serves mostly to draw attention to the problem – and to him.

TOP TIP

Apart from at the RSC, there are no permanent companies of actors in theatres any more, so there is no justification for writing spear-carriers into the script. Even the police officer who delivers the bad news needs to be more than just a stock character. Can you justify paying an actor to come on and say one line? Is it fair to the actor? Could another character fulfil the same function?

QUESTION

Are the actors finding it hard to learn their lines? It could be that they aren't very well written. Is the character simply there to fulfil a function in the plot, with no driving, dramatic argument or logic to their words?

CHARACTER EXERCISE 1

Over time, collect portraits of interesting-looking people from magazine and newspapers. When you have a good selection of them, lay them out and pick one that draws you strongly. Give yourself five minutes to jot down some basic information about them as you imagine it:

their name,
age,
where they live,
how they live,
where they come from,
what they want in life,
what's in their pockets,
what's their secret.

Then for fifteen minutes write a monologue for them, based on their expression and situation in the picture, and the information above.

Once you've done this, pick a second picture. Do the same process: create a quick sketch in words of who they are. But instead of then writing a monologue, write a dialogue between these two characters. How does each one's aim in life conflict with – or complement – the other?

TOP TIP

If you get stuck with what a character would do, or say, or if you lose hold of their voice, spend half an hour writing a monologue for them. Often writing a monologue from their childhood will help you understand them and find their voice.

CHARACTER EXERCISE 2

Get into the habit of writing down the idiosyncrasies and character traits of the people you meet, and ideally a line of dialogue which captures it:

- The person who always apologizes for themselves ('Sorry about the birthday present, you've probably got one of those already …').
- The person who has to have the last word, win the argument, and who cheats at board games ('I don't care what it says in the dictionary, common usage is always spelt like this …').
- The person who protests too much ('No, I'll definitely be there, there is literally no way I'm going to let you down on this one, trust me …').

Dialogue

Clare Bayley

As a young playwright with his first big success on his hands, Arthur Miller bumped into a favourite uncle, Manny, who had snuck in to see a matinee without telling him. Manny's son, Buddy, was the same age as Miller, but had never been as successful – and Manny had always felt competitive with Miller on behalf of his son. The first thing Manny said betrayed exactly the opposite of what he was really feeling: 'Buddy is doing very well', he blurted out.

Miller recounts this painful and moving encounter in his autobiography, *Timebends*, as a key moment in his understanding of what dramatic dialogue should be.

'How wonderful, I thought, to do a play without any transitions at all, dialogue that would simply leap from bone to bone of a skeleton that would not for an instant cease being added to, an organism as strictly economical as a leaf, as trim as an ant.'[2]

To achieve this stripped-down economy while imbuing the words with resonance and meaning is what we're all trying to achieve. It's already

[2] Arthur Miller, *Timebends, A life* (London: Methuen, 1987), p. 131.

been said that dialogue is action: in this one line Manny is simultaneously resenting Miller's success, lamenting his own son's ordinariness, concealing his real feelings from his nephew and unwittingly revealing the true nature of those feelings. He's showing a lifetime's relationship with both his son and his nephew, and betraying his own failure as a father within it. No wonder the story sends shivers down the spine.

This one line of dialogue obeys all the rules that dramatists are attempting to follow when writing dialogue. Like a true professional, Miller not only recognized the fact but was sharp enough to write it down and remember it.

Dialogue, not real speech

The playwright Steve Gooch says:

> To imagine that the simple representation of people speaking to each other constitutes a play is false.[3]

The way that people really speak, if you transcribe it, is not going to make good dialogue. People repeat themselves, take a long time to get to the point, say the same thing in different ways, procrastinate, interrupt, exaggerate, evade, digress, conceal, pause and forget what they were going to say. The way people really talk is very undramatic.

Good dialogue takes all of these tendencies, and reproduces them in an artful way. Good dialogue will certainly have pauses, interruptions, repetitions and non-sequiturs – but they are fashioned by you, the artist, and so they are very different from what real conversation sounds like. What you are required to produce is a facsimile of real conversation.

You may not even be aiming for naturalism. You may be writing in a poetic or lyrical voice. But if you're doing this, you also have to pay attention to the conventions of naturalistic speech, and then adapt them to your own uses. In poetic speech, the use of pauses, interruptions, repetitions and non-sequiturs can be extremely powerful. You just have to look at debbie tucker green or

[3] Steve Gooch, *Writing a Play*, 3rd edn (London: A&C Black, 2001), p. 63.

Enda Walsh to see how the same tropes of natural conversation exist, but in a heightened form.

> **TOP TIP**
>
> All the great dialogue writers allow their characters to speak only when it's absolutely necessary. Some will say that speaking dialogue is the very last thing a character should do, when all other means of expression have been exhausted. In this way you can avoid the slack lines that are just passing the time, which in turn produce longueurs in the theatre.

Dialogue as action

Each line of dialogue has multiple functions to perform. The more it achieves, the better it succeeds. Each line has to be active and propel the plot forward; it has to reveal something about character, perhaps even convey information, as well as amuse and engage the audience – and all without ever seeming to do any of these things.

David Mamet's writing so clearly fulfils all these requirements that it acts as a primer for dialogue writing. In *Speed-the-Plow*, for example we first meet junior movie exec Fox in the office of his superior, Gould. Fox arrives full of urgency – the biggest break in his career may have just arrived. But Gould's status is such that Fox makes no less than five attempts to gain his attention. All he says, and repeats four times, is:

'Bob … '

– but each time Gould's own unstoppable monologue prevents him going any further. Even after Fox manages to blurt out 'I have to talk to you' it takes seven more lines of dialogue before he finally asks the key question:

'How close are you to Ross?'

In the whole of this exchange, Fox is vigorously striving to put his career-changing proposal to his boss, while Gould is equally energetically pursuing his own engrossing tangent. We want to know what's so important to Fox, so we are on the edge of our chairs until we know. The fact that the pay-off is so protracted is comic, but it also predisposes us to have sympathy for the underdog Fox.

The rest of the play sees Fox's increasingly desperate attempts to overcome the obstacles that life, fate and Gould throw in his way. We may be partly repulsed by Fox, and yet we can't help wanting to find out whether he prevails or not. As Mamet says, 'Dramatic storytelling [consists] exclusively in making the audience wonder what happens next.'[4]

Jump right in

Dialogue begins at the point where a scene becomes interesting, not at the point where the protagonists come into the room, take off their coats, exchange banal pleasantries of 'How are you' etc. When you go back and reread your scenes, think about where they really start. The first draft will often include a leisurely build-up to the action. You can often cut the first few lines – sometimes the first few pages – of tedious set-up.

Don't let them tell us

The main enemy of good dialogue is explaining too much. The listening and watching brain is much cleverer and quicker than the writing brain. An audience is capable of making emotive and instinctive leaps of understanding far quicker than you would believe.

Sometimes you have to write something out in order to know it; but after that you have to go back and cut the explanations and the links. As Miller said, all you need is the bones, and the audience will do the rest.

Stating the obvious should be avoided at all costs. Take your cue from Samuel Beckett: the only real justification for a character telling us they are about to leave, rather than just leaving, is if – as at the end of *Waiting for Godot* – they say 'Let's go' and the stage direction is 'They don't move.'

[4] David Mamet, Great American Plays and Great American Poetry in *Theatre* (London: Faber and Faber, 2010), p. 115.

People don't say what they feel

And if they do, it doesn't make for good dialogue – or satisfying drama. Somebody who is very upset or jealous or angry doesn't normally say they are. They yell, 'I'm NOT SHOUTING', or 'No, go ahead, I don't mind at all'. In the TV comedy about the Olympic planning committee, *Twenty Twelve*, Sally Owen doesn't say she is in love with her boss Ian Fletcher. She just goes to absurd lengths to research his holiday for him, including phoning the owners of the bar in the piazza opposite the hotel to check their hours.

> SALLY They say it closes at ten but basically they said they'll stay open till whenever you want to … till you're ready to go, really.
>
> IAN Well, that's my kind of – hang on! You've spoken to them?

Emotive language

Not allowing your characters to tell us their emotions doesn't mean that your language can't be emotional. In theatre, language is valued and lyricism is possible, in contrast to film and TV where image is dominant. And while this doesn't mean that you can justify long screeds of poetic ramblings, the quality of the expression is important. Mamet again: 'The dramatic poetry (the text) … must possess all the fluidity, rhythmic forces and tonal beauty of which the author is capable. This is to say it would be good if the playwright could actually write.'[5]

TOP TIP

Make a habit of reading your words aloud to yourself as you write. You will immediately start to hear the clunky bits, the lines that are hard to get your tongue around. Before you hand in your first draft, gather a group of actors – or just your friends – to read the script aloud. Rewrite accordingly.

Revealing character

Dialogue should be able to embody the voice of the character so completely that you could cover up the name tag on the left-hand side of the page and

[5] Ibid., p. 73.

still know who's speaking. In *Love and Information* Caryl Churchill actually does dispense with giving characters names – or situations, or character descriptions of any kind. If you read the text, they present themselves in your mind's eye. The clues are all there for us to decipher – the vocabulary, the syntax, the idiom, the subject matter, the preoccupations, the way they are relating to the other people in the scene. The audience will then flesh out the rest themselves.

Rhythm, pace and tone

Playwrights tend to have (or develop pretty fast) an ear for the rhythms both of the language itself, and of the types of language as they appear in the script. An hour and a half of one rhythm or one tone of voice would begin to grate, however skilful and beautiful.

Accents, patois, vernacular, idiom

debbie tucker green has developed a unique voice in the theatre which is both lyrical and authentically, humorously 'street'. The sister of the boy who is killed in a random attack on the street opens the play *Random* waking up on that fateful morning:

> This ent a morning to be peaceful
> and the something in the air –
> in the room –
> in this day –
> mekin mi shiver –
> even tho my single duvet
> is holding onto me like my man –
> who still don't phone –
> should be[6]

It's poetry of a sort, and not strictly speaking dialogue at all. It's deployed in the play to provide an impressionistic yet forensic reconstruction

[6] debbie tucker green, *Random* (London: Nick Hern Books, 2008).

of the day of a teenager's death. But within it, each of the characters comes through with startling clarity, with all their wit, vulnerability and idiosyncrasy.

Capturing the idiom, the vocabulary, the slang and the rhythm of your characters is a particular skill, and when a playwright succeeds it transports us instantly to a very particular time, place and personality. A playwright doesn't have to have a perfect grasp of the grammatical rules of the English language, nor do they have to have a talent for descriptive prose. But they have to have a real love for the way that people express themselves, and an attention to the detail of the language they use.

DIALOGUE EXERCISE 1

Practise the actioning technique, which many directors use, on your own dialogue. For every line you have to find an active verb which describes what the character is doing with that line. Are they persuading, threatening, pleading, intimidating, mocking, seducing? If all the lines in a scene are doing the same thing, would a little variety improve the dynamics? If you can't think of a relevant active verb, should the line be cut?

QUESTION

Has a character just told another character something they already know, just to inform the audience? How can you change things so that the audience still finds out the information?

TOP TIP

Read Timothy West's spoof radio drama *This Gun That I Have In My Right Hand Is Loaded* for an object lesson in how NOT to write expositional dialogue.

> **DIALOGUE EXERCISE 2**
>
> Rewrite a scene using only fifty words of dialogue. It will reveal to you the 'bones' of the scene – what is essential, and what is not. You can then rewrite with this in mind.

Place and situation

Clare Bayley

The question of where to set a play or a scene is more than just a decision about location. Sam Smiley expresses it like this: 'If the writer envisions a scenic metaphor that visually represents the overall dramatic image, then the setting will tend to suggest, intensify and sometimes compel the action.'[7]

Within your chosen milieu, you need to decide whether the action will play out in one defined location, or in a number of different settings. If you want to use a unified space, the key is to choose somewhere that will offer the greatest dramatic possibilities.

> **TOP TIP**
>
> The first place you think of isn't always the best. Sometimes you have to disregard the most obvious setting, and think instead about the most dramatically interesting place to place your characters.

> **REALITY VS THEATRE**
>
> In reality much of the drama of our lives plays out in sitting rooms and offices; many of our life-changing conversations happen over a kitchen or restaurant table. But how interesting is this for an audience to watch? Could these conversations be heightened by putting them in a more challenging environment?

[7] Sam Smiley, *Playwriting: The Structure of Action* (New Haven, CT: Yale University Press, 2005), p. 259.

Some playwrights consider that putting your characters in a place is less important than placing them in a situation with dramatic potential. In other words, that the setting is entirely subordinate to and determined by the action of the scene.

It's always useful to consider how the space acts upon the character. Do they feel nervous or relaxed, nostalgic, claustrophobic or confident in that place? The more 'stuff' that is going on for them, the more active and dramatic your scene will be. Even better if the location suggests activities the character has to perform. How can that develop? Does their sense of competence wax or wane, does the task in hand become more or less easy for them? If the dialogue is happening while one character is trying to conceal their lover behind a screen (as in Sheridan's *The School for Scandal*), or to do some DIY with an electric drill (as in Ayckbourn's *Just Between Ourselves*), the potential for the playwright is infinitely richer than if they were simply sharing a cup of tea.

Unity of place

As Alan Ayckbourn cannily says, 'Unity of place is always very satisfying and economical, not just financially but dramatically.'[8]

His plays frequently take place in a liminal space, which unites what could have been several different sets. So his comedy *Season's Greetings*, for instance, is set in the hall of Neville and Belinda's suburban home, with a view into both the sitting room and the dining room. The story kicks off during a Christmas Eve party being held in the house. During the party, the characters must go through the hall to get to either of the other rooms, while – satisfyingly – they can also catch sight of people in those rooms (and be seen by them).[9]

[8] Alan Ayckbourn, *The Crafty Art of Playmaking* (London: Faber and Faber, 2003), p. 29. Ayckbourn also recounts how he was commissioned to write a play (*Bedroom Farce*) for the newly completed Lyttelton stage: 'I could not for the life of me think how to fill that big wide stage. So I divided it into three and wrote a play set in three different bedrooms.'

[9] In the National Theatre's lavish production in 2010, the set showed the whole three-storey house, which Michael Billington in his review considered actually reduced the comic impact of the play (*The Guardian*, 9 December 2010).

In the nineteenth century the unity of place became popular in naturalistic theatre, and Ibsen was a master of the technique. *Hedda Gabler* is entirely set in Hedda's drawing room, which has a smaller room off it. Hedda's force of character and her magnetism are such that characters are inevitably drawn to visit her; her problem is that she's trapped in her life and her marriage, and, despite herself, rarely leaves. Despite her destructive power over others, she has failed to escape from her own literal and figurative confinement in this house. When she finally leaves the room, it marks her departure from this life.

To set your play in one room requires considerable technical discipline. You have to get characters on and off stage and develop the action without any of it seeming contrived. You have to suggest the past history and the wider world of the play while never stepping outside. However, whether the space is a prison cell, a drawing room or an underground bunker, when successfully achieved this technique is highly satisfying for the audience, giving them a heightened focus on the drama.

Linked but unified settings

There are times when a single setting is too restrictive for the story being told, though there is still a unity about the places chosen.

Rona Munro's 2002 play *Iron* takes place fifty years into Fay's life sentence for murdering her husband. At the beginning of the play, her 25-year-old daughter Josie has come to visit her for the first time since she was sent down. You might expect all the scenes to take place in the prison visiting room; but in order to afford us glimpses of the characters alone, or talking to prison officers, there are also scenes in a waiting room, an interview room and Fay's cell. Expanding the settings in this way prevents them becoming restrictive, while still keeping the characters – and the audience – firmly within the prison system.

Setting which determines action

In some cases the setting can determine the action of the play.

The advantages of setting a play in a place intended for a specific activity are manifold; a gym, for example, or a betting-shop, or the rehearsal room for a play. You can exploit these expectations for stage business; but more importantly, you can use the activities to comment on the thematics and symbolism of the play.

Roy Williams' *Sucker Punch* takes place entirely in a gym where the characters Troy and Leon are learning to box. This setting includes a ring (which in breakout monologues stands in for the rings where Leon's fights take place), as well as lockers, punchbags, the trainer Charlie's offstage office, the permanently blocked and flooding toilets. It's a public place, so that characters can come and go, and turn up unexpectedly. The activities they engage in (sparring, romancing, arguing) reflect the action of the whole play and the setting becomes a metaphor – it's a place where disadvantaged black kids can go and try and make something of their lives; where they may find love, but will also encounter racism and learn that corruption is rife – even the ambiguous father figure Charlie is involved in match-fixing.

Multiple settings

For epics, history plays – all kinds of dramas unfolding across time and space – playwrights from Shakespeare to Brecht have needed the freedom to roam. *King Lear* takes place in court, on the blasted heath, in a hovel, outside castles, in dungeons, on clifftops.

The settings are conjured through the verse, most wonderfully in Act Four, scene Six, where Edgar, in disguise, leads his blind father Gloucester to a hill which he claims is the top of the cliffs at Dover. Edgar knows that Gloucester will try to throw himself off the cliffs, and to save him he deceives him:

> Come on, sir, here's the place. Stand still: how fearful
> And dizzy 'tis to cast one's eyes so low.
> The crows and choughs that wing the midway air
> Show scarce so gross as beetles…

The ensuing scene – where Gloucester jumps on flat ground, believing he is on top of the cliff, and lands in a faint, so not realizing his mistake – is both arresting and poignant. Moreover it mirrors the story of Lear, and shows another great fall from grace of a self-deceiving parent.

Timberlake Wertenbaker's *Our Country's Good* tells the story of a group of convicts arriving in seventeenth-century Australia. Their enlightened Governor in Chief encourages them to produce a play, in an attempt to create a civilizing effect and 'change the nature of our little society'. Because Wertenbaker's play is about the staging of a play, there are certain activities which immediately suggest themselves for scenes, such as an audition, line learning, rehearsals and the performance itself. In these scenes the situation or activity is sufficient to give context to the scene, and the playwright leaves the choice of location to the director/designer. But in other scenes, where the action is more abstract or emotional, the setting is specified, and the action is conceived to reinforce its meaning.

There's a scene between Harry, the part-time hangman, and his convict-mistress Duckling, set in a rowing boat. Duckling was condemned to hang in Newgate prison until Harry took a fancy to her and managed to get her sentence commuted to deportation. She sees this as merely exchanging one prison for another, however. Harry's love is unrequited; the more he tries to win her round, the more she feels stifled by him:

'I wake up in the middle of the night and you're watching me … JUST STOP WATCHING ME', she exclaims.

Harry intends this rowing expedition to be a romantic treat for Duckling; she sees it as just another situation she can't easily escape from. She longs to be free of him; he longs for love; in a moment of truce and compromise they agree she can take part in the play. He ruins it all with the last line of the scene:

'I'll come and watch the rehearsals', he says. And they row off together in their unhappy little boat.

EXERCISE FOR CHOOSING A SETTING

1. Make a list of brilliant settings for plays you have seen, and write each setting on a separate piece of paper, for example:

   A clifftop near Dover

   A DIY enthusiast's workplace

A boxing gym
A rowing boat
A ladies' toilet
A tattoo parlour
The swings at a local park
A bedroom with a screen to conceal somebody

2. Pick one setting at random.
3. Rewrite a troublesome scene and set it in this location. What do you discover about the characters, the play, the action from this forced relocation?

TOP TIP

Keep a stockpile of interesting settings in a list. Each time you are starting a new scene or a new play, look through the list before you begin writing.

Action and plot

Fraser Grace

That fact that a drama travels through the time span of the play, and also travels 'unstoppably' through actual time, makes watching a play an almost unique experience.

Martin Esslin points up this essential difference between a play text and, say, prose intended for private reading:

> While it is possible to interrupt or put down a literary text [...], one of the chief distinctions of a dramatic text in performance is its relentless and irreversible progression from situation to situation within each of its basic structural elements (scenes, acts, sequences). A dramatic performance thus becomes a very definite 'structure-in-time-'.[10]

[10] Martin Esslin, *The Field of Drama: How the Signs of Drama Create Meaning on Stage and Screen* (London: Methuen, 1988), p. 87.

That phrase 'relentless and irreversible progression' is well chosen.

> Does my script suggest a play that will feel relentless (in a good way)?

The above is a good question to ask of any new play, particularly at first draft stage. If the answer is 'no', then it's worth examining how the action is structured in your play. You can address this in two ways:

- Are the characters in my play genuinely *in action*?
- What is the action of the play itself?

As Aristotle points out in his *Poetics*, the Greek word from which the word drama is derived is *dran. Dran* means 'to do'. Dramatic action then is about people doing things, but not just anything; the thing done must be linked to a purpose – an internal drive.

S. H. Butcher, a specialist on Aristotle, defines this dramatic action as an inner need: 'psychic energy moving outwards':[11]

> The πρᾶξις[12] of the drama has primary reference to the kind of action which, while springing from the inward will, manifests itself in doing.[13]

What begins as an impulse in a character (cause) has to find expression in action (effect), which includes speech. This triggers further events, and so on.

This in fact is how character is revealed in a play; we only know what a character is really like because we see what they say and do.

---

[11] Quoted in Stuart Spencer, *The Playwright's Guidebook* (London and New York: Faber and Faber Ltd, 2002), p. 37.

[12] 'Praxis' – the ancient Greek word for action.

[13] S. H. Butcher, *Aristotle's Theory of Poetry & Fine Art* (London: MacMillan and Co Ltd, 1902), p. 334.

TOP TIP

Be clear about what each of your characters wants. If you have a draft to work from, examine every line your character says, notice everything they do. How does this line or that action relate to the goal they are inching towards?

For Lin Coghlan on different kinds of wants, see Part 2 'Tips and Tales'.

- Like many of us in the real world, some characters only have a dim sense of what it is they really want (much less need), and an even dimmer notion of how to get it. They may tread water, act tentatively, follow false trails, get easily distracted.
- Other characters have a strong sense of what they intend to get, and can swiftly calculate the best route to getting it.
- In drama 'the best route' does not always mean 'most direct'.

A philanderer – let's call him Ben – may want to both bed the boss's wife and keep his own wife oblivious, so a circuitous path, characterized by disguise, denial and manipulation, is called for. And besides, the boss's wife, Karen, has intentions of her own; who's to say she is remotely interested in Ben? And Ben's wife, Amy, is not stupid either, despite what Ben thinks of her. Together their respective goals may place significant obstacles in Ben's path.

In fact, what seems to be the story of how comically sly, determined Ben cleverly seduces a woman who protests her indifference too much, might turn out to be the rather pleasing tale of how a devious and arrogant man ends with nothing, while Karen and Amy finally achieve happiness as life partners.

The plot

The sequence in which our imaginary drama above presents its unlikely story will necessarily be full of twists, turns, revelations and reversals, one thing leading to another, until a crisis is reached and a new reality is born.

> This is the plot – a story revealed in an intelligent sequence of cause and effect, each 'episode' driven by the dramatic action of its participants, but also presented in a sequence that feeds the Action of the play.

The action *of* the play

As George Bernard Shaw puts it, 'Plays are about believable people doing believable things' – driven, as we've seen, by their desires and needs. But dramatic action is also in operation in another way:

> Every play has ambitions of its own, a thing or things which the play's design is endeavouring to deliver, and which all the action in the play will combine to accomplish. This 'achievement' of the play is the play's Action.

This idea has its roots in Aristotle's idea of the unity of plot: an effective play (he is talking specifically about tragedy) has one or more driving sequences – plots – which constitute 'the imitation of the action'.

As Bentley notes, 'What is the Action? Aristotle forgot to tell'.[14]

Theorists ever since have offered their own definitions of the action of a play. One of the most writer-friendly formulations is offered by the French dramatist and critic Pierre Aimé-Touchard, quoted by Bentley:

> The general movement that brings it about is that something is born, develops, and dies between the beginning and the end.[15]

It's important to note that a claim is being made here that a play can and usually does have a trajectory over and above that of any of the people within it; the play is greater than the characters; it has needs of its own.

---

[14] Bentley, *Life of the Drama*, p. 15.

[15] Ibid., p. 15.

Determining a play's action

British playwright David Edgar develops the idea of a play's action by suggesting that it can be encapsulated in a single, focused statement – 'a brief encapsulation of the narrative progression of a play structured to reveal its meaning'.[16] He enlarges on this with the following formulations:

> A dramatic action consists of a **project** (usually described in the form of a subject, verb and object: someone sets out to do something) followed by a **contradiction** or **reversal** (as like as not a clause beginning with the word 'but').[17]

He then defines two variations of the encapsulating statement, which we can paraphrase as:

A project followed by reversal

and

Despite … nonetheless …

The first of these applies to a more tragic play, while the second is more optimistic or comic.

So Shakespeare, in Henry IV Parts One & Two, begins with King Henry both facing a rebellion and despairing of ensuring his succession. The main cause of the latter is that his son Hal is off playing the wastrel with his dissolute pal Falstaff. But then Hal performs a handbrake turn, revealing hidden depths by first defeating the rebellious Percys in battle, and then reconciling with his dying father. All this happens in the nick of time, as yet another rebellion is gathering. Hal's rise to the fearful and lonely challenge of monarchy is then, never simple. But the action that binds the two plays embraces all of this. We can summarise it as: 'Despite Hal's wastrel ways, England nonetheless discovers the king it needs in the prince it thought was lost'. For the people in the play – and for us the audience – this transformation is made all the more remarkable by Hal's necessary but still cruel-seeming rejection of Falstaff. The drama on the other hand knew where it was going all along; it has an action. All the plot had to do, was find a way to achieve it.

---

[16] D. Edgar, *How Plays Work* (London: Nick Hern Books, 2009), p. 17.

[17] Ibid., p. 25.

Why is this useful to a playwright?

- Having identified a play's action, we can see how any playwright we admire structures their play to both pursue and (sometimes) disguise the action.
- For our own plays, either at a pre-writing design stage (if you go in for those) or at first draft, working out a possible action for the play may help us decide which scenes are essential to the drama and which must be pared away.

> **TOP TIP**
>
> If a play seems to lose impetus:
>
> - check that your characters are genuinely *in action*;
> - check that every scene advances the play's central action.

Unlike the novelist, a playwright can rarely risk digression.

Summary and direct actions

The above formulations work well if a play has a clear protagonist, but what about plays which don't?

A useful refinement to the notion of action is to distinguish between plays that have a direct action, and those whose action is best described as summary.[18]

The direct action

In some plays, the entire drama is driven by the progress of the central character, the protagonist. David Mamet's play *Edmond* is an extreme, almost unique example, but useful for clarity's sake. Here's a quick outline:

A consultation with a fortune teller in the prologue-like first scene initiates the action of the play, when she tells Edmond 'You are not where you belong.' If this is the cause, the effect is not long in coming. In scene two, the

[18] The term 'complex action' is unfortunately already taken: Aristotle speaks of a 'complex' action – by which he means one which contains a reversal. In the discussion that follows, both direct and summary actions will ideally satisfy this need for an element of reversal.

eponymous anti-hero breaks out of his comfortable (and suffocating) white suburban existence with a single line: 'I'm going.' Excitingly, it immediately transpires that Edmond doesn't mean he is popping out and can helpfully bring back some cigarettes (as his wife understandably assumes). He means he is leaving her, the apartment, all of his present life, irrevocably, for good. In the twenty three short scenes that follow (each in a new location) Edmond pursues his existential goal; he wants to live what he thinks of as an authentic life. Without the protections offered by his affluent existence, however, he quickly sinks to the bottom, entering New York City's 'underworld', a world in which he comically lacks survival skills. He tries to pay for a strip-show with a credit card. He gets beaten up, and buys a knife. He takes a hooker back to his room and ends up stabbing her. When he is later arrested, his wife visits him in prison and asks if there is anything he needs. He says there isn't. Next we see him sharing a cell with a physically intimidating black cellmate, whom he is clearly expected to serve sexually. This is especially ironic since the only reason Edmond gave his wife for leaving in the first scene was that 'You don't interest me spiritually or sexually.'

Mamet does give us a tiny bit of uplift at the close of this downward spiral: following what seems like a breakdown, we see Edmond in what is almost an epilogue, as he conducts a stumbling philosophical conversation with the Prisoner, ending their chat with a peaceful goodnight kiss. This may indicate that Edmond has achieved a version of the fulfilment he sought, even if it has cost him his liberty in a physical sense. Whatever we make of that, the entire action of the play has been dedicated to getting him to this point – and at breakneck speed. There is barely room in the play for anyone but Edmond.[19]

Less extreme examples of a direct action abound – less extreme insofar as they contain scenes in which the lead character does not appear, or where other characters are developed to a far greater degree than the functional labels – 'the Chaplain' 'Prisoner', 'Man', 'Wife' – of *Edmond* suggest. Buchner's *Woyzeck* (a clear prototype for *Edmond*) also has a direct action, while more

[19] For incisive analysis of the scene construction of this play – and plays in general – see Steve Waters, *The Secret Life of Plays* (London: Nick Hern Books, 2010), Act One.

recent examples include David Lindsay-Abaire's *Good People*. It would be almost impossible to describe the action of these plays without reference to their central characters, because each is in fact the only character *in action* in any sustained way in the whole play. Even though Prince Hamlet's main action is *in*action, the play bearing his name also has what we might call a direct action, since the meaning and energy of that play is invested almost entirely in his journey.

By contrast, many other plays – such as *The Cherry Orchard*, or more recently Tracy Letts' *August: Osage County* – have a summary action.

The summary action

> Whenever playwrights combine a group of separate actions into some sort of whole, they establish a summary action, and that becomes the overall form of the play.[20]

Who drives the action of *The Cherry Orchard*? A case can be made for Lopakhin (he is, after all, the only one who does anything about the situation in which the Gayevs find themselves). However, he is not the central character in any conventional sense, and most of what he does in relation to the main plot happens offstage. Madame Ranyevskaya usually gets top casting/billing – but she does nothing effective in the play, and like Lopakhin is absent from the stage for much of it. Chekhov's intention, as has often been discussed, seems to be to treat the fate not of an individual, but of a class. Likewise Letts' play is not about only Violet (though again the matriarch gets top billing); it is about a whole family and its hangers-on, and perhaps about the patriarch Beverley whose unexplained disappearance triggers the play. The meaning lies in the aggregate of the actions of all the people on stage, and the energy is spread around – including, in the case of *August: Osage County*, in the attic bedroom of the mysterious Native American housekeeper, Johnna. Any attempt to describe the action of either of these plays would have to involve collective terms, rather than simply the name of a protagonist.

[20] Smiley, *Playwriting*, p. 74.

Action: the playwright's arrow

A play's action is a direct channel to the design and intention of the playwright or, in a devised piece, of the playmakers, and a key *locus* of meaning.

The action of a play is one way in which structure carries meaning: to slightly misquote Sophocles, knowledge comes through action.

TOP TIP

- Decide what kind of action best suits your project (direct or summary) and work out a possible action statement, based on your initial ideas.
- Write this 'action statement' on a strip of paper and stick it on the wall.
- As you write your first draft, keep a weather eye on the statement: does every scene and act add something to the prosecution of the action?
- If not, either the action statement needs refining or you are wandering off-piste. How much exploratory 'wandering' you allow yourself will depend on the tightness of the deadline, and the clarity of your intention.
- If your first draft is very exploratory, determine the action once you've completed it. It will help you decide what, out of all the material assembled, is truly vital. To quote a New York City billboard, the more you know, the less you need.
- Above all, a strong action gives a play drive.

EXERCISE

- Think about the very first paid job you ever had – e.g. a Saturday job as a teenager.
- Presumably money was an important motive in turning up for work. But unless you were a coin fetishist, this would be just an instrumental want: why did you need money?

- If it was to save up for something special, what was that thing? Why was it so important? What did it represent?
- If it was for a ticket of some kind – for a bus, for a football match – who, or what, might it bring you closer to?
- If it was to buy something simple – like sweets or cigarettes – was it comfort you needed? Or power in the playground? Or to be seen as an adult?
- Maybe money was almost irrelevant – perhaps it was a workmate you wanted to be near? Or did you need to prove to someone you could hold down a job?
- Was this your first step in taking on the world? What were the others around that time?
- Perhaps it was less pull than push; did being at work mean you could escape from home, or the street? Why did you need to get away?
- 'To be loved', 'to be independent', 'to be comforted', 'to be respected', 'to be safe', 'to be free', 'to be needed' – these are the kinds of needs that can drive a character and set them in action.

Units of energy and convenience 1: Acts

Fraser Grace

The most obvious units of a playscript are labelled at the top of the page. Large blocks of action are badged as 'Acts' (or 'Parts'), and smaller ones – if used – are frequently called 'Scenes'.

Given the modern fashion for one continuous stretch of action, it's not surprising that some plays – and play scripts – are marked by neither scenes, nor acts.

Why do some writers use acts, some scenes, some both and others neither?
How big does a scene have to be to become an act?
What do playwrights get out of writing in scenes and acts?

Two things to note:

- The terminology, and the actual nature of these units are functions of convention; it is just what playwrights working in the English-speaking theatre (and some others) have become accustomed to doing.[21]
- As the above variety of approach indicates, there are plenty of ways to divide a script.

Here's a quick list of benefits for the playwright of working with acts and scenes:

- **Rhythm**: repetition and variance – combined with escalation, climax and reboot – provide the pulse of any play. Breaks in the action can help reinforce this. In *Waiting for Godot*, for instance, having two acts opens up the possibility of seeing (to use the famous gag) nothing happen, twice.
- **Progression and focus**: no need to plough through every second of real time (just as well – we only have two hours); a break in the action allows the dramatist to focus attention only on the vital bits.
- **Shifts in time/location**: follow the action from the dockside in Southampton in 1957 to the mountains of South America ten years later, if that's where your drama leads.
- **Dynamic shifts of pace and mood**: setting a play at a party makes it easy to introduce characters, and may deliver plenty of bracing action – but it's not the best place for quiet soul-searching. The morning after, or 'Later, alone in the kitchen', is another matter entirely.
- **Radical shifts of perspective**: one moment we are absorbed with how a battle looks to the generals, the next we're a universe away, in the hapless world of the poor bloody infantry.

The shifts mentioned above frequently work together – a change of time often heralds a change of location and of mood. All refresh an audience's attention.

Most of these shifts can happen between scenes or between acts – so how are these units different? In the rest of this section, we concentrate on acts. In 'Units of Energy and Convenience 2' the focus is on scenes, and the relationship between these two common units.

[21] In the French playscript by contrast, a new scene number is given with every entry or exit.

Acts

Acts are an endangered species. At one time plays came in seven acts. Over time, the number has reduced – to five, four, three, and now often just two acts (sometimes called parts), split by a single interval.

The key distinguishing features of the act are as follows:

- An act is one of two or more bits of action that together compose a play.[22]
- Each act is composed of one or more blocks of action. If more, those smaller units are usually called scenes. There is no absolute rule about how many scenes an act can or should contain, or how long either should be.
- Crucially, each act represents a new state of being, or condition, with its own relationship to time. It can be set in any period, and can progress at any pace. The act begins when the playwright, via the action (split into smaller scenes or not), begins exploring this particular state of reality. The act ends when that condition comes to an end (or its end is in sight). An act can even present a condition that takes place outside of natural time, e.g. in a distorted memory.
- Each act also has its own relationship with physical space; it can take place in one location, or skip across several locations, scene by scene.
- Each act of a play can ask an audience to read the action in a different way. All of a play's acts *may* operate according to the same conventions, and may take place all in the same location, and in the same historical period, BUT crucially (again) they do not have to. In one act the action may be presented in a naturalistic style, and be tragic in tone; in another, the tone may be farcical, and the action fantastic. We may find that we are being asked to read the second act as a parable, or a dream, or as a darkly comic version of the tragic first act. In short, each act can assert its own 'way of seeing'.
- This leads to a further point – second and subsequent acts do not have to follow in time or link causally with the previous act at all. Act Two may pick up the story begun in Act One one hour later, or a thousand years later, on the same continent or a different one, but it does not have to. The link between acts may be thematic instead. In this, as we'll see, acts are fundamentally different to most scenes.

---

[22] The 'One Act Play' is a separate subspecies, comprising a single unit of action, possibly divided into scenes, with a duration of less than 60–70 minutes running time.

- The precise purpose of each act is related to its place within the whole, and the leap to the next act is a major part of the playwright's bag of tricks.

> Each act is a different state of being, played out either through one sustained period of action, or through a collection of scenes, until that condition has been thoroughly explored.

Using acts

Lope de Vega, who sailed with the Armada before becoming a playwright, was the author of several hundred plays, many of which are still performed almost 400 years after his death. He offers this advice about the use, and usefulness, of acts:

> In the first act set forth the case. In the second weave together the events, in such wise that until the middle of the third act one may hardly guess the outcome. Always trick expectancy; and hence it may come to pass that something quite far from what is promised may be left to the understanding.[23]

Apart from anything else then, acts are a major means of springing surprises.

Time and space shifting in naturalistic plays

Because they follow the stories of a few chosen characters over a greater length of time than the two to three hours running time of a play, even the most naturalistic plays will often compress the action by shifting in time and perhaps location between acts.

Mike Barlett's *Love Love Love* is a good example of this: we see the same characters in three acts labelled simply 'One', 'Two' and 'Three', taking place on '25th June 1967', 'Spring 1990' and '2011' respectively. The action is naturalistic throughout. In 'One', set in a 'North London Flat', we witness

[23] Lope de Vega, quoted in Lajos Egri, *The Art of Dramatic Writing* (New York: Simon & Schuster, 1960), p. xiv.

Sandra seducing her boyfriend's brother Kenneth, in a single (very efficient) evening. The second act picks up in 1990, in the house that Kenneth and Sandra share with their teenage kids Rose and Jamie. 'Three', in 2011, finds the family – now all adults – living in a large country house. Time and location are new for each act, and each act clearly presents a different 'state of being'. The 'sense' or narrative meaning of the play clearly lies in what endures, and what changes, through the sequence.

Often the progression between acts in a naturalistic play will be more subtle than this. But dig away: the change of condition is there.

Changing the lens between acts

Good examples of plays where the conventions of the play – the way we view the action – also change radically between acts include the following:

- Caryl Churchill's *Top Girls*. Act One presents a fantastic dinner party attended by women from myth and history. This may be a dream, or at any rate, may be happening inside the central character Marlene's head. The following two acts are by contrast to be understood in an entirely naturalistic way (although the sequence in which we view the action is highly inventive).
- Max Frisch's *The Fire Raisers*. Here the play is constructed in six scenes, with the action flipping between the living room of a bourgeois home, and the attic of the same house, where the Fire Raisers of the title – with the unwitting help of their catastrophically over-polite host – are stashing their explosives. Frisch also throws in a Greek-style chorus. The action ends when we learn that Biedermann has also kindly loaned his 'lodgers' a box of matches – cue noise of explosions, and blackout. Throughout Frisch's play, a very comic satire on the compliance of his countrymen, the action is preposterous yet still rooted in a naturalistic world. The play is followed by an 'Afterpiece', effectively a second act, which finds Biedermann and his wife, and their arson-inclined 'lodger', in an afterlife, where other characters include 'a long-tailed monkey' – who seems to be a doctor – and Beelzebub.[24]

[24] Max Frisch, *The Fire Raisers* (London: Methuen Drama, 1990).

This brings us to a final thought about acts. As we've seen, the link between them is determined solely by the writer (rather than *necessarily* being the result of cause and effect within the drama). The implicit contention that these things are indeed connected thus becomes part of the play's argument. To put this another way, The act is linked to narrative (the story about the story) rather than to plot (the sequence in which the story is told).

> The shift between acts is one of the chief ways by which a playwright can communicate his or her vision.

Units of energy and convenience 2: Scenes

Fraser Grace

The term 'scene' is so much part of everyday conversation, we hardly think about what it means. At its simplest level it can just indicate a setting, location or view – 'imagine the scene'. Another way we often use the term – someone *made* a scene – is more active; it implies incident and action, suggesting an episode that was notable but fleeting. Somebody did something significant which made an impression, and then the episode ended. At the time the 'scene' took place, we probably didn't understand everything that happened, or why, but the chances are we'll spend considerable time trying to explain it to ourselves.[25]

Put all this together and you have, in a nutshell, the regular scene; what goes in it, and how it relates to scenes that come before and after. A scene shows us people in a particular time/place doing things of consequence in every sense (even while often pretending to show us the exact opposite). In the process it solves some mysteries, creates others and makes further events inevitable – and so drives us into the next scene.

[25] This is yet another way in which drama is superior to life: in the theatre, we not only *want* to understand what we have seen, we have confidence that by the end of the play some of that mystery will have been solved.

TOP TIP

Use scene and act breaks to achieve the following:

Compress time, space, action and contention into a single evening at the theatre.

Duck the irrelevant bits – cut and keep to whatever you believe to be the chase.

Deepen your involvement in the great game of connections, juxtapositions and disconnections – these contribute so much to this act of mimesis, or representation.

When working in these chunks of action, the gaps start to feel almost as important as the content. For the audience, the game of momentary disorientation with which every play begins is repeated at the beginning of every unit. Where are we now? Who's this? What's happened since the last scene or act? This makes us – the audience – work, and if we're working we're engaged.

Downsides of division

- Any interruption in the action which allows time for reflection also provides opportunity for attention to wane.
- Less obviously, breaks in the action betray the hand of the maker. Briefly, we realize again that what is being presented is an edited reality. The bigger the shifts, the greater the writer's shadow. This feeling of being locked in a debate with another intellect can be bracing for an audience – but will almost certainly erode the audience's sense of immersion in the play, their identification with the characters as people.[26] It is this desire to maintain the immersion of an audience – and perhaps the influence of cinema – that lies behind the modern trend towards continuous action.

[26] As noted in Part 1' Reflections on the History of Playwriting 2', the shattering of sympathetic immersion is what Brecht deliberately set out to achieve in his epic theatre. This is why he shapes his scenes almost as mini acts; disrupting the cause-and-effect flow of the action, and drawing attention to the shaping hand of the author.

A few more things about acts and scenes, and then a confession:

- If you are remotely mechanically minded, the relationship between acts and scenes can be compared to the way derailleur gears work on a bicycle. Often there are five (or more) smaller gears on the rear wheel hub, and two (or more) large gears at the front of the bike, fixed to the crank. After working up through the five smaller gears, it's time to shift to another level of power. By shifting the chain to the next large gear at the front, you can now run through five more gears at different ratios. The shift from one cog on the rear hub to the other is like the change from scene to scene – but the shift between the larger cogs on the front wheel hub is like the change from act to act; a different level of energy is now in play.
- As well as being technically helpful in the construction of the drama, acts and scenes are also practically useful in the rehearsal room. If acts and scenes are not marked, the director will have to 'unit' the script in some other way in order to focus attention, group actors and schedule rehearsals. In fact, you'll also often hear directors and actors refer to the 'beats' of the play. These are smaller unmarked subdivisions within an act or scene, or within a play that has no formally noted acts or scenes, representing a small unit of the flow of action.
- Scenes and acts are also audience-friendly constructs: if rightly constructed, they will parcel out the action so the audience receives a small moment of satisfaction (something is born, blossoms and dies), followed by a small respite (the scene change, lights down or curtain), and a renewed hunger for the next act or scene to begin.

THE CONFESSION

As a playwright starting out, my sense of a scene – what it was, what it needed – was instinctive. Maybe I'd absorbed something from the few plays I'd read and seen. I would think about characters, hear voices, start writing – and feel that a scene was beginning to emerge. I tried to stay with it, keeping the characters interacting as long as I could, creating reasons why they couldn't or didn't want to escape. I'd then think about what would be an interesting next development, and who might cause it. The same goes for the bigger structure of my plays – I busked it, and hoped that when I got to the end of the play, I'd recognize that a good finishing point had been reached. I then had to work out why the journey to that point felt so unsatisfactory, go back and fix it. Nowadays, I plan more – working out how I will compass the play in a few blocks of action, and then playing around with the grouping and ordering of those blocks until it starts to feel efficient and pleasing (to me at least). Even so, with every play, by the time I reach that point, I already have pages of dialogue. Planning a play need never stop you listening to the voices, 'seeing' the images, that will ultimately drive it along.

EXERCISE

- Write out the story of your play as fully as you can on one side of a sheet of A4 paper.
- Crumple the sheet into a ball and roll it to the other side of the desk.
- Now take four small pieces of paper no bigger than the size of a postage stamp, label them A, B, C and D.
- Divide what you remember of the story into four major events that together encompass the story – one event per stamp-sized page.
- Place the four 'stamps' a foot apart horizontally along the front of the desk.
- Now give yourself three Post-it notes, labelled 1, 2 and 3 respectively, and place them between the four 'stamps'. Imagine these are your 'acts'. Think about what series of smaller steps will get you across these Post-its, from one 'stamp' to another, i.e. from A to B, B to C, C to D.
- Fix more stamp-sized pieces of paper onto each Post-it, one per 'step'. Fill them in with what happens in each step. These are your scenes.
- When all the Post-it 'acts' are full of notes divided into three or four stamp-sized 'scenes', push the pieces labelled A, B, C and D higher up the desk, so you have two rows – A, B, C, D and beneath that line 1, 2, 3.

- You now have two outlines of the story – one where the major events happen between the acts (offstage), and one where every chunk of the play nails a significant moment, but there are big gaps between.
- Which seems more interesting to you? Is the kind of play you want to write best expressed in A–D or 1–3? Or do you need a mix of the two?
- What happens if you mess up the sequences: D, C, B, A or 3, 2, 1? Does each 'play' get more complex, or just more complicated? How might you signal the changes in time if you went that way?

Image and symbol

Clare Bayley

> *A play is a woven tapestry of images, and it creates a strange, often magical image of life.*[27]

The difference between writing a play and writing prose is that the images and characters the writer invents take physical form on stage. Having been conceived in words, they will be conjured using lights, costumes, props and the choreography of actors on the stage. Those images have to make sense in the context of the drama, as well as conveying meaning on a more universal level. If the fictional stage world has been successfully created, it can miraculously transform to represent something far greater than itself alone.

The magic happens when something occurs onstage, which the audience understands on a deeper level: when the lights dim to denote nightfall in the world of the play, but the audience knows it also signifies an imminent death, for example, Tim Crouch writing in the *Guardian* quotes the Austrian writer Peter Handke: 'Light is brightness pretending to be other brightness; a chair is a chair pretending to be another chair.' Crouch goes on to say:

> Theatre can't do real. As soon as you put something real on stage, it stops the theatre – or, more likely, the thing itself stops being real …

[27] Smiley, *Playwriting*, p. 292.

> Art's power is its ability to contain the idea of one thing inside something else .... If we work too hard to make everything look like the thing we say it is, then we're also removing any sense of the game of art.[28]

TOP TIP

Think carefully about the objects you write into your play. You might be tempted to mention a dead seagull, for example, or a glass ornament. You can be sure that during rehearsals the assistant stage manager (ASM) will be sent out to source and buy or make that very thing. This will have budgetary implications (bear in mind it also will affect the aesthetics of the play).

When the audience can read an object's significance beyond its function, its place in the play is justified, and the audience's experience is enhanced. Tennessee Williams achieves a compelling synthesis of imagery as stage prop and stage metaphor in his breakthrough play *The Glass Menagerie*.

- There really is a case of glass animal ornaments on stage, which belongs to the narrator's crippled sister, Laura.
- The 'menagerie' represents the fragile, brittle little family as a whole, each unusual in their own rarefied way, but ill-equipped to survive in the rough and tumble world of Depression-era St Louis.
- One ornament in particular represents Laura – a glass unicorn, a rare and beautiful beast. Its mythical beauty suggests her spiritual loveliness, while the oddness of its horn echoes her deformity. The glass unicorn is more than mere decoration; it has a key role in the development of the plot.
- When the gentleman caller, Jim, comes to visit, Laura's mother contrives for.them to be left alone together, on the pretext of her showing him the glass ornaments. Everyone is hoping that Laura will find love – or at least a husband. But when Jim accidentally breaks off the unicorn's horn, it's an act of destruction as devastating symbolically as the way he leads Laura on, only to abandon her for the fiancée he hasn't previously admitted to. Laura, like the unicorn, will never be the same again.

[28] *The Guardian* 18 June 2014, http://www.theguardian.com/stage/2014/jun/18/theatre-reality-adler-and-gibb-tim-crouch-playwright (accessed: 11 May 2015.).

Allegory

Lynn Nottage's play *Ruined* tells a very specific story about the women who have been horrifically and permanently scarred by rape as a weapon of war in the Democratic Republic of Congo. Ostracized and unmarriageable, in the play their only option is to become sex workers in Mama Nadi's brothel. If their scarring is so bad that they are unable to have intercourse, they can be employed to sing, dance and procure punters for their colleagues.

Inspired by interviews with rape survivors in the DRC, the play self-consciously refers back to Brecht's *Mother Courage*, which was written to reveal the brutal truth that war is merely another profit-making opportunity for powerful interests. The play offers a bleak insight into what war means for the millions of non-combatants (predominantly women) whose lives are devastated by conflict. Mama Nadi's brothel offers a precarious safety predicated on grim compromises.

The play works as

- a story about a particular time and place,
- an allegory for the destruction that all wars wreak on civilian populations,
- an allegory for the DRC itself. Violated and abandoned by successions of foreign and domestic plunderers, irredeemably damaged from one generation to the next, its citizens have little choice other than to painfully, resiliently carry on their daily lives.

Imagery

Sometimes an image can itself be the starting point of a play. Lucy Kirkwood's *Chimerica* dissects the iconography of the well-known image of the 'tank man': the Chinese citizen standing in front of the tank in Tiananmen Square, at the time of the massacre of protesters in 1989. Taking this image as its starting point, the play explores the relationship between China and the West (specifically the US) in terms of politics, economics, culture and global influence. The play tells the story of the (fictional) photographer who captured the image, and his hunt for the real man in the picture. He has his own personal and professional reasons for wanting to find him; his newspaper and the Chinese government have equally compelling reasons for wanting him *not* to. So does the tank man himself. The photographer's simplistic notions are constantly challenged by the realities he uncovers. The image and its story come to illuminate the complexity and contradictions of the relationship between the two superpowers.

Non-visual symbolism

In Brian Friel's *Translations*, language itself is both the subject and the engine of the drama. The central character Yolland is an English sapper in Gaelic-speaking Ireland who has been sent to anglicize the place names and redraw the boundaries. It's an act of blatant cultural imperialism, but Yolland defies expectations by becoming interested in the local culture and enamoured of a local girl, Maire. The play's brilliant device is to represent both English and Gaelic on stage with English: in scenes where one character is speaking Gaelic and another English, we hear it all in English. This allows us to understand both parties, even when they can't understand each other. We see that they are all human beings with their own hopes and frailties.

This device reaches its apogee in the iconic love scene between Maire (who speaks no English) and Yolland (who speaks no Gaelic). They speak to each other in their own language, which is incomprehensible to the other, and though they are speaking at cross-purposes, each has the same intention. They find common ground in simply reciting the place names they both know. It's symbolically important that the central scene should be enacted through language, as well as being an ingenious dramatic device.

Form and meaning

Tom Stoppard famously wrote *Jumpers*, a serious play about moral philosophy, as a surreal bedroom farce featuring a troupe of acrobat-philosophers in yellow jumpsuits, one of whom is dead for most of the play. They cunningly dramatize the philosophical questions, and challenge the audience's belief about what is real and what is not. The use of comic characters and absurd situations to symbolize lofty academic arguments made the subject comprehensible to the general public and ensured the play's commercial success.

Nick Payne has been hailed as Stoppard's heir, for his ability to write popular plays about abstract academic subjects. *Constellations* demonstrates quantum multiverse theory, the idea (as explained in the play) that 'every choice, every decision you've ever and never made exists in an unimaginably vast ensemble of parallel universes'.

The relationship between a beekeeper and a quantum multiverse academic is related in a series of scenes which are repeated with variations of memory and intention, and therefore come to illustrate the theory themselves: each scene may or may not have happened, and so the couple may have had a life together, betrayed each other, ended their relationship or died. The formal structure of the play embodies its subject matter; you could almost say that its form is its subject.

EXERCISE 1

If you're teaching a class, you can collect an array of interesting objects – the quirkier the better. Alternatively, you can ask each of your students to bring in a significant object. Lay them all out on a tray or a table.

Each student then has to think of a character, and pick an object which is symbolic of them. They can't pick their own object.

They then write a short scene in which the object they've chosen has a significant narrative role. Often the fact of having to pick an object can unlock something in the writer's mind and reveal a new facet of their character, or crystallize a trait in a tangible and dramatic form. Often these objects remain in the play beyond the exercise; but even if they don't, their function in understanding character is still useful.

Next, get the students to choose an object which symbolizes their whole play. They can then write a scene in which this object features. The same process applies.

EXERCISE 2

If you're working alone, write a list of all the props used in your three favourite plays, and in the last three plays you've seen in the theatre. Pick one, and follow the steps above.

TOP TIP

Look at Nick Cave's Museum of Important Shit website (www.2000daysonearth.com) for a wealth of inspiration from objects that have symbolic power in our lives – from our children's milk teeth to the discarded chewing-gum of our idols.

Onstage and offstage worlds

Fraser Grace

We are very rarely asked to believe – except perhaps in the plays of Samuel Beckett – that what we are seeing on stage is all there is of the world of the play. We are always aware that 'this, here' is a token of a much bigger reality.

The offstage world exists beyond the edges of the stage:

- It is intimately connected to the onstage world.
- It is quite distinct from our own.

The offstage world is a strange place when you think about it – an imaginary world made necessary and summoned into existence purely by the world of the stage – which is itself imaginary. Without the world on the stage, we would have no glimpse of this offstage world at all. And this is the first thing to say about it: that the offstage world is *implied* by what is on stage, and we are only provoked into consciousness of it by what is revealed to us on the stage.

> If the onstage world is a token of the offstage world, what kind of token is it?

The onstage world is usually read in one of three ways:

- **The onstage world is a microcosm of the offstage world**: the onstage world represents a typical example of the offstage world – in fact, it *is* that world, writ small. Change that happens here is symptomatic of what is happening, or could happen, more broadly in the offstage world (and perhaps, by extension, in our own world). The onstage worlds of Ibsen's plays operate in this way. Similarly, the onstage world of David Mamet's play *Glengarry Glen Ross* is the particular world of a set of small-time realtors standing in for the general world (underworld?) of that industry. Moreover, as noted in *Image and Symbol*, in some plays, onstage and offstage worlds combine to create an allegory; in *Glengarry Glen Ross* a suggestion is surely being made that this small world of hustlers is a metaphor for the larger culture and economy of America.
- **The onstage world is an outpost of the offstage world**: a world that is so far from the centre of the offstage world that the grip of the 'normal condition' is weaker.

> EITHER change happens here first
>
> OR change that has already happened in the offstage world arrives here belatedly.

The outpost is Chekhov's onstage place of choice in both *Three Sisters* and *The Cherry Orchard*. In Act One of Zinnie Harris's *Further from the Furthest Thing* the island in the Atlantic that constitutes the onstage world is an outpost of the British Empire for which 'H'england' is a venerated offstage point of reference. Act Two reverses the picture, as the inhabitants find themselves evacuated to a Southampton jar factory. Steve Waters' diptych of plays *The Contingency Plan* similarly shows us the onstage/offstage worlds from each end of the telescope in turn, the onstage world of each play to an extent operating as the offstage world for the other.

- **The onstage world is antithetical to the offstage world**: the onstage world is an indigenous or peculiar world, with its own rules and culture, invaded by agents of the offstage world. This is particularly clear in plays about colonialism – colonialism being, in one sense a visitation of one world on another. Shaffer's *The Royal Hunt of the Sun* and Friel's *Translations*, for example, both depict an 'innocent' world, threatened or corrupted by an invading force. But the same is also true, more subtly, of Harold Pinter's *The Birthday Party*, or *The Homecoming*. Even *Waiting for Godot* can be read like this, as pointed up by the Baxter Theatre's production that played at the Old Vic in 1981. This 'anti-apartheid' production cast Estragon and Vladimir as black Africans, Pozzo as an Afrikaaner Boer and Lucky as his mixed-race lackey.

How can a playwright best manage the onstage/offstage relationship?

First, what happens or appears in the onstage world has only to imply the existence of everything else, while it is itself bolstered by it.

- The magazine pictures of the Queen on the wall of Mill's shack in *Further from the Furthest Thing* establish a whole offstage world, and offer a testimony to the power it exerts over the imaginations of the onstage characters.
- Martin McDonagh's play *The Beauty Queen of Leenane* likewise plants a surprising number of such tokens around the simple single set. Some are in open view from the outset (an embroidered tea towel). Some are hidden, to be revealed by the action (a swingball confiscated from children playing outside, a poker, later related to battles with policemen).

Second, timing the moments when the offstage world further impinges on the onstage world is crucial – the juddering rumble of the volcano in *Further from the Furthest Thing*, which will eventually precipitate the evacuation of the islanders, for instance, or the letter to Maureen from her lover Pato in *Beauty Queen* .... This letter is sent from what is – for Maureen – the unreachable offstage world. It is delivered by the 'messenger' – in this case Pato's younger brother, Ray. In a reversal of the case in most Greek tragedy, the tragedy here is caused by the messenger's failure to deliver good news (rather than success in delivering bad) allowing the letter to be intercepted by Maureen's mother. This is fantastically economic writing, not only serving up a savage twist of plot, but intensifying our consciousness of the offstage world, full as it is of possibilities for freedom and love, even as the antithetical onstage world is confirmed as a trap from which Maureen may never escape.

EXERCISE

Find a play you like, and (if it has more than one onstage location) choose a particular scene.

- On a piece of paper, draw a series of concentric circles.
- Mark the centre as the onstage world, whatever it is; junk shop, birthing pool, minefield.
- Note all the phenomena indicated in the text that establish this place for what it is – the tea towel mentioned above, for instance, or a radio announcement.
- The next ring out represents the rooms or other spaces we can't see, but are adjoining – the beginning of the offstage world.
- Further rings move outwards still, to embrace the neighbourhood, town, country(ies), world, and the people in them.
- Keep going until you exhaust all you know about the geographical and historical worlds of the play.
- How does information about the offstage spheres pierce the onstage world? Much will come via recollection, or reporting. As we've seen, some may come via intrusions into the immediate space – the rumble of the volcano, a message being delivered (or not). A technical device – radio, television or phone – may also be the conduit. Other intrusions may be effected by the introduction of a character from the outer spheres, with orally delivered news (as in the case of *Antigone*'s Messenger). Perhaps something is observed from a window.
- Write or draw such phenomena in the sphere in which they originate, draw a dotted line to the centre and note the means by which they travel from the offstage world to the onstage world.

- Notice the complex picture of the offstage world(s) of the play, and their/its influence on this present, onstage world, and the variety of means by which the influence is effected.
- Note too how the picture is a dynamic one, growing ever more complex, and how the worlds become more interdependent, as the play progresses.
- Finally, study the obverse:

Reread Beckett's *Endgame* and see what fun the dramatist has as Clov positions his step ladder before each of the windows in the '*Bare interior*'. Gazing outwards, into what the stage directions comically refer to only as '*the without*', Clov can see nothing, even with a telescope, apart from, at one point, what looks like a small boy. Inevitably, Hamm and Clov decide against investigating further.

This is a philosopher bleakly emphasizing his characters' existential isolation, but also a dramatist, joyfully toying with the conventions of theatre. By divorcing the onstage world from any possible impact on, or effect from, an offstage world, Beckett the master dramatist taunts us with how little he needs to make a play.

The rest of us must content ourselves with being as economical as we can.

Drafting and redrafting

Fraser Grace

Good scripts, according to Paul Abbott, aren't written, they're rewritten.

For many writers, rewriting is a vital process, and some – Michael Frayn included – claim to prefer it:

> I get more enjoyment out of rewriting, I think, than writing the original. The great difficulty is getting from nothing to something; going from something to something else is always easier.[29]

[29] Interview with Maddy Costa, The Guardian G2 7 March 2012, http://www.guardian.co.uk/stage/2012/mar/06/michael-frayn?INTCMP=SRCH (accessed: 27 September 2014).

For 'writing the original', we can read 'producing the First Draft'.

> What does a first draft look like, and how do you write one?

The First Draft

Whenever a playwright starts a new play, he or she invariably has some of the pieces of the jigsaw already in the bag – some characters, a setting, a subject. For some, the writing of the First Draft is a major means of discovering the other pieces. For others it is mainly about how all the pieces assembled are going to work in concert. Either way, it is the element of discovery that can make the writing of a first draft such a ride.

You know you have a first draft when ...

- the play is an identifiable whole, at the very least reducing Aristotle's 'thousand mile creature' into something which can be appreciated as a limited entity.
- the play has become firm about what it is *not*. If you've discovered that your play, set in a US TV station in 2012, is ultimately about honesty in an age of political expediency, you will now know that there is no room in this play for that other story you've been thinking about – the musical about the teenage love triangle in 1930s England. One can never say 'never', but most likely that idea will have to wait for another commission.
- the play has found both its subject, and its angle of attack – you now understand the major dramatic strategy by which this subject is to be treated.
- the play has generated its own world, subject to light and heat and time and space and governance and feeling.
- the play has summoned all the characters it needs, or most of them. You may sense other characters tugging at your sleeve, wanting to be let in to the next draft – be careful: how will they help?
- the play has the beginnings of its verbal and visual language in place. Even if these elements are not yet fully formed, consistent or honed, the play is starting to look and sound like – and yet quite unlike – other plays you've written.
- the play still casts a spell, draws you to it; it still has something of the enigma about it.

The First Draft is a vehicle for exploration – finally, it will be a product, but getting there is a process.

The First Draft is also a writer's prototype, an attempt to assemble or grow an imagined or felt thing into something tangible – and see if it works.

The First Draft creates employment for the writer. Up until the completion of a first draft, the playwright is working *towards* a play. From here on, the writer is working *for* the play; the play has only to become more itself, and the playwright is the one who must help it.

So what's it like, working for a play?

In a second draft, and all the drafts that follow, the choices and sacrifices you must make are in the interests of this particular play – in terms of both its cohesion and its chances in the market place. No play can be all things to all men – or even everything you want to achieve as a playwright. Some lofty ambitions may have to be parked, to be picked up in your next play. And you'll have to axe some good material, as well as bad, to make this play the best it can be.

A play succeeds moment by moment, yet its *intention* depends on the achievement of the whole; the job from now on is to find that balance, whatever it costs.

What happens to a play when it is rewritten?

- A play that is being rewritten sheds unnecessary material (see the section on 'Cutting') but also gathers more to it, and deepens its enquiry.
- A play generally gets smarter, and wiser – both in terms of knowledge (see the section on 'Research and Planning') and of tactics: now the play has discovered it can throw a few punches it can get better at disguising and timing them, so catching us unawares.
- A play gets better at making connections – both with the world we live in, and internally with itself, one part resonating with another.

> I revise in order – generally – to further unearth theme as new connections are discovered. You want to find the centre of the web where all the threads meet.
>
> Arthur Miller[30]

- Once a play has discovered its 'truth' (in the First Draft, hopefully) you can work backwards in the Second Draft, making sure all the clues or steps towards that truth are in place, and suitably disguised.
- A finished play wastes no time. It often starts later into the story because you are no longer wondering what this play is all about. A new draft can hit the ground running, and express itself more succinctly.
- A rewritten play is usually more focussed, more purposeful. It begins to throw its weight around.

Goals for second and further drafts

1. To fully realize and embed discoveries made in the First Draft.
2. Ensuring the play's structure is fit for the purpose you've discovered – think about urgency, and scope (see the section on 'Action and Plot').
3. Clarity and orientation – put aside for a moment your own interests: what's this play like as an experience for the audience? How are they to find their way through it?
4. Coherence – consistency – muscularity – sufficiency. Working on these elements will make a play more like itself, more efficient, and better equipped to assert itself.
5. Considering form and genre: has this play started to reveal similarities to a certain *kind* of play? Check out what the conventions are that make those plays work so well.
6. Considering the play as a staging proposition: is it as economical with cast as it can be? Can a character really exit that late, and still reappear a moment later? Is the play fit for the venue or scale you have in mind, or have been commissioned for? Are you making the most of your opportunities?

[30] Arthur Miller, in George Plimpton (ed.), *The Paris Review Interviews: Playwrights at Work* (London: The Harvill Press, 2000).

7. Nailing particularity: are all the characters distinctive in speech and action? Think about contrast, rhythm and syntax.
8. Making space for actors to work: does everything that is said in the play need to be spoken? Can action or silence do the same job? Or a single glance?

REWRITER'S PRINCIPLES

- The seed of what makes a play wonderful is in the First Draft. Hang on to it.
- The whole and the parts are mutually dependent. Only if a play succeeds moment by moment will anyone care about the whole.
- Don't be tempted to drive all the mystery or strangeness out of your play – but make sure those elements earn their keep.

TOP TIP

- Take a well-earned break after completing the First Draft.
- Read the draft again, several times, 'through different eyes', e.g. the minor character's play, the audience's play, your mum's play, the stage manager's play, etc.
- Don't expect to solve all a play's problems in a single draft. Be glad to get a few things fixed in each draft (eight drafts is not unusual for a professional script).
- 'Making it less rubbish' is not a sufficiently specific goal. Note objectives/questions for each draft, and stick to them; i.e. have an achievable plan.
- If working on a computer, always start a new file for a new draft and back it up.
- When you think the new draft is complete, print it in hard copy and read it aloud to yourself – with a tea/gin break as required – and don't forget to time it.
- Develop a pool of trusted private readers to whom you can send your Second Drafts. Over time, you'll learn what to expect from each of them.

Your friend the teacher may be excellent at spotting emotional truth, but is not necessarily acute on structure, or politics.

- Join a writing group where you read and comment on each other's work. Learn to be conscientious, supportive and analytical – and expect the same in return.
- The insights of a literary manager, dramaturg or director can be valuable, BUT they are especially valuable if they are already committed to producing the play.
- Try to not *react* to criticism, e.g. by immediately charging into a new draft. Weigh the comments you receive carefully, and then respond in the new draft as you judge fit; this is your play, you're its guardian as much as its slave.
- Respect the writer who began the process; without the insight and instincts of a month ago, you wouldn't have a play to work on.
- Beware the phantom play: while a play exists only in your head, it can be many things at once. Once committed to paper, the play becomes one thing, or one collection of things, one iteration of your vision – but not another. It's the other play it could have been that can haunt you – the phantom play. (Answer? So haunt me. It's better to have written and lost ... etc.)
- Each time you feel disappointed with your play, meditate on Samuel Beckett's dictum:

> Ever tried. Ever failed. No matter. Try again. Fail again. Fail better.

EXERCISE ON REDRAFTING

- Find a short scene you're happy with.
- Rewrite every statement as a question, replace every question with an action, every action with a statement.
- Is it recognizably the same scene? What changes?

Stage directions

Clare Bayley

The approach to stage directions has varied over the centuries, though they have always existed as a practical indication of the stage furniture and the mechanics of bringing actors on and off stage. They can also offer an indication of how the actors say their lines. While in screenplays everything that isn't dialogue conveys plot, atmosphere, character and mood, stage directions in a play are simply mechanical instructions about where things go. In contemporary times there is a tacit understanding that they should be kept to a minimum, to allow the director and designer free rein to visually conceive the production, and the actors to do their job. The dialogue should convey the intention and the emotional state of the characters. If you have to include lots of adverbs to convey your meaning, you probably need to have another look at the dialogue.

Stage directions are indicated by italics.

Keeping them minimal

Shakespeare, writing for the Globe which didn't use sets, kept it very minimal, rarely more than a statement of when a character entered or exited; from time to time including a prop (a letter, a rapier), a 'flourish' or an 'alarum', and only once a bear.

Excessive detail

By the nineteenth century, however, and in naturalistic, single-set plays in the twentieth century, playwrights went to elaborate and precise detail with their specifications. Terence Rattigan, Noel Coward, Oscar Wilde virtually took on the role of interior designer; and as for George Bernard Shaw, he happily offered suggestions on landscape architecture (in *Mrs Warren's Profession*):

> *Summer afternoon in a cottage garden on the eastern slope of a hill a little south of Haslemere in Surrey. Looking up the hill, the cottage is seen in the left hand corner of the garden, with its thatched roof and porch, and a large latticed window to the left of the porch. A paling*

completely shuts in the garden, except for a gate on the right. The common rises uphill beyond the paling to the sky line. Some folded canvas garden chairs are leaning against the side bench in the porch. A lady's bicycle is propped against the wall, under the window. A little to the right of the porch a hammock is slung from two posts.[31]

The actor's job

Having laid out in some detail the design for the show, Shaw goes on to detail not only what the characters should look like, but every move the actors should make, and how:

> VIVIE [*striding to the gate and opening it for him*] Come in, Mr Praed. [*He comes in*]. Glad to see you. [*She proffers her hand and takes his with a resolute and hearty grip. She is an attractive specimen of the sensible, able, highly-educated young middle-class Englishwoman. Age 22. Prompt, strong, confident, self-possessed. Plain business-like dress, but not dowdy. She wears a chatelaine at her belt, with a fountain pen and a paper knife among its pendants*].[32]

This is to be avoided. It's the job of the actor to interpret your words, and lots of instructions are generally frowned upon, and ignored.

Provocations

For other playwrights, stage directions can be something of a provocation – or an indication of a wish – depending on your point of view. Strindberg unapologetically included in *Peer Gynt* snowfall, mountains, storms, shipwrecks, troll palaces and the unforgettable stage direction:

> *THE TROLLS take to flight, amid a confused*
> *uproar of yells and shrieks. The palace collapses;*
> *everything disappears.*[33]

[31] Project Gutenberg.

[32] Project Gutenberg.

[33] Project Gutenberg, end of scene six.

Some directors love to be given this kind of a challenge – this is the part of the job that really excites them. But not all.

Precision and control

There is nothing vague or hopeful in Samuel Beckett's stage directions. His 35-second play *Breath* consists of nothing but a stage direction (the playwright tried to put a stop to the first New York production when this was not strictly followed). In *Footfalls* he even delineates the compulsive pacing of the performer, down to '*starting with right foot*' … (and the Beckett estate will ensure that this is carried out to the letter).[34]

Pinter was equally fastidious with stage directions, notably the pauses and beats between speeches. This was because he could 'hear' the dialogue almost like music, and had 'scored' it with great precision so that the meaning was accurately conveyed. Pinter uses 'pause' liberally, but in a highly controlled way which raises tension and galvanizes the pace. Overuse or lazy scattering of 'pause' can just slow everything down in an unhelpful way – make sure you really need a pause before including it. Commonly a 'beat' is used to indicate something more significant than a pause. (See below.)

Typographical tips

If you have a very clear sense of the rhythm and pacing of the dialogue, there are typographical ways of conveying this:

- A 'pause' is a way of punctuating dialogue, to suggest a moment of hesitation, a change of tack or just to give a character a moment to absorb what's been said or plot their next move.
- A 'beat' is usually used in the script to indicate something longer than a pause, often suggesting a decisive moment, a tacit realization or a significant revelation.
- Caryl Churchill pioneered the use of the / (slash) to indicate interruption in dialogue. She specifies at the start of a script how it should be interpreted (*Top Girls* contains a page of explanation about four types of overlapping dialogue).

---

34 *Footfalls* – Deborah Warner's 1994 production with Fiona Shaw moved some lines from the Mother to the Daughter. The estate threatened to put an injunction on the production if she didn't retract her decision – three hours before the press night.

In general, the person talking is interrupted at the /. This is now the generally accepted use of /, but it's best to clarify at the start of the script exactly what your intentions are.

- There are different ways of indicating when a character is present but actively keeping silent, rather than just not speaking. They may be sulking, resisting, resenting or dissenting, but it's a different kind of silence than just not saying anything. debbie tucker green indicates this by including the name of the character with no dialogue. Other writers include the name of the character and then .... you can also add a stage direction telling us: '*Character X does not respond.*'

Physical and visual staging

Some types of play require specific and detailed stage instructions, notably Lucy Prebble's *Enron* which develops its own visual language to explain complex financial transactions and proceedings. Prebble's stage directions include this scene on the trading floor:

> '*Above us somewhere there is a twinkle of gold. And then another of silver somewhere else. And then more – commodities like stars in the sky* ... '

She also uses singing as a way of indicating the thrill of trading:

> '*The sound of singing, each their own different song. It builds to an atonal babble of commodity prices and bids. It's a musical cacophony of the trading floor* ... '

This very specifically indicates her vision for the way something so abstract can be communicated, while still allowing plenty of scope for a director to find a particular way to represent it on stage.

Use of sound effects

Sound can be a brilliantly effective and cheap way of communicating anything from the arrival of a car or an aeroplane passing overhead, to a rainforest setting. Tom Stoppard memorably uses the sound of crows at the end of Act One of *Arcadia*: '*The light changes to early morning. From a long way off, there is a pistol shot. A moment later there is the cry of dozens of crows disturbed from the unseen trees.'* In Act Two the sound is repeated and we discover the reason for what we've heard.

Sound can also evoke more than objects, places and actions. In Act Two of *Three Sisters*, Chekhov famously specified a haunting but mysterious sound cue: '*Suddenly there is a distant sound, as if from the sky: the sound of a breaking string – dying away, sad*'. Much has been written about the underlying meaning of this melancholy sound, but its effect is to evoke an emotion rather than any particular object – and it is more powerful as a result.

GENERAL TIPS ON STAGE DIRECTIONS

- If you don't imagine a naturalistic production, but include a direction such as 'She takes a letter out of the formica kitchen unit', you could be in trouble. In general you're expected to specify the minimum of essential furniture and props required by the script, and leave the director and designer to do the rest themselves.
- There's little need to specify whether characters exit left, right or centre unless there is a good reason to do so. Rather, you need to establish where they are exiting to – outside, or to another room, for example – and the logistics of what lies where can be decided upon in rehearsal.
- This doesn't mean that you shouldn't think through the logistics of staging your work. It's good practice to plot it all through in your mind quite minutely, to avoid presenting physical impossibilities or what in the film industry is known as continuity errors. A character can't 'enter skipping' if in the last scene he's been up to his thigh in a plaster cast; equally if a character exits one scene wearing a bikini and is immediately required in the next scene wearing a wedding-dress and veil, you're not allowing the actor enough time for a complex costume change.
- Make sure that you have sufficient information in stage directions to clarify basic points. If you do away with them completely your script could be puzzling to read. Remember that as a bare minimum you need to give an idea of how you imagine the space on stage and in the world of the characters.

Cutting

Clare Bayley

For many writers the first draft of a play is a way of discovering through writing who your characters are and what their story really is. However much you plot and plan beforehand, for many of us there are still anomalies, complications and discoveries to be found along the way. Often your first draft will be overlong, discursive, rambling (there's no shame in that – August Wilson's first drafts often ran to four-plus hours). The work then is to extract the essential parts, the bones, and enough meat to make the script sufficiently fleshed out to be attractive without being flabby.

Terry Johnson once sprang a revealing exercise on us unsuspecting writers. He asked us to write a scene from the play we were working on as well as we possibly could, giving us plenty of time to get it right. Then, when we were all sitting feeling smugly pleased with ourselves, he told us to cut it by 25 per cent. After our initial protests, it was surprisingly easy. And the scene was certainly improved by the cutting. We were starting to feel smug again, when he told us to cut it by another 25 per cent. That seemed like an impossible task. We all made quite a fuss. But of course, that too was possible. Later, I had a look at what had gone, with a view to putting back some of the bits I hadn't wanted to lose. The strange thing is that once something is cut, it very rarely needs to go back in. A play is invariably improved by cutting.

How to tell if a line can be cut

Each line of dialogue needs to be doing more than just one thing, and should never just be conveying information. You need to find out first of all what the purpose of a line is. Ask yourself:

- Is this line advancing the plot?
- Is this line conveying information? If so, do we need to know this information at this moment? Do we already know it?
- Is this line revealing character?
- Is there any subtext to this line?
- Can this line be replaced by an action?

If it's not doing any of these things, it must be cut. If it's only doing one thing, can you make it work harder for you by combining it with something else?

There's nothing like hearing your work read or performed to help focus your mind on which part of your play can be cut. An early play of mine contained a line which I realized at the dress rehearsal ought to go, but there had been a lot of changes to the script and I didn't want to burden the actors with further last-minute line relearning. Every time I heard the line in performance I winced. Now I will always tell the director if a line is sounding wrong. The director can take the decision about when to tell the actors it can be cut.

An emergency is also very good for stiffening the resolve. At a full run on a Friday evening of a play that was going to start previewing the following Tuesday, I realized that it was almost half an hour too long. There was just too much script and it was holding up the action. At the end of the run, the director and I looked at each other, and I knew we were both thinking the same thing. There's nothing like the pressure of a deadline. We took ourselves off to a quiet room, where I found that I was able to slash whole speeches that a few days before I hadn't seen a problem with. In fact I got too carried away, and in the end she was restraining me and putting lines back in.

Have you cut too much?

Sometimes you can get over enthusiastic and cut too much from a script. This sometimes happens when you are trying to write your first draft as your second – you are trying to shortcut the process, and fail to establish enough from the beginning to guide the audience through the story, either because you don't know enough yourself, or because you haven't succeeded in communicating what you do know. There's also an argument that you have to include lines in a first draft which you know will ultimately be cut, but are necessary for actors and directors to fully understand your intentions. Once everyone is at the same of understanding, the line has done its job and can go.

When you are being very scrupulous about cutting it can also happen that you forget some basic things that the audience needs to know. It may be that you've forgotten to include a key bit of context or information which clarifies everything else. When you've been working and reworking your scenes it can become hard to remember what the audience knows at what point in the play. The best solution is to get a trusted person to read the play or scene for you. If they come back to you with a slightly puzzled expression and lots of questions, that's a good indication of what key information you've forgotten to include.

EXERCISE

1. Take a scene, and then cut it down to no more than fifty words. The result isn't necessarily going to be naturalistic, but it must convey the essence of what the original scene was intended to do.
2. Once you've done that – can you reduce it further, to ten words only? If you can, you will certainly have discovered the bones and sinews of the scene. Now you can be selective in putting back the muscle and fat on those bones.

Formatting and layout

Fraser Grace

Whatever the mechanics involved in writing your play, eventually it will have to be laid out and printed in such a way as to make it look and work like a theatre script. This is formatting.

A script can be formatted after it's written, but there are obvious advantages in formatting as you write.

Again, there are a number of ways this shaping can be done.

- Do it yourself, manually, as you write.
- Use an off-the-peg computer programme to do the donkey work for you. Free packages include the basic version of *Celtx*, though some writers report problems when transferring scripts, e.g. into an email attachment. *Final Draft* is a more sophisticated package, but you'll have to pay for it.

> Many writers (I'm one of them) appreciate the convenience of a simple word processing programme for writing, editing, reproducing and distributing a script, but like to handle most of the formatting aspects the hard way. The time it takes to type in each character name at the left hand margin every time they speak, then render the name in bold, stick a colon after it and hit the tab button, can be invaluable; it allows thinking and adjusting time, and this becomes a vital part of the rhythm of composition. The same is true of manually turning stage directions into italics, single spaced. Slow is sometimes good.

As the above implies, the finished script will need to possess certain qualities. This is not to say that there is only one way of laying out a script for theatre – there isn't. But every script must

- present the work in a professional-looking way,
- aid the *use* and *comprehension* of the script,
- quietly but clearly present the work as your intellectual property.

> A play script is above all a working document.

Unlike the BBC, who will reformat a script for radio drama for instance, few theatres will go to that trouble. What is used in a reading or rehearsal will almost certainly be a photocopy – not always a good one – of your own 'rehearsal draft'. It's in your own interests to ensure the formatting of the script makes your intentions clear. What's more, some of the information you supply in the script will be referred to when contracts are drawn up, so clarity of presentation and accuracy are vital.

The script you present will need to observe the following rule:

- Use standard A4 paper, printed on one side only, minimum 12-point font in a clear typeface.

The script then has two parts:

Title pages

This is where most of the legal and informational material belongs. Title pages generally comprise:

- A title page, bearing a clear title (even if only a working title) and the name you wish to be known by as a playwright. This in effect asserts your legal right to the material that follows.
- Also contacts, for your agent and agency if you have one, your own contacts if not.
- A character list with *brief* indication of type – gender, age, ethnicity – where crucial.
- Time and place where the action is set (optional, but helpful).
- Any *brief* notes you want to add about background to the play, historical accuracy, etc.
- If your script uses unusual punctuation as an indication of the desired mode of delivery – for instance, backslash (in place of forward slash) to indicate an interrupted or overlapping line, or material in brackets to indicate what is not said but implied – your peculiar convention should also be explained here, to avoid confusion.

Body of the play

The part we're really interested in – the play text – needs the following:

- Page numbers – obvious, but if a literary assistant drops the script between the printer and the artistic directors' desk, your play will stand a much better chance of appearing cohesive if the pages are reassembled in the intended order. Also invaluable when discussing the script with, e.g. a literary manager, director, designer or actors. Setting a 'footer', so that every page bears the title and author, is a further failsafe.
- Wide margins – more a courtesy than a requirement, but useful for all who might need to make notes.
- Double spacing of all dialogue.
- Clear attribution of dialogue to character. This can be achieved either by rendering the speaker's name in bold immediately preceding the line:

  Stevie: Keith, get that toxic waste you call your sister out of my house.

or by capitalizing the speaker's name at the left-hand margin, or by placing the name (centred or at the left) above the dialogue, so we only get to the dialogue through the character's name:

Lindi

I have got a name, y'know. (*To Keith*) Come on dipstick, we're going.

- Clear distinction between dialogue and stage direction. The latter is usually single-spaced and italicized:

  Lindi exits upstage, followed by a furious Keith.

  Pause.

  Stevie is about to clear away the detritus of the drinks party when Lindi weaves her way back into the room, snatches the bottle of vodka, pulls Stevie's face toward her and kisses him full on the mouth.

  She exits as before, a stunned Stevie staring after her.

  As you see, terms like 'pause' and 'beat', if used, are also usually given in italics.
- The conventions of 'Upstage' (away from the audience) 'Downstage', 'Stage left' (right for the audience) and 'Stage Right' can be used, especially if, as here, the fact that Lindi exits away from the audience, watched by Stevie, means something important – i.e. that Stevie is facing away from us, and his reaction is therefore hidden.
- Reference to 'lights' or 'fade lights' or 'blackout' are often used to indicate the end of a scene:

  We hear the outside door slam shut. Stevie waits until he's certain they've gone, then flops onto the sofa, bewildered. Then a smile spreads across his face, and he punches the air.

  Stevie: O Yes, geddin!

  Music kicks in. Blackout.
- A new act or scene (where those units are used) usually begins on a fresh page, and the units are numbered sequentially.
- It's customary to clearly indicate the end of each act, and of the play:

  End of Act One.
- Adding your name at the foot of the play, accompanied by the copyright symbol ©, further asserts your rights to the work.

TOP TIP

ALWAYS print out your script in hard copy and check it over thoroughly before sending it by email. Errors in format are frustrating for reader and writer – and this is the best way to catch them.

Write on 2: The industry

Finding a suitable theatre

Fraser Grace

If you don't have anyone banging on your door begging to produce your new play, then some activism on your part is required. You are for the time being the play's only advocate, and in the words of one of Shakespeare's more hapless kings, 'nothing will come of nothing'.

Take heart! At the same time as you are dreaming of getting your play produced, there are theatres out there bent on discovering new playwrights. A marriage made in heaven is just around the corner ...

Theatres in search of writers

> A fairly reliable piece of conventional wisdom among playwrights is that theatres, if they are interested in new writing at all, are generally more concerned to find a writer than to find a play.

The old model of the writer lobbing an unsolicited play into a theatre – where it gets picked out from the pile, miraculously strikes a chord with first one reader, then another, then a literary manager and finally a director – is largely obsolete. Fewer and fewer theatres have the infrastructure in place to process unsolicited scripts, and some – even new writing theatres – are honest enough to admit it. 'No unsolicited scripts' is now a common policy.

Writers' programmes

It is much more likely that a theatre will 'find' a writer through its writing groups or schemes. Such a company will play a part in 'developing' a writer through smaller opportunities and readings, and may eventually come to believe in that writer's ability and vision to the extent that they are willing to invest some precious commissioning money in this 'undiscovered' talent. This may be in the form of seed money to further develop an idea, or (the dream scenario) the invitation to propose a new original idea for a full-blown commission.

> **TOP TIP**
>
> The big trick is getting on a theatre's radar. Start by identifying a theatre that produces new work that excites you; find out about their new writing or writer development programme, and work out how to access it.

If you manage to get involved, you will find a listening ear, some helpful training and advice, and a few resources (actors, directors, dramaturgs, possibly even a photocopier) put at your disposal. The theatre will have found a candidate, and maybe, eventually, a play. (For more on this, see the section on 'Theatre Writers' Groups'.)

Competitions

The exception to the 'playwright-before-play' rule is that other, well-proven means of sourcing a new play – the open competition.

- These are sometimes funded through a small entry fee, but are often linked with a theatre, and can therefore include a production, as well as a cash prize, as a reward for the winner.
- Even if you only make the short list, you have introduced yourself to the theatre – you're a blip on that radar.
- If attached to a festival, the competition may offer of a range of levels of 'production' – from scratch readings, through workshops and rehearsed readings, to full production.

> **TOP TIP**
>
> A single reading of a new play may not attract the attentions of agents, directors or critics.
>
> A competition announcement, or a festival's glut of offerings, frequently does.

Current competitions

The constant churn of competitions (and the funds that back them) means that the list of hot competitions, their deadlines and the terms under which they operate, are constantly changing. Many have an online entry process anyway, so the best thing to do is put the name of the competition into a search engine and get the latest accurate information. Alternatively, go for the broad sweep and search for 'play competitions'. But read the rules carefully; some will effectively tie up your script for a couple of months or more, as they demand that no entry has been 'offered for production elsewhere'.

The chances of winning such a competition are naturally small, but increase with the size of your talent and luck – and winning guarantees both press attention and a tiny bit more of that precious commodity, credibility. Not every playwright likes the idea of press attention – much better to let the play to speak for itself – but that's just a cross you may have to bear; the 'award-winning playwright' tag has a habit of sticking, and with a production, a playwright's education can finally begin in earnest.

Titles of a few open competitions to get you started:

- *The Bruntwood* – the most valuable new play competition in the UK, run biannually in association with the Royal Exchange Theatre, Manchester.
- *The Verity Bargate Award* – one of the most influential and long-established open competitions, run by Soho Theatre Company in memory of its late, great, founding director. Beating off the 800 or so fellow entrants wins a cash prize representing an option on production.
- *Hotbed Festival* – run by Menagerie Theatre in Cambridge, this new writing festival offers a range of small commissions for new plays, and takes new work to various levels of production, including full production and occasionally, national tours.
- *Hightide Festival* – another festival based in the East of England, and a growing power in the new-writing landscape. Readings, workshop performances and full productions are given to a small number of new plays of promise.

Plays in search of theatres

To have written a play, and to find that a theatre is not really interested in it, but keen to see the next one, can be frustrating. In that situation, getting involved in the 'process' (any interest is better than none) still leaves you with a play in your back pocket, to which you may decide you owe the chance of life. The play now has to find a production, and that means getting it to someone else – but to whom? And how?

A few possible routes suggest themselves:

- Via a developing relationship. The theatre in whose new writing programme you are now involved may have 'passed' on your play, but there may be directors or dramaturgs around – even within your writers' group – who have relationships with other theatres or companies, to whom the play might be of interest.
- Via the passage of time. You have to be patient with this strategy, but once your new venture finally works its way into production, you may attract the services of an agent who can be tasked with 'placing' the older play. You may also get interest direct from another theatre or director who has seen the new piece. Often, a company that cannot afford to commission a new play from a writer they like will be willing to look at a play already written.
- Via your own production. Many playwrights are also actors, directors, producers. Many more do not see themselves as any of these things, but find themselves operating in one or other of these roles as a way of getting work to the stage. Remember, not only is a production an end in itself – a way of giving life to the script in which you have invested so much – it is a door-opener. It could be time to swallow your pride, call in favours, and get to work. However humble the level of production you can muster, it will be a chance to practise your craft, in every sense.
- Via approaches to other theatres. If you don't have the time and patience required to take the routes above, you can still send out the play to any theatres you'd like to work with. If a theatre has said 'no' to the play, but 'yes' to you as a playwright (by inviting you to be part of their writer development programme) this can be used to establish a bit of credibility with other theatres, in other towns and cities, or even in other countries. Maybe this 'old new play' will fit better with their programme – and then you'll have two productions on the go.

TOP TIP

Do your homework on any theatre to which you send a play. Check the theatre's programme. If a theatre is committed to producing contemporary epic plays from across Europe in translation, a heart-warming comedy about four young office workers in Tewkesbury before the Second World War is unlikely to hit the mark.

Some plays work as 'door openers', while never themselves attracting production. Every playwright – even the most successful – is familiar with this kind of tragedy. A play that has earned a meeting, or access to a theatre's circle of writers, or even a commission, nonetheless remains stuck on the shelf. If a script succeeds in winning you other opportunities, it owes you nothing. Whether you still owe it a chance of life, and how much you are willing to sacrifice to 'do right by' the characters you love, only you can decide.

Pitching

Clare Bayley

The theatre world is nothing like the brutal film industry, where you will be expected to deliver your brilliant idea in a pitch of no more than one sentence, or during the time it takes to reach the executive floor in the lift. In theatre you will generally be in a meeting with a director or literary manager which at least has the veneer of a friendly chat. You still have to find a way to enthuse them very quickly with your idea. Remember that they will be hoping that it is inspiring and original – everyone wants an exciting new idea to take forward. But equally, remember that these people spend their lives listening to writers' brilliant ideas, and they've heard most of them before.

So to prepare:

- You probably need to come up with a quick encapsulation of the idea, and also be able to expand on it articulately, fluently and concisely.
- Don't get bogged down by explaining the entire story – it's incredibly hard (and boring) to follow garbled plots as explained by nervous writers.
- Concentrate instead on the broad themes, the major plot points, the dilemmas and conundrums.
- If it helps, think about your character the protagonist, and talk about their journey, the obstacles they will face, and what is at stake.

> **REMEMBER**
>
> The higher the stakes for your characters, the better your pitch.

One line with irony, twist or reversal

As observed in the section on 'Action and Plot', the greatest stories can often be encapsulated in a single sentence which contains an irony, twist or reversal.

For example:

- 'The aged king hopes to avoid disharmony among his daughters by dividing his kingdom between them, but by doing so splits both the kingdom and his family irrevocably' (*King Lear*).
- 'The hero seeks to right an ancient wrong and find his long-lost parents, but by doing so unwittingly murders his father and marries his mother' (*Oedipus*).

Not every play can fit into a neat formula like this – but if yours can do so, it will make your pitching job much easier. It can also indicate an idea with real depth, complexity and dramatic potential.

What's your USP?

Only you know the answer to this question. You're not selling washing machines or TV advertising, but you do need to have a Unique Selling Point. That could be a subject matter that is ripe for treatment, a quintessentially dramatic scenario, or just something that's been germinating in your imagination for years. They say there are no new stories under the sun, so somebody else has quite likely come up with the same or a similar idea; the USP is your specific take on that subject/scenario/seed of an idea. As Rufus Norris says in the Foreword to this book, the most important aspect of any play is 'the nucleus of the endeavour that is indisputably yours: why does the realm you are exploring need *you* to reveal it?'

Why now?

This is the question you will always be asked. You may have an idea that is driving you wild with desire to write it, but it has no contemporary relevance or echo, and sheds no new light on our present-day situation. This is hard for a theatre to sell, and so it will be hard for you to get commissioned. This is a bleak truth, the more so since it's often not until after you've written the play about your relationship with your adopted brother that you realize it works as a metaphor for immigration tensions in the UK/USA. But unless you can find some answer to the 'why now' question, that commission may be elusive.

Why you?

Authenticity counts for a lot in theatre, because great dialogue is about capturing the essence of how people reveal themselves through speech. It's hard to fake. You may have an idea which can be contained in a single line with a twist, it may have urgent contemporary relevance, but if you, a young atheist from downtown Baltimore, want to write a play about an ageing community of Glaswegian Muslims (or vice versa), you might encounter some skepticism. On the other hand, even if you've never been to Glasgow, but your uncle is a pillar of the Muslim community there, it's a completely different story. Still, you certainly shouldn't let your background and circumstances limit your imagination. If you can convincingly embody your characters, whoever they are, you have every chance of success. His background never stopped Derbyshire-born Fraser Grace from writing his award-winning play for the RSC about Zimbabwe's President Robert Mugabe, his wife, and the white psychiatrist summoned to deal with his demons.

Will they be able to get an audience?

Literary managers don't all like to admit that this is a factor in their decision-making, but they'd be foolish if it didn't have some bearing. Some theatres are more gung-ho about supporting the work, embracing the art and believing that the punters will follow the talent. It shouldn't be your first consideration, but there's no point making things hard for yourself.

TOP TIP

Don't pitch a dark one-hander in verse about suicide among the under-sixteens to a theatre well known for its populist comedies and middle-aged core audience.

How committed are you really to this idea?

- Your enthusiasm – if genuine – will be infectious, and you want the director to get carried away by it. So if you've only come up with the idea on the train on the way in to the meeting, or if you only pursued it because you think it's what they are looking for – in short if you haven't thought it through, or if you don't have much appetite for it and couldn't really honestly be bothered to write it even if you got the commission – that will communicate itself instantly and negatively.
- Even if they do get carried away with enthusiasm, they will be trained to seek out all the shortcomings and pitfalls at this stage in proceedings. They will probably have to pitch the idea themselves to someone else before long, if they take it on. So they will be trying to anticipate possible objections, and they will hope that you have a good rebuttal. When the questioning gets very tough, and yet you continue to give persuasive answers, that can be a very good sign indeed.

High-concept or high-execution?

In Hollywood they like the kind of pitches/ideas that can be summed up in a single sentence: 'Jaws on paws' is a personal favourite; Robert Kosberg's pitch for a horror film about a rampaging dog. This is the epitome of the high-concept pitch. If you can boil your idea down to something that could go on a poster – give it a try. But the whole point about theatre is that it isn't formulaic, simplistic or reductive, so generally your idea is going to be high-execution – meaning that the full glory of your idea and writing will emerge in the finished script, and not in a single sentence. In this case it helps if the person you're pitching to already knows and admires your writing and is prepared to go along for the ride. It's hard to persuade people that your brilliant execution will make a wonderful script; but if you can talk about it in a way that excites and intrigues, they may be convinced.

The golden moment

There sometimes comes a golden moment when your credit is high in the industry, and the theatres want you more than you want them. Pretty much whatever you pitch they are going to enthusiastically greenlight. Sometimes you don't realize you've hit this point until afterwards. But if you are aware that it might be approaching, don't squander the moment.

Question

> What do you really, really want to write? Don't just pitch them something you think will be a goer – go for your dream project. But just make sure that what you think is your dream project actually is something you want to devote the next weeks/months/years to. Sometimes you can accidentally land yourself a stinker.

Caveat

In direct contradiction to all of the above, there is the story of Matt Groening getting his commission for the first incarnation of *The Simpsons*. He had spent some time preparing an elaborate and well-thought out idea, only to catastrophically lose faith in it as he sat waiting to go into his meeting with the studio execs. He quickly conceived a new idea, basing the characters entirely on his own family (his father's name is Homer, his mother's Marge). He was going to call the main character Matt after himself, but thought it made it too obvious where the idea was coming from, so changed it to Bart at the last minute. The rest, as they say …

Literary manager or dramaturg?

Fraser Grace

> A director once told me that she was excited and determined to produce my play, but didn't 'do dramaturgy'. If I wanted that, I'd have to go elsewhere – although if necessary they could 'get someone in'.

Apart from making dramaturgy sound like something you might normally obtain in a plain brown bag from under the counter, the story points up a general nervousness about this darkest of arts, even among those who rely on it.

The fact is that if you've fallen into the embrace of one of the UK's largish regional theatres, a dedicated new writing company such as those on London's fringe, or one of the national companies, the chances are your chief link to that theatre will be via the Literary Department and literary manager, or the dramaturg in particular. So what do they do?

The interchangeability of these titles in the English-speaking world is based on an overlap of duties, but also on uncertainty and debate about the roles implied. In fact we could throw a couple of other job titles into this particular hat – 'writer in residence', say, or the Elizabethans' 'ordinary poet' – all figures with dramaturgical functions. But what are those functions exactly?

> The word dramaturg (hard G in German pronunciation, soft in French) should not really frighten us so much, since the Greek derivation simply means 'playwright'.

This points to the origins of the role. The 'ordinary poet' for example was the chief text expert in the Elizabethan theatre, responsible not only for writing new plays of their own, but for 'scouting' other playwrights, taking on translations of foreign language classics, or cutting old plays to fit the resources of the company or the will of the theatre manager.[1] While UK theatre in modern times has generally preferred the term 'literary manager' for the overseer of all things textual, the influence of both European and American models means that 'dramaturg' is becoming an increasingly popular title even here.

There are currently two models of dramaturgy, best explained with reference to the theatres of Germany and America.

The German model

In Germany, the theatre is a much-respected part of a town or region's civic society, and has civic responsibilities to go with it. In addition to mere artistic

[1] Direction at the time was usually the lot of the lead actor, comparable with an orchestra's first violin.

or commercial priorities, a town's (well-subsidized) theatre is expected to provide a programme of plays over a cycle of several years that will ensure all the citizens of the town have the opportunity to learn the classics. Citizens must also be kept abreast of developments elsewhere in the world of theatre, and be exposed to the newest voices of their own generation. The dramaturg – or more often the dramaturg and his or her staff (the office can be almost as big as the brief) – is responsible for seeing that the theatre's programming succeeds in this duty, and also for explaining and defending that programme to the town's authorities.

The chief dramaturg in Germany should also choose a programme that provides opportunities for the existing ensemble, and perhaps for enticing new talent to the company. Finally, the chief dramaturg appoints a 'production dramaturg' for each play in the programme.

The production dramaturg

Some of the responsibilities of this lesser text expert (textpert?) are much more like those of the 'writer in residence', working alongside the playwright to further stimulate development of the playscript (in the case of a new play). They must also, however, provide research materials for the company; commission or source essays from academics on the play in hand for inclusion in the programme (a far more serious document than the UK's often feeble collection of adverts for nearby curry houses); and compile, design and produce that programme.

> As in theatre and film schools throughout Eastern Europe, dramaturgy is likely to form part of the core curriculum taken by all students in equivalent German institutions, regardless of their specialism as actor, designer, director, technician, etc.

The US model

In America, where the civic burden on the theatre is less onerous, dramaturgy has come to mean a less public but still influential role. This consists of creating and resourcing a research environment for the company, but also, more controversially, working alongside the playwright (if living) to help them develop their play as a vital, more rounded piece of theatre text. This will include organizing readings and workshops, and generally testing the strength and impact of the piece. Prestigious courses in dramaturgy are run at top universities such as Yale and the University of California, their graduates fanning out to the literary departments of theatres across the country.

The UK fudge

Whatever the post-holder is called, the activities of the dramaturg will be performed by someone – or several 'someones' – in a UK new writing theatre, at least at the text-development level in which the playwright is so closely involved. They are though currently less likely to hold a post with that title. Courses in universities are correspondingly low-profile.

Despite this, if you have had help from a theatre in the form of private readings, script reports, consultations with literary managers and directors, public readings or workshop performances, then you have already experienced some form of dramaturgical support. A few very specific results of this kind of support that I have found valuable include the following:

- The acute observation that my issue play was becoming a thriller, and that a useful way forward might be to try redrafting it in that direction (literary manager).
- That suggestion that some of my lines – specifically noted – were over-compressed, too tightly constructed for an actor to articulate the lode of meanings I was hoping they would communicate in that moment (director).
- That notion that there might be a scene missing in the play which robbed the audience of the chance to fully appreciate the central character's journey (actor/director).
- That in an era bursting with staccato-rhythm plays, my nascent effort stood out because I dared to write extended speeches; and that this was not a failing but a strength – even though those same speeches had just died a death in a scratch reading (writer in residence).

TOP TIP

Rather than thinking about the dramaturg as a post, it's probably best, in the UK at least, to think of dramaturgy as an activity or process which might be contributed to by the director, as well as by those whose job description is bound up with it. At its best, this is a process of making the play fitter and more itself, through having it reflected back to you.

This brings us to perhaps the most important question for the playwright: am I allowed to disagree with any recommendations?

The best people operating in the dramaturgical role, whatever their professional title, will employ the following Wills and Will Nots:

- *Will* accept that the play belongs to the playwright; that it is a unique vision. The person responsible for it, and so best equipped to find solutions in it, is the playwright.
- *Will Not* pretend that there is one objective way to develop a play. Any script commissioned by a theatre will find its final form partly because of the context in which it is being developed and (hopefully) produced. This is a context forged from the needs and capabilities of the theatre, the tastes of the director, the size and shape of the space, the sophistication of that particular theatre's audience, and many more components – in addition to the steely vision of the playwright.
- *Will* work chiefly by asking open questions, working outward from the play's strengths to encourage thought about alternative choices or untapped opportunities, all intended to enhance the play.
- *Will* be clear about their part in the process and honest about who they themselves are working to (in almost every case, the director of the play, though the artistic director of the theatre may also have a say).

This last is particularly important. No playwright who has taken a play through several drafts to the satisfaction of a literary manager, only to find that the artistic director has no appetite for it, will want to go through the experience a second time.

TOP TIP

- If the dramaturgical input you're offered seems 'open-ended', aimed at helping you make the play the best it can be, and acknowledging the circumstances in which you are working, why not welcome it?
- Try to ascertain at the start of the process how the chain of command/ decision-making in that particular theatre works, and the likely timescale of this development period. This is particularly important if the theatre has yet to commit to production. Is there a commissioning round in February, by which time the play needs to be in shape?
- If, after commission, you are asked to develop the text with someone other than the play's eventual director, find out at what point the script meetings can go from two people to three. Generally speaking, the sooner the better.
- Make sure, if you can, that everyone involved shares the same vision of the potential your script represents. If the artistic director is interested in only that part of the play that is set in Ireland, while you – with the help of the dramaturg – have developed it into a transatlantic epic (however polished), you may just have written yourself out of a slot in the theatre's programme.

Agents

Clare Bayley

In your dreams, your agent is someone who rings you up to tell you how talented you are. They take you out for boozy lunches to discuss the finer points of your latest oeuvre, and send you vast bouquets on your opening nights. The rest of the time they are tirelessly working to promote your genius, negotiating staggering amounts of money for you and arranging meetings with high-end producers and directors. In your dreams.

It's not that they don't do all of those things from time to time – but agents can only survive by having lots of clients, the majority of whom earn them small, incremental amounts of money. They are subsidized by the Big Fishes who are raking it in – and demanding lots of time and attention. When you are first embarking on a relationship with an agent, it's best to have realistic expectations. I wish somebody had told me this.

Do you need an agent?

It's definitely an advantage to have one. Above all, an agent releases you from having to negotiate money with the people you are trying to work with. If there's ever any problem about money, it's wholly advantageous not to have to spend time and anxiety sorting it out yourself. And in a cash-strapped industry, even the nicest, most generous-hearted theatres and commissioners will try and get you cheap if they can.

How much do agents take in commission?

Generally agents take 10 per cent of everything you earn through writing, whether you've got it through your own efforts or theirs, so long as they handle the contracts. Some agents take off VAT on top of that. Therefore, it's not a disaster if you don't have an agent when you are starting out. If you're earning very little, at least you'll get to hang onto it all.

How do you choose an agent?

First you have to decide what kind of agent you want. You may want someone to act as a professional friend, who admires and promotes your work, reassures you when your career seems to be going belly up, and tips you off about interesting opportunities. It's very valuable to feel you have someone who is backing you up.

Alternatively, you may want a Rottweiler of an agent, who won't give you tea and sympathy but will net you large amounts of money for any deal you get, because they are generally as much feared as respected in the industry – even by you. Ideally, you want someone who is both these things; but I wouldn't recommend having an agent who is so scary and high-powered that you're afraid to phone them up.

Generally a very grand agent with a famous name and many celebrated writers on their books is unlikely to give you as a fledgling very much time or attention. It's knackering to have to fight to get the attention of your agent – you've got enough battles to fight without that one.

How do you get an agent?

Get recommendations from people in the industry whom you trust and who know your work – other writers, directors, dramaturgs, literary managers. Have a trawl through all the major agencies to see which agents represent the kind of writers you aspire to be, and/or who are at a similar level as you. It's often more strategic to target a junior agent who is hungry to build up their list and needs you to make money for them, rather than an established agent who already has more writers than they can manage. When you've got a shortlist of three or four, wait until you've got something on. It doesn't have to be a full production; a student presentation or a rehearsed reading will do, and is certainly better than trying to send in an unsolicited script.

Yes, but how!

Approach the agent with an email. Tell them why you want them specifically (because you love the writers they represent). Tell them in no more than a line the type of writer you are, and any credentials you have (winner of a competition, a previous production, an existing commission). Then ask them if they would very kindly come and see your latest work when it is produced/given a reading/showcased. If they don't reply, follow it up. If they keep ignoring your emails, don't assume it's because they think you're beneath contempt – it may just be they're busy and you're not top of their priorities. Phone the office. Phone again. Persist until you get an answer one way or another. It's common for people who are being besieged by prospective clients to say no, just because it's easier than to say yes. Don't let it be easy for them to say no to you.

TOP TIP

Invite agents to see your work in the afternoons. Theatrical agents don't have many free evenings, because they are always out seeing existing clients' work, or scouting around for new talent. But they love to get out of the office – so inviting them to see a rehearsed reading at teatime could get a better response than you imagine

What can you expect once you've got an agent?

- At the start of your career, don't expect agents to be running around trying to impress you. The reverse is true: once someone has taken a gamble on you, it's up to you to impress them, and convince them that you are the next great talent to hit the stage. Once you've convinced your agent, they will be more able to convince others on your behalf.
- Don't expect your new agent to get you work. You must be proactive, show that you have initiative, pulling power, contacts. Once you're bringing money in – albeit in little dribs and drabs – then you become interesting to them.
- Nothing succeeds like success. When you're starting out and most in need of any and every opportunity going, they go to people more successful than you. When you do hit that elusive run of good luck, and have plenty of work – suddenly everyone wants a piece of you (as Britney so perceptively sang). Once writers become successful, they get offered more work than they need or even can handle. Ironic, but true.
- Do keep in regular contact with your agent – let them know what you're doing, what you're aiming at, what you're hoping for. Email is good for this, and phone calls. Make sure your agent knows about your successes, and the work you're doing to try and get commissions. It's good to meet up on a fairly regular basis so that they know what kind of ideas you're pursuing. But don't just ring them up to moan – they haven't got time and it doesn't make you look good.
- I know of one writer who was able to phone their agent and say 'I can't pay my mortgage this month – what can you get for me?' It's a delicate balance between being demanding enough that they don't forget you are there, and being so demanding that they stop taking your calls.
- Discuss with your agent how much of your work they want to read. They have an impossible amount of professional reading to do, so you can't expect them to look at every draft and every treatment. But find out what they expect so that you don't either offend them by not showing them enough, or annoy them by burdening them with too much.
- You are entering a long-term relationship with an agent. You have to give a little and take a little, if you want them to see you through the long haul. But ultimately it is a business arrangement, not a love affair. They will love you most when you are most successful and earning most money. You can't blame them

for that. And if it's not working out, you have every right to find someone else to represent you.

What do you do if you want to change your agent?

While it's entirely your right to do so, this is a delicate process and should be approached with caution. You can't just start contacting other agents willy-nilly, because of course they talk to each other – and your agent will take a dim view if they feel you're being disloyal or underhand. Equally you don't want to leave your current agent before finding a new one, or you could be left without representation. You need to make discrete enquiries, and avoid being rude or ungracious about your current agent. New agents are going to be most interested in you when you've got a successful production either in the pipeline or in production right now. When the time comes, be upfront with the agent you're leaving – and make sure they find out you're going from you, not from anyone else.

Getting your play published

Fraser Grace

The value of having a play published cannot be overstated. A published script can be:

- stumbled upon by influential people in far-off places
- read by journalists in advance of interviews
- used as a calling card to theatres
- bought by people attending productions and workshops for years to come
- used to generally enhance your career.

If a play is published, it can also be studied; the libraries of many schools, colleges and universities carry multiple copies of successful plays, and are read by bright minds that in some cases will soon be joining the industry or forming opinion about it.

That said, getting a play published, at least in the UK, is not an easy business.

It would be churlish not to admit that, along with all the business advantages, a published script is a beautiful thing; it will be stocked in the British Library in London, delight your family, and look good on your bookshelf – if not quite so nice in the bargain bin.

Publishing in the UK

Playwriting in the UK is a much less respected business than elsewhere in Europe, and getting published – if it happens at all – invariably *follows* getting your play produced, rather than being seen as a work of literature in its own right.

TOP TIP

If you want to be published in the UK, write a play that someone wants to produce in a 'reputable' theatre – and the rest may follow.

Even when a production is secured, the going can be tough. There are currently very few UK publishers committed to publishing new plays by unknown playwrights, but those that will publish new playwrights are run by enthusiasts. What's more, they tend to have mutually beneficial relationships with new writing theatres. This has a couple of upshots:

- Sales of new plays by new writers are small, and distribution for these independent publishers to bookshops can be patchy. Consequently the smaller publishers generally rely heavily on a tie-in with a theatre's production. But these enthusiasts do like to discover a new voice – so even if this is your first production, if the publisher likes what they read, you could strike publishing gold.
- To make the most of footfall in the foyer, copies of the playtext sometimes double as a programme, complete with the original cast and creative team listed.

- Many scripts produced this way remain available after the run – sometimes only on a publish-on-demand basis, but good bookshops do carry small drama sections where notable modern plays are stocked.

> One consequence of the production tie-in is that in order for the playtext to be prepared in time for the first night, the about-to-be published playwright will have to surrender the script sometime in the early stages of rehearsal. This in turn means the published version can end up enshrining some of your less finished lines and scenes, rather than the polished glories that characterize your play by the end of its run – but you might well judge that a price worth paying.

Lending credibility?

In straitened times, few public libraries carry new playscripts unless by very famous writers, so unless you donate copies, it's unlikely you'll be borrowed into a higher public profile. For the time being, it'll have to be bookshops, theatres or colleges where your work in written form will meet its audience.

Royalties

Extremely tight financial margins for publishers mean that advances for new plays by new or newly established playwrights are vanishingly small, and like all advances are offset against royalties. Most publishers offer copies of the script at a discount to the writer, which though a small thing, means you can always have copies to hand for your own use, or to press on others. On the whole, though, be warned: you are unlikely to get rich from publishing your plays. The rewards are less direct, or of a different kind entirely.

Publishing in the US

In America, in addition to the regular publishers of scripts aimed at bookshops, colleges and libraries, several 'stock' publishers specialize in producing scripts for the many amateur and semi-pro companies that operate in virtually every town across the country. These stock scripts are fairly humble publications – deliberately cheap to buy, in plain cardboard covers, with basic paper and print quality – but the North American territory (to use the contractual term) is huge. If each amateur production sparks the buying of a dozen copies for rehearsal, the royalties can mount up. This again is quite apart from the pleasure and value of having your work quietly disseminated and considered by all kinds of people you may never meet.

The publishing revolution

> The step-change in publishing represented by the internet has had a major impact on the opportunities for publishing theatre scripts, including those scripts yet to be produced.

At the simplest level, the online bookstore allows some publishers to maintain their lists once the production is over, by printing-on-demand, and responding to orders placed remotely. This means that even plays which rarely sell a single copy remain available almost indefinitely. At the other extreme, many scripts can now be obtained instantly in an e-reader version. But it is in the marketplace for unproduced scripts that the biggest new publishing opportunities are opening up.

Recent years have seen a proliferation of online bookstores that, in addition to selling hardcopy published playscripts from traditional publishers, also undertake to publish the unproduced or barely-produced scripts. Type 'publish my play' into a search engine and you'll find the latest sites where (sometimes for a small upfront fee to cover e-formatting) you can get your script published as a buyable download. The better sites even offer to refund your money, once a half-dozen copies have been sold, and to split the proceeds of any further sales.

You may decide that the risks that accompany any online transaction are best avoided, or that selling your artistic capital cheaply like this is not for you: you'd rather hang on for a relative 'hit' production and a publishing deal that will sweep up your back catalogue. But as a way of making a cruelly overlooked script work for you now, by putting your play into the hands of general readers or potential producers to whom you don't have a direct route, it could be the outlet you are looking for.

Upload to the marketplace

At the other, less-commercial end of the spectrum, the BBC's Writersroom also maintains a site where scripts, including theatre plays, can be uploaded. The Script Room, which is open for various categories of scripts for limited 'windows' of time, is one of the places where the BBC's producers and others in search of new talent allegedly turn. Putting yourself in the shop window like this is not publishing, but fulfils many of the same functions – even if it doesn't help fill the gaps in your bookshelf just yet.

Professional bodies

Fraser Grace

Writers' Guild of Great Britain

The Theatre Committee of the WGGB was boosted in 1997, when the Guild amalgamated with the Theatre Writer's Union. The Theatre Committee now represents the interests of all those within the 2,000-strong Guild who write plays for theatre.[2]

Contracts

One of the most significant things the Guild does is negotiate with management associations over the terms of the contracts used when almost any theatre buys or commissions a play. If you have signed a contract offered to you by a theatre affiliated to the Independent Touring Council (ITC), the Theatre Management Association (TMA) or any of the following: National Theatre, Royal Shakespeare Company, Royal Court, Theatres National Committee (TNC), then you have already benefited from the Guild's activity.

---

[2] For more on the history of the Guild, see Nick Yapp's book *The Write Stuff*, published in 2009 to celebrate the first fifty years of its existence.

The terms of these contracts establish not only the minimum you will get paid for your script, but the stages during the development of the play at which you will receive that money, and many other essentials you may not have considered. These include the extent to which you can be obliged to rewrite your script after acceptance; your right of approval over the appointment of a director; the size of the typeface used on any advertising to name you as the playwright (relative to that used for others involved in production); when you can attend rehearsal; and so on. It also limits the rights the theatre management has over your play in terms of:

- time – after which the rights revert to you, and can be offered elsewhere
- space – the territories to which you are free to sell your play even while it is in production in the territory covered by the agreement
- medium – retaining TV/film/radio rights for separate sale

All these factors can obviously make a huge difference not only to your pocket, but also to your working life. If you're feeling overworked, or unsure whether you can attend auditions for your play, the contract is the first thing to check in order to establish your ground. The fact that the terms have been negotiated by your fellow playwrights ensures that the contract is not only clear but fairly comprehensive, and sympathetic to the playwright's situation.

Conscious of the constantly changing scene, particularly in the age of script development programmes, seed schemes and devising processes, the Guild also publishes advice about working in the theatre in circumstances *not* covered by the standard contracts, and will even check over any ad hoc contract for you.

Advice, membership, other benefits

Full membership of the Guild obliges you to pay a subscription which you work out yourself as a percentage of your annual earnings from writing, with a fixed minimum fee and a maximum ceiling.

However one of the key distinctions of the Guild is the recognition that the time when a playwright is most in need of help, and least likely to be aware of 'best practice', is at the beginning of their career. With limited experience of this new world, with paltry funds and probably without an agent to intervene or haggle on your behalf, you are then at your most vulnerable. Membership of your professional body might suddenly seem a necessity you can't afford to be without, but a luxury you can't afford. The Guild therefore offers a Candidate Membership at a reduced rate. You don't get access to all the services, but enough to protect you in the marketplace and in the theatre itself.

Gratitude for all this might be enough to persuade you to join the Guild as soon as you can – even though experience shows that playwrights are not great 'joiners' of anything, and fiercely value their independence. But like any union or professional body, the WGGB also offers a range of other services and advice that can be of great importance.

These include a pension scheme, a welfare fund and also free membership of another body, the Author's Licensing and Collecting Society (ALCS). This organization exists to collect royalties, often small amounts due to you for the use of your work in far-off places, in return for a small cut. I still treasure learning I have earned a few pounds from a Swedish radio station for broadcast of a radio play – a broadcast I knew nothing about – or for the repeat broadcast of a half-forgotten piece written for TV ten years ago. Put enough of these together and the annual ALCS cheque soon mounts up.

Beyond all the financial and workplace advantages of belonging to the Guild – or any professional body – there is also the strength-in-numbers lobbying power created when you join forces with your fellow writers. The Guild in turn regularly coordinates with Equity and other professional bodies such as the Scottish Society of Playwrights when the issue is one that affects the sector as a whole.

When a poorly informed cabinet minister makes an unsubstantiated claim about the theatre sector, or a policy initiative threatens to undermine the industry's future, it's likely to be the Guild and its partners that are turned to for comment. The bigger the membership, the stronger the voice.

Representing the US ...

In the US, the Dramatists Guild of America boasts a membership of more than six thousand playwrights, librettists, lyricists and composers, and is governed by an elected council of huge stars in the theatrical firmament.

'[E]stablished for the purpose of aiding dramatists in protecting both the artistic and economic integrity of their work', the DGA offers model contracts aimed at helping members negotiate with managements in an intelligent and comprehensive way. These are different from the 'minimum terms' contracts offered by their British counterpart, or by the much bigger Writers' Guild of America, which serves mainly screen writers. Like the agreements offered by those associations, however, the DGA's contracts do aim to limit the management's rights to the writer's work, as well as ensuring that agreement is made on all relevant aspects, helping to make sure playwrights get adequate compensation for their efforts.

The DGA offers three levels of membership, at fixed fees, and is also open to playwrights and student playwrights in Canada and elsewhere for a small surcharge.

The vast size of the US territory presents some particular problems to playwrights trying to carve out a living from their work. The National New Play Network was founded in 1998 and now counts more than twenty regional theatres in the USA as core members, plus associates. One of the group's chief objectives is to help protect playwrights – and managements – from a play's catastrophic loss of cachet once it has received its 'world premiere'. Under the aegis of the NNPN, not only are productions shared or advertised across the group, but a play can have up to three 'rolling premieres' within an eighteen-month period. The NNPN also offers bursaries to support residencies, commissions, and collaborations.

Theatre writers' groups

Clare Bayley

New writing theatres often run writers' groups as a way of supporting young or emerging playwrights. It's a statement of encouragement, a means of inviting writers inside their doors even if they are not able to fully commission them. These groups are often led by the theatre's writer in residence, if it has one, or coordinated by the literary manager. They vary in terms of their remit, from inviting writers in to see their productions at discounted prices, to running workshops and masterclasses, and hosting regular meetings at which work-in-progress can be shared and peer-reviewed. They are usually by invitation only, and if the offer is extended it can be a great opportunity for a writer.

Some famous writers' groups – such as the one at the Royal Court – have been fertile breeding-grounds for successive generations of writers. They allow writers to get close to the seat of power, to become personally acquainted with the people running the theatre, and to begin to understand the culture and aesthetic of the building.

Regular meetings are great for encouraging a writer to write, and to get used to the sometimes uncomfortable process of sharing your work with other writers. In a genuinely collegiate environment, the honest and constructive feedback of your peers can be very valuable. Ideally you'll also have the wisdom of a more experienced writer running the sessions to guide you through and offer exercises and strategies.

Inevitably, though, if badly run these groups can turn nasty. There can be a feeling of competition among the writers, made worse if the theatre dangles limited opportunities for progression in front of the participants. In this case the law of the jungle can prevail, with only the strongest/loudest/pushiest surviving. Some writers thrive on competition, but many don't.

Form your own writers' group

The alternative is to form your own group. Network among playwrights and friends (though if you invite only your friends, you aren't certain to get an objective and helpful response to your work). You can draw on writers from other disciplines, though here the specialist playwriting knowledge is lacking. It's great to ask actors along as well – not only will they be skilled at reading work aloud, but they will often be a source of insight into the work itself. Directors are similarly invaluable at providing insights into where the work is going wrong and how it might be fixed.

As with all such enterprises, you're well-advised to clearly define your intentions and parameters of activity:

- How often you meet.
- Where you meet.
- When you meet – during the day (which may exclude some people) or during the evening (which may exclude others).
- Do you circulate work before the meeting, or read it cold on the day?
- Does everyone present work at every meeting, or do you concentrate on one person per meeting?
- What type of feedback are you looking for?
- How structured do you want the feedback to be? Do you want people to write anything, or just talk?

THE MONSTERISTS

David Eldridge and Moira Buffini were working at the National Theatre Studio, when they became aware of how few plays were being commissioned for large spaces from writers like themselves. In 2003 they vowed to address this by forming the Monsterists, a coalition of writers demanding bigger spaces, including Richard Bean, Rebecca Lenkiewicz and Roy Williams among others. Within seven years Eldridge (*Market Boy* 2006), Buffini (*Welcome to Thebes* 2010) and Lenkiewicz (*Her Naked Skin* 2008) had all had plays produced on the Olivier stage at the National Theatre, while Bean's *Harvest* (2005) at the Royal Court had a cast of twelve.

The Antelopes

The Antelopes is an invitation-only informal group of playwrights which was originally set up by David Eldridge. It sometimes acts as a pressure group to promote playwrights' interests; but its main function is as a private network where playwrights can meet in a London pub to discuss their industry, 'without danger of pissing anyone off'.

Membership is by request to an administrator. Real names must be used and not pseudonyms. The group is open to all playwrights currently working in the UK: the only criterion is that you must make at least part of your living, however small, by writing plays for the stage. There is also an Antelopes email list you can join by sending a message to the.antelopes.group@gmail.com, which will send around occasional messages, for example when a new meeting has been scheduled.

Playwriting UK

A public Facebook group for everyone who writes plays for the theatre in the UK. The idea is for writers to share tips on:

- How to get funding
- Who you should send your plays to and at which theatres
- Writing opportunities – competitions, prizes, etc
- Useful websites
- Quality, dynamic new writing companies
- Useful courses/schemes

And anything else which will help and support writers.

Other places to try

London

All the major London new writing theatres – though these mostly run groups by invitation only: Royal Court, Bush, Soho Theatre, Theatre 503, Finborough, Arcola, Tricycle, Hampstead, Old Red Lion, Lyric Hammersmith, Battersea Arts Centre.

Festivals and touring companies

Paines Plough, High Tide Festival, Out of Joint.

Regional theatres

Contact your local theatre. If they don't already run a writers' group, perhaps they ought to – you could suggest setting one up: Birmingham Rep

Liverpool Everyman

Manchester Royal Exchange

West Yorkshire Playhouse

Hull Truck

Live Theatre, Newcastle

Sherman Cymru, Cardiff

Traverse Theatre, Edinburgh

Abbey Theatre, Dublin

Lyric Theatre, Belfast

National Theatre of Scotland

National Theatre of Wales

Writing courses and degrees

Clare Bayley

There's some debate in this book over the value of teaching writing. I studied for an MA in Playwriting Studies from the Birmingham University course that David Edgar set up, and which has since been run by playwrights (including Fraser Grace). When I was accepted onto the course, I was sent a letter addressing me: Dear Playwright. At that point I'd only had one or two rehearsed readings of my work, and I'd never have presumed to call myself a playwright. If you're fortunate enough to have the confidence and certainty to know early in life what you want to do and how to do it, then perhaps you won't need to take an MA or a degree course in writing. But for most of us, it's more of a fumbling process of discovery and reinvention. Daring to call yourself what you want to be is the first important step towards gaining the confidence to do it.

Studying for the MA itself was nourishment. For a year we were fed with ideas, debate, speakers, readings, feedback, writing exercises, peer support, a community of writers. The professional life of a writer often feels like the reverse – you are there to feed the hungry producers, directors and commissioners. All those ideas, pitches, proposals and plays have to come from you, out of you. The MA was like having a long, slow drink before setting out on a long journey. You need to stock up before you embark.

Now I also teach creative writing at BA and MA level. When I was going to university, the belief still reigned that you were either born a writer, or you shouldn't even try. Genius would shine through, and no amount of working at it could improve something that wasn't innately there. As a teacher, you do come across writers with natural talent. But there's no doubt that you can help people to understand form, technique, craft. The view that only genius will prevail forgets how important the sense of entitlement can be – and how destructive its opposite. If the craft is properly taught, it isn't a process of reproducing clones of the teacher. Nor is it about giving false hope to non-writers. It's about supporting writers to make their own discoveries and hone their existing talents.

There are playwrights who have failed their English Literature A-level, who can barely string a prose sentence together, and yet who can capture, in scintillating dialogue, a culture, a milieu, a character, an era. The way people speak is the stuff of playwriting – not just the vocabulary they use but the rhythms, the inflections, the verbosity or the brevity, the silences and the jokes, the meaning behind the words, the threats hidden in the pleasantries, the seduction underneath the banalities. These aren't people who necessarily understand how to get their work produced, or how the industry works, and they certainly don't have a feeling of entitlement about their place in it. Many people can benefit from degrees and courses, and thanks to the proliferation of such opportunities, there are increasing numbers of writers emerging with confidence, experience and a realistic understanding of the industry they are going into.

Write on 3: Rehearsal and production

Casting

Fraser Grace

A playwright can expect to be consulted on casting, but not necessarily to be present for auditions. This last can be a blessing, as the process may go through several rounds, with each audition wedged between a director's other commitments and a casting director's availability. It may also suffer sharp turns of fate, when a preferred candidate turns out not to be available after all, and the process backtracks or starts all over again.

Whether it's worth the playwright going through this sometimes frustrating and gruelling process, and whether that playwright has anything useful to contribute, will depend upon their experience and curiosity, the time available to them, their relationship with the director, and the scale of the production.

What if there are no auditions?

This is rare, but can happen in some cases:

- In the repertory ensemble: most if not all the parts will be played by actors well known to the director, so formal auditions may not be held, except for those actors brought in to cover a part for which there is no candidate within the company.
- In the small permanent company: you may have known which actors you will be working with before writing a word of the play.
- In star casting: if the part is very big, and the actor in the frame very starry, the part may simply be offered on the basis of their reading the part privately and discussing it with the director. All you have to do is nod.

These extremes apart, the 'normal' condition applies: a production must audition for every part, because

- the company is so large that the ensemble can put up several candidates for any role,

  or more usually

- the company has no ensemble, pulling actors together on a production-by-production basis.

In the case of a very small company especially, the director may appreciate having a second pair of eyes and ears in the auditions, and the playwright – with a good grasp of the vision of the play – can play a helpful role.

Who is in the room?

Auditions are generally run by the director (or for lesser parts in larger productions, possibly the assistant director). In Europe, or in some theatres in America, the dramaturg or literary manager may take a hand.

If the production depends on group work, there may also be tried-and-trusted actors present – or those already cast – to help conduct the audition.

Depending on the set-up (e.g. if there is no dramaturg) the company's casting director may also be present. An independent casting agent may be brought in where no casting director is available. Members of this key but low-profile profession are famed for their little black books, full of contacts for actors and agents, but also prized for their grasp of the current scene – who's in town or out, who is ready to move up to a bigger role, who is a hot name or the next thing, or who is just about to emerge from a drama school and might be available. It is the casting director's or agent's job to provide the director with options beyond the director's own list of regulars or contacts.

Finally there is, of course, the actor to be auditioned.

Let the right one in ...

> The actor making it to audition has already got through the first round: the hours the director has spent checking their own lists, or scouring online talent sites, and consulting with the casting director over likely candidates.

That said, in this cruel world many very good actors spend an inordinate amount of time shuffling around from rehearsal room to auditioning suite, having been called for audition only to be rejected repeatedly, often for reasons quite beyond their control. They are too tall, too old/young, not quite as they looked in the photo, and so on. Then there are the things which are more to do with training or lack of it: they are too mannered, not vocally strong enough, insufficiently fit physically, technically lacking in some respect. Or perhaps they seem poor at responding to direction, or come across as temperamentally brittle, unlikely to fit in well with the other members of the company.

Reasons for rejecting an actor for a part, in the hope that someone more suited might be out there, always seem to be in good supply.

Who gets cast, and why

It goes without saying that in the end, the actor who will be successful is the one who seems interested in the role, with some intelligent grasp of the journey ahead, technically proficient, a good and generous team player, a good balance to those already cast, and most likely to discover something rich and wonderful in the role.

> WARNING – the director can make choices that seem to fly in the face of the obvious, to the bewilderment of the playwright.
>
> That's because the director is at the beginning of their process, while you have at last sighted landfall ...

A true story

A director, casting agent and I once auditioned three women actors for a solo play. The part had been successfully developed with, and superbly played by, a company regular who had had to withdraw for family reasons (she was starting one).

The first actor gave a fairly flat reading, showed no signs of being greatly enthused by the part, but demonstrated enough technical ability to suggest the part would be in safe, if slightly uninspiring hands.

The second was a completely different proposition. She was reputedly destined for great things, and the casting agent made it clear that such a small company was lucky to be seeing her for audition at all. The moment she walked in, this actor looked the part. When she read, I was stunned by how much she seemed to grasp the 'voice' I had in my head. She had prepared well, and knew how to 'work the room' with positivity too.

The third was, I thought, physically quite a stretch for the part. She was technically talented for sure, but quirky. Her reading was not particularly fluent, and I couldn't really see how what I was seeing connected with the character in my mind, let alone with the performance by the heavily pregnant colleague who'd had to withdraw.

Even if you're not a playwright, you've probably guessed how this story ends. Once alone, the director, the casting agent and I all agreed there was one outstanding candidate; the decision had been made for us. The director then said he would go with number three.

After the casting agent had withdrawn, wounded, I spluttered my confusion: what could possibly be wrong with number two, and surely she was a slamdunk for the part? What was the director thinking of?!

He said that while it was possible he could cast the second actor, he could not imagine how we would spend the next four weeks of rehearsal. With number three, he had no idea what the new version of the part would turn out to be, but the journey to it would be unusual and surprising – and that's what, as a director, made him tick. The obvious route is not always the best.

I now know he was right.

TOP TIP

- If you are encouraged and/or willing to attend auditions, try to go with an open mind.
- DO be alert to what's interesting and surprising and offers the prospect of a journey (though hopefully a successful one, that can be achieved in a few weeks).
- DON'T look only for what conforms to an end result – that's a destination arrived at far too soon. A questing spirit is better than a closed book.

Actors

Clare Bayley

As a writer, you should have the greatest respect for actors. Very often, they deserve the credit for successful productions. Brilliant actors can produce an outstanding performance from what is merely a good script. They can bring out aspects of your characters that you yourself may hardly have been aware of. In the rehearsal process itself, intelligent and experienced actors can sniff out a duff line of dialogue, an implausible reaction in a character, a false note in the plotting – and you should always listen to their suggestions.

A production is an act of trust on their part. The rehearsal period is only the tip of the iceberg for them. They have to go out there on stage, night after night, even after you and the director are sitting at home or working on the next project. If the production is a flop, if the reviews are bad and the audiences stay away in droves, it's the poor old actors who have to keep on going out there, night after night.

TOP TIP

Actors deserve your sincere gratitude and highest regard. Give it to them.

The relationship between writers and actors

The closeness and intensity of the rehearsal process often means that you form lasting friendships with actors.[1] It's of clear benefit to writers for many reasons – not least the fact that actors are generally very good company indeed. As the industry works so much on personal contacts, actors are usually happy to keep in touch with writers. If they like your work they can be amazingly generous about offering to do informal readings or rehearsed readings of new scripts or work-in-progress. It's always useful to hear your script read aloud by somebody else, and actors always ask the questions which show up the weaknesses in the writing – the whys and the hows. So if actors are willing to do it, it's of great benefit to a writer.

If or when they become big names with pulling power in the industry they can be useful in other ways. Many scripts have attracted the interest of a prominent actor, and then proved more attractive to theatre managers. Jez Butterworth has written candidly about his play *Jerusalem*, which had got caught in development purgatory, and despite draft after draft there was never a production in prospect. Then Mark Rylance fell in love with the character of Johnny Rooster, and pushed for it to be put on.

In rehearsal

For an actor the process of rehearsing a new play is one of huge and steep learning. The world you've created has probably been living inside your head for months, if not years, before you get to the first read-through. The actors have a short time to get familiar with the themes of the play, understand their characters, learn their lines, get their heads around the blocking and props, and not least navigate all the relationships within the company, both on and off stage.

In order to do all this, actors need to feel supported and free to make mistakes. Mostly this is the director's job, but the writer has a big part to play

[1] Clearly it goes further than that sometimes – Chekhov famously fell in love with his leading lady, Olga Knipper, while you only have to think of Arthur Miller and Marilyn Monroe, Tom Stoppard and Felicity Kendall …

too. Just being courteous, open and receptive to their ideas is helpful. Equally, you have to be circumspect about becoming too chummy with your cast. Their principal relationship has to be with the director, and it's ill-advised to do anything to undermine that. (See also 'Rehearsal Room Etiquette'.)

Directors

Clare Bayley

> **TOP TIP**
>
> You need to form a good, open and strong collaborative relationship with a director.

Ideally a director is a writer's natural ally, champion and conduit to the world. It's through their commitment and enthusiasm that your work will be seen. Through them, your ideas will be realized. They may see in your work insights that you yourself are only dimly aware of, and their skill can tease these out to full expression. But in order for them to do all that, you have to hand your work over to them and trust them to do it.

That can be hard. It doesn't always go according to plan. Their motives might not be entirely to do with honouring the genius of your words, but with furthering their own career, and using you as a useful (or even an unpleasant but necessary) stepping stone. But a strong relationship gives you the best chance of it all going as well as possible.

The power of the director

The job of the director in the rehearsal room, and in trying to get productions off the ground, is to convince people to do things they don't necessarily want or feel able to do. Directors have to be persuasive. They have to know how to wield their power. They have to bring their will to bear on other people.

That includes you. You may not always want their will to be brought to bear on you. You have to know where your boundaries are, and where you need to make a stand for your work.

Not all directors are megalomaniacs, of course. Most of them get a long way by being extremely clever, charming and good at their work. Often the more experienced and confident they are in themselves, the more open and easy-going they are. But no successful director ever got to where they did by being a pushover. In *Theatre of Blood* Michael Blakemore talks of the 'fantastic deviousness and treachery of ambitious directors behind the essential theatre mask of affability', and tells hair-raising stories of savagery and ruthlessness. On the other hand, there have been famous lifelong collaborations and friendships between writers and directors. Those are the luckiest writers.

The writer–director relationship

Generally you first meet a director when they have already decided they want to direct your play, or when they have seen enough of your writing to know that they want to work with you. In that case you are starting from a good place, where you can assume a mutual respect. But even if the director has only been 'assigned' to your play by the theatre's artistic director, and there wasn't much of an element of choice in the matter, it's in everyone's interests that you have a good relationship.

Good communication with the director is the most important thing to establish from the start. If you can talk openly and honestly, your collaboration has the best chance of succeeding. If you can avoid either party being defensive or overbearing, and if everyone is prepared to compromise a little, your collaboration will be fruitful. As the writer you will also have to know where to draw a line; but don't start from that position.

Letting go of your script

In the rehearsal room (and see also' Rehearsal room etiquette') the director has the power. They have a direct relationship with the actors and with you, and their job is to navigate between the two.

A Very Important Point

Once you're in the rehearsal room the script is no longer your property, and it no longer has single authorship. The creative intelligence of the director, the actors, and the set, lighting and costume designers all work on it to make it something far greater than you the writer could do alone. And the director is in charge of the whole process.

Some directors are brilliant at building a generous, collaborative company spirit, so that everyone feels confident, able to give their best work and combine their talents to the benefit of the production. A surprising number of directors, however (if we are to believe what actors tell us in private), lack this kind of social skill, and rely on dominating proceedings, imposing their vision on everyone else, concealing their own feelings of inadequacy by playing unhelpful games of divide and rule.

I've never worked with anyone like this. But I have heard stories of writers being banned from the rehearsal room, actors being bullied, actors walking out halfway through the production, rewrites being demanded at impossibly short notice and changes being imposed against the wishes of the writer. If things do start going badly wrong, and you don't feel able to resolve difficulties alone, you should get in touch with your agent as soon as possible. You shouldn't attempt to deal with a situation like this on your own.

The great majority of rehearsal processes, however, are the icing on the cake for the writer. After all those lonely months sitting in your room writing, you finally get to emerge from your solitude and spend time with clever, funny, professional entertainers who are devoting all their energy to your work.

The great skill of the director lies in enabling the actors to understand the text in both an instinctive and an intellectual way, so that they can portray your characters truthfully and vividly. This is not a straightforward process. It requires a lot of playing, trying out, testing, revisiting. During this mysterious process, the director has to hold the uncertainty of all the others in the room, and project calm, certainty and reassurance. Sometimes they may not be feeling that themselves. But the last thing they need is for you to be panicking. It's not your job to fix anything, other than problems with the script. So you are well advised to leave the actors to act and the director to direct. Sit back, and enjoy witnessing a process which is sometimes painful, occasionally alarming, often hugely enjoyable and always, ultimately, miraculous.

Designers

Fraser Grace

It may be that you will have the chance to meet the designer and talk to them about the play early in the process, though since the designer works (like everyone else) directly to the director, you might not get that opportunity. If not, the designer will work from your text and from discussions with the director.

Chances are you won't see much of the designer around the rehearsal room either – they will be working on designs for two or three other shows by this time, leaving their vicar on earth, the production's set builder, to actualize the vision for the show.

However, if you only attend one rehearsal, try to make sure it is the morning when the designer shows the model box to the company. This is a moment of pure magic, when the world that has so far existed only inside your head suddenly finds visible (if miniature) form. As the designer talks the company through the evolving set, you'll realize how the design cleverly solves all sorts of problems you thought might trip the production up, or slow its flow.

A good designer will have absorbed an amazing amount from the script (and if you were lucky, your earlier conversations) and not just the play's technical requirements. The model box will be pregnant with both the play's spirit and its underlying narrative – all subtly worked into design, props and costume. You will be smitten with the care and genius of it all. The actors, naturally, will be worrying about the steepness of the rake, or whether that door should be opened with their left hand or their right – and is that table *really* going to be *there* in Act Two? ...

Stage management team

Fraser Grace

By the time rehearsals arrive, you will already know the literary manager and/or dramaturg, you will have met the director and picked over the play with them; you will also undoubtedly have been introduced to the marketing and publicity personnel, and been asked how much you want to be involved in promoting the show.[2]

As soon as you enter the rehearsal room itself, and work begins on the script, it will become clear – if it isn't already – which actor has been cast to play which of your characters. You may even, as we've seen, have had a hand in auditioning them. There will still though be a number of people around the rehearsal room or the playing space whom you may not recognize. What do all these people do?

Company manager

Not strictly speaking a member of the stage management team, the CM handles the business affairs of the company, including both contractual and financial matters, and the company's welfare. They will also liaise with front of house (FOH) and with the marketing and publicity departments once rehearsals are underway. As a link between the theatre's management and the company, the CM's is an even more crucial role when it comes to touring a show. Who liaises with the tour venues, arranges transport? Who sets up accommodation (and sorts out any problems with the same)? That would be the CM. When 'the ghost walks' (on pay day) chances are the ghost will look remarkably like the CM.

Stage manager

As team leader for stage management, the SM has responsibility for overseeing the production process, and for coordinating communication between the

[2] If you're unsure of the role of any of the above, and how the playwright relates to them, see separate sections on 'Directors', 'Literary Manager or Dramaturg' and 'Actors'.

rehearsal room and all production departments – those technicians and designers that will make the show actually function in the theatre.

Together with their assistant stage manager (ASM), the SM has to work within a tight budget to source and supply all props and anything else required to support rehearsals. The technical rehearsal, where safety and smooth running are vital considerations, also falls under the SM's auspices, the designer and director relying on the SM to deliver a production that fulfils the original concept, without injury to life and limb.

Talking of props, do you know your 'actual' from your 'practical'? The SM will put you straight.

Deputy stage manager

The DSM represents the production team in rehearsal. It is down to the DSM to compile The Book (alias the Prompt copy, or Bible), maintaining an up-to-date copy of the script alongside a meticulous record of all cues for lighting and sound, and equally tight notes on blocking. When an actor is called for a costume fitting, or given a call for the next rehearsal, it is the DSM who issues that notice.

During performance, the DSM can be found at the prompt desk from where all the technical cues are issued, alongside backstage and FOH calls.

After the show, the DSM produces a daily show report, keeping production personnel and the director informed about audience size, technical or performance glitches, the need for running repairs and so on. This alone makes intriguing and useful reading (see 'Press Night and Reviews').

Assistant stage manager

The ASM's role is to support all aspects of the rehearsal and performance – effectively a right-hand person for both the SM and the DSM in resourcing, preparing for and running rehearsals from a technical point of view.

Once the show tips into performance, the ASM sets the stage and runs the backstage area – keeping nervous playwrights from cluttering up the wings, among other things.

Rights in rehearsal

Fraser Grace

The right to attend rehearsals of your play is one enshrined in any contract worth signing, and certainly in all those negotiated by the WGGB.[3] How often, and which, rehearsals you will attend is something you will agree with your director.

> Some directors might be happy for the writer to be present throughout, or whenever you feel like dropping in, but most will want some time to work without you present, and will certainly prefer to know in advance when you intend to come in.

There's nothing sinister about this, simply a recognition that the presence of the playwright, while a positive asset at some stages of the rehearsal process, and a necessary 'test' of progress at others, can also have a slightly distorting or disruptive effect on the company's exploration.

> Probably most playwrights can recall incidents when, the director having answered a question or issued a note, the cast shifted their gaze to see whether the writer was nodding or cringing.

Actors are remarkably un-self-conscious in rehearsal, except where the hallowed author is concerned; the question 'Is that how you wanted it?' is not a useful one when addressed to the playwright, especially when the exploration of the play is meant to be an open-ended process.
Two questions are useful here:

- Why be present?

[3] The question of how to behave once there is covered in the separate section of this book 'Rehearsal Room Etiquette'.

My favourite book about the rehearsal room, not least for its subtitle, is Susan Letzler Cole's *Playwrights in Rehearsal: The Seduction of Company*. This, in a nutshell, is one of the big attractions of the rehearsal room for the playwright: it's a break from all that isolation, a chance to watch others work (always a pleasure) and a chance to enjoy good company. As Clare Bayley confesses (see 'Rehearsal Room Etiquette'), the warm glow of adoration is much underrated.

- As a playwright myself, driven by curiosity, eager to see and learn how actors work, what they need, how they are helped by the director, how my text helps or hinders the search for meaning and the creation of a vital experience for the audience, I cannot imagine not wanting to be present for at least some rehearsals. These are some of the biggest learning opportunities I'll ever have.
- There are playwrights who hate the exposure of rehearsals, and would prefer to 'do a Salinger' and remain thoroughly detached from the whole process.

Even I have other stuff to be getting on with, I like to be useful, don't like being a spare part, and certainly don't want my presence to mean the company is engaging with me, instead of with their own craft or with the text.

- When *should* the playwright be 'in'?

Together with the directors I have worked with most frequently, we've established a mutually agreeable pattern of my attendance (based on a four-week rehearsal), which goes something like this:

Week 1 – Playwright attends all rehearsals.

- Absence by notification. I start when they start, leave when they leave.
- If the director does a lot of 'table work' – sitting around said table interrogating the text – it's likely to be in this week. This is clearly a time when having the playwright around is a useful resource – if only to reveal that he/she does not have all the answers, and to demonstrate the relationship of trust and respect for independent thinking shared by director and playwright. If you've worked with the director before, and the cast are all new to both of you, then yours is the best-established relationship in the room, and can help set the tone in those nervous first days of rehearsal.

Weeks 2 and 3 – Writer generally away from rehearsal, but on call.

- Available to discuss by phone/Skype any questions/ideas/problems the director encounters with the text.
- Available, subject to other commitments, to be present at any run-through. The timings of these, and the playwright's presence, by notification.
- Present at designer's presentation of set model (see 'Designers').
- Available also to marketing/publicity for interviews etc., reducing demand on acting company where necessary.

Week 4 – Writer in for dress rehearsal, and preview/first night.

- Playwright not available for tech run!

> Can I be excluded from rehearsals?

> **TOP TIP**
>
> - Absence from rehearsal does not mean you can't be in contact. Make sure you have a channel of communication with the director that is two-way (plus a back-up channel).
> - Being told by the director it might be best if you weren't present at certain points is not the same as being excluded. If you have a good relationship founded on trust and respect for each other's craft, this is just working together for the good of the play.
> - If your determination to enforce your right to attend any rehearsal clashes with a director's determination to exert their power to ask you *not* to be present, then it's time for arbitration; the company's Artistic Director (if not directing the play) the Literary Manager, and most importantly, your Agent if you have one, are the names on the doors on which you should knock.
> - Your rights of consultation – over cast changes, over cuts or other changes to the text, remain sacrosanct, and any reputable director will take care not to contravene the terms set down in the contract. In the event that you do feel these rights are being traduced, recourse is through the channels above, or through your professional body.

Rehearsal room etiquette

Clare Bayley

The collaborative nature of theatre means that in the rehearsal room you should be afforded respect as the writer, and your words should be treated accordingly. But you are only one of a number of collaborators who are there to transform your script from words on a page to a theatrical event. You are no longer the most important person in the room.

Check your contract

It's useful to be clear about what you're entitled to in terms of casting, attending rehearsals and of course, allocation of free tickets to the production. (See 'Rights in the Rehearsal'.)

- Generally you will be at least consulted on casting, if not actively involved in auditions.
- You should have the right to attend some, if not all, rehearsals.
- You will be given a certain number of comps for the first preview, and/or the press night, and for other performances during the run.

Before rehearsals start

You can expect to have a number of meetings with the director once the production has been secured, before rehearsals actually begin. These are very important as a way of establishing your all-important working relationship with the director before you enter the pressure of the rehearsal room. This will also be the time when you will be discussing cuts and rewrites to the script.

Since the director is already committed to doing your play, you can assume that they are in good faith and want the best for your work. Listen to any comments they have about rewrites or cuts. At this point they want to go into rehearsals with the most robust script possible. Not only is it a waste of valuable rehearsal time if there are lots of rewrites, but it can unsettle the cast. If actors begin to suspect that the script isn't good enough – or just that any line can be open to negotiation – they may lose confidence in it. This will be bad for morale, and an unhappy or uncertain cast is the last thing you need. It's not beneficial for you or the director if there is a feeling that the script is infinitely changeable.

Establish ground rules

Before rehearsals begin, it's good to discuss with the director how you're going to handle questions about the script generally, and about individual lines.

- In the early stages, and especially if you've already worked together on some rewrites, it's best to get the actors to find their way into lines, rather than assuming they can just be changed. The company's confidence in the script is important, and if you start rewriting willy-nilly, they're going to start assuming that everything is provisional, and that's not a reassuring place to be.
- If actors are asking direct questions about the meaning of the play, or the journey of their character, again it's wise not to jump in with explanations too quickly. The rehearsal process is one of discovery for the actors: they have about three to six weeks to catch up with the thinking behind the play which may have taken you a year of intense involvement. It's tempting, but it doesn't work to just try and tell them the answer, to short-circuit their learning process. They have to work it out for themselves. Sometimes being told a writer's intention too early is positively damaging – if the actor hasn't understood in their own instinctive way, they will end up trying to deliver something they only know intellectually. Acting doesn't work like that.
- One of the skills a director has that a writer may not is the ability to tell actors things about the play in a way that helps them to perform it better. This is most often not about literal explanations. It's a mysterious process and one which takes experience. A lot of the time it can look as if everyone is just mucking about and having a laugh, and not getting the point about your script at all. Sometimes, this is precisely what's happening. But it's all an important part of the process. Often, that's the moment when breakthroughs happen. As the writer you just have to zip it, and trust the process.

> Bear in mind that Pinter, Beckett and Churchill all refuse point blank to explain their work, to actors, journalists or anyone. They insist that the answers are embodied in the words. Remember too Jack Thorne's advice about 'the power of moo'.

The first rehearsal

After initial introductions, maybe some warm-up exercises and games, the first rehearsal usually involves the first read-through. The whole company will sit around a table and you will hear the script read by the actors for the first time. This is an exciting moment for the writer – the first time you hear it really come to life. Sometimes the read-through is so exactly how you hoped it would sound that you can hardly see the point of weeks of rehearsal ahead. Quite often you may immediately become aware of lines that don't work and cuts that you want to make. Very occasionally your heart may sink because you are disappointed in one of the actor's interpretations of your character. The truth is that this is only the first read-through, and during the course of rehearsals many things can and will change – for better, and for worse.

Avoiding the pitfalls

Writers of scripts are the only kind of writers who ever get to work collaboratively. The most social contact that poor lonely novelists ever get is signing books for members of the public, and possibly the odd lunch with an editor if they're lucky. Perhaps some people become writers of scripts because they're more gregarious than other types of writer. In any case it can turn a playwright's head to get into a rehearsal room.

You've spent all this time bringing your characters to life, and now here you are in a roomful of people who are as interested in them as you are. And you are the Expert in the room. You are the Creator of this little universe. You've spent a lot of time leading up to this on your own, and now people are sidling up to you in coffee breaks and openly in rehearsals, asking you insightful questions about your play. The temptation to bang on at length is almost irresistible. Resist. You have to rein yourself in, not get overexcited, be judicious in your replies.

Of course it's tempting to tell everyone what you really meant when you wrote a line, or a scene – especially at that moment when you can see director and actors all happily barking up the wrong tree. One of the hardest moments for a playwright is when you are sitting witnessing the whole company careering headlong down a blind alley, enthusiastically cheering each other on. The desire to stand up and shout: 'STOP! You've got it all WRONG!' can be almost overwhelming. But you shouldn't do it. It won't help.

Instead, have a quiet, calm word with the director at the next break. The director may not like this very much. They may be on a roll and not want to hear that the roll is the wrong one. But it's better to speak up now before they go even further down their road to perdition.

Remember that the process of discovery in a rehearsal room is mostly about trying out different ways and approaches to the text, and seeing how they fit. Often it's important to try out the 'wrong' way in order to find the 'right' way. Rehearsals are about being in a constant process of change and flux. Hopefully this moment will eventually evolve into rightness and certainty. When things seem to be going in completely the wrong direction, your relationship with the director is the key. If you have a good relationship, and can talk openly and honestly, it will see you through any of these potential tensions and difficulties ahead. If you don't, they will most likely ask you not to attend rehearsals at this point.

Stages of rehearsal

As mentioned in 'Rights in Rehearsal', at different points in the rehearsal process, you as the writer may be less useful a presence. It doesn't imply that they're planning to commit horrible crimes against your work. So be gracious; let it go. Distract yourself with starting work on your next play or getting on with other projects.

There comes a point in every rehearsal process, much as during the process of having a baby, when the situation seems impossible and doomed. Women at this stage in labour commonly demand drugs, cry, swear, try to leave the hospital or just curl up in a ball and refuse to go on. Similarly in rehearsals there is the moment when it appears to you, the director, all the actors and the creative team generally that the whole enterprise is a complete disaster, which it will not be possible to salvage before the opening night. There seems to be no way forward, no way back and – worst of all – no way out. It seems that there can only be pain, public humiliation and ridicule ahead, and quite certainly the end of your career. However, be assured that this is an entirely natural and almost inevitable part of the process. Keep the faith. It usually comes just before a massive leap forward.

The technical rehearsal

The tech is a hellish process during which the actors and creative team have to be locked in the theatre in the dark for hours and hours on end, while all the lighting, sound, costume, set, props and cues have to be finalized. It's not a creative process, but it's essential. It's extremely stressful, especially for the director, who has to oversee everything. And for the actors it is exhausting, simultaneously boring and nerve-wracking at a time when they are aware they need to conserve their energy for the opening night. In general, unless you are specifically asked to be there, it's best to absent yourself entirely.

Actors' dressing rooms

All actors prepare for performance in their own way. Most have to be quiet and alone after 'the half', the half hour before curtain up. You shouldn't invade their personal space or visit them in their dressing room at this point unless you've been specifically invited.

The first night

Traditionally, cards and even presents and flowers are exchanged among the cast and creatives on the day of the first night. After the traumas of the tech, it's a good way for everybody to give each other a lot of love and appreciation for all the hard work they've endured, and to boost their confidence for the beginning of the run. In small theatres this is just a matter of handing out cards in the dressing room. But in bigger venues the management will set out a table for your company. From about midday onwards, envelopes, bottles of champagne and bouquets start appearing. It's quite a thrilling sight. The stars of course get the biggest piles of presents and flowers from their admirers outside the company. But often the cards you get from your team are the most moving and precious. As the playwright, you might even get a bunch of flowers yourself (especially if you prompt your partner, or exert heavy pressure on your agent).

Marketing, press and publicity

Clare Bayley

Marketing

If you're running your own company, you will probably be involved in all of the above. Marketing includes designing the poster and any fliers you're going to produce (and handing them out on the street if you're unlucky).

When your play is produced by a big theatre with a marketing department they may not even consult you on the poster design, and they'll be surprised if you express any interest in it. That's their job, and you are expected to let them get on with it, which in itself can be something of a shock. If you like what they choose, of course, it's a relief not to have to worry about it. Otherwise, it can be difficult to let go. Pick your battles.

Press

You need to let the press know about your production so that you can get previews, listings and reviews. A press release is a simple enough document to write. You should think of it as primarily a document containing information about

- what's on,
- why the journalist should be interested,
- where it is,
- when – dates, times,
- who's doing it.

You should give a bit of background about the main creatives, a brief account of what the play is about, and anything unusual about the production. It's not the place for a mad attempt to sell the production with purple prose and hyperbole; that's more likely to put people off than attract them.

TOP TIP

Don't be afraid to chase up your press release. Arts editors and theatre critics receive dozens of them every week, so unless you make sure they've noticed yours, it's likely to get lost under a pile. You can try phoning or emailing to ask them politely whether they'll be attending the press night (and of course, offer them two complimentary tickets for any performance they want to come to).

Promoting the production may also involve talking to journalists about the play and how you came to write it. If it's an original play, it makes sense that it's you who has to talk, since you know as much as anybody about its origins and meaning. Don't be shy about doing this – the more publicity you get the better it is for everyone. But don't assume the journalists have done their research ahead of time. Many will have done, but others won't have a clue. You need to have in your mind the key things they need to know, and make sure you get them across. You're a writer – you know what to do.

Press Night and reviews

Fraser Grace

Press Night is an undeniable watershed in the life of a production: the secret work of the company is over, and the critics are free to publish their opinions. This in turn may have a major impact on the length of the run, the positivity surrounding the theatre, the future of the play and, conceivably, the careers and reputations of everyone involved.

So, no pressure then.

> Most theatres will make a bit of extra effort on Press Night, keen to give the production every chance of success.

This could extend to the following:

- The theatre's senior personnel turning out as a 'show of strength'.
- 'Papering the house' with free tickets, to guarantee an audience.
- Providing a glass of wine and a few nibbles for press before, during and/or after the show.

> **TOP TIP**
>
> The last is generally thought to encourage the critics to turn out, possibly based on experience. However, experience also shows that it will have absolutely no impact on what gets written; theatre critics, like all reviewers, fiercely guard their independence, and rightly so.

Still, creating a celebratory atmosphere on the press night does no one any harm, and helps compensate for the sheer nervous energy filling the house.

The power of critics

The sight of a well-known critic in the bar during the interval is enough to induce nerves in most writers, no matter how much free wine has been supplied – and with good reason.

> In some cases, in some towns (New York City is famously one of them), a good review from certain critics can ensure extended runs and make likely further productions. The opposite can mean a show closing before the current run is even completed, or at least peg back the rush for tickets. This is because these critics have earned the trust of audiences, who book tickets on the strength of what they write.

At the opposite extreme in terms of glamour and scale, reviews are equally vital to a festival like the Edinburgh Fringe. Here, it's almost impossible to choose from the thousands of shows on offer without the aid of reviews. A good notice helps a theatre glutton, with limited means, target just those shows that are – in that famously coveted word – 'Unmissable!'

So how should a playwright respond to the pressure of the press night, and to the reviews themselves? Here are a couple of options:

- Stay away – at least for the performance itself. Attend rehearsals and previews, when there is still a chance you can spot something you can help fix, but when it gets to the Press Night, save yourself the grief.

> A director I know always has dinner during the performance on Press Night, timing his return to the theatre so that everyone assumes he's been there all along.

- Practise fixing your face – the sense of responsibility for the play, the desire to be present at the birth itself, plus loyalty to the company may mean you have no option but to be there. If you have invited 'significant people' – other literary managers, potential agents, old tutors (for whom that free glass of wine is also apt to work its magic), you have no alternative but to be present.

> **TOP TIP**
>
> - Try not to grimace, tut or grumble if nerves get the better of actors and lines get mangled or missed, if the set sticks yet again, if a cue is missed. Prepare instead to sit, smile, and suck it up – and if you can, try to learn.
> - Don't be surprised if, in stark contrast to fears stoked by the previews, your play suddenly grows wings and flies, borne up by the extra adrenalin of the company, and the tangible pleasure of the audience's response.

For more extrovert playwrights, the press night is the icing on the cake: a chance to see the play at a time when everyone is likely to be positive about it (at least to your face) and to bask in the affirmation of friends and family who can scarcely believe all that bad-tempered redrafting has finally borne fruit. If that is you, lap it up – but don't be deceived; more sober judgement is heading your way …

On reviews

The age of intelligent reviews from respected critics with wide knowledge of classical, modern and contemporary theatre is largely over. The democratizing power of the internet and social media may have many positive effects, but means – as has often been noted – that everyone is a critic. Having your work intelligently critiqued is one thing; seeing it dismissed with ill-informed or unsubstantiated contempt is another.

Sensible companies avoid posting reviews of any kind inside the theatre while the show is running. For one thing, it can be divisive if one actor gets all the attention, and for a second, some actors wish to avoid reading anything – positive or negative – that might throw their performance. If actors do want to read 'the notices' they can do it in private – and still retain what US Defence Secretaries like to call 'deniability'.

TOP TIP

Some companies will compile a file of the major reviews and send them on later, after the show has finished. There is therefore no need for anyone, including the playwright, to personally scour the papers or their online versions, where reviews are published within hours of the performance.

No need, of course, and yet …

For playwrights, it's especially difficult to ignore what is being written as it is published; for one thing, you are now spending virtually all your time outside the theatre, and separation anxiety will draw you to any news of your play, wherever it comes from.

> **TOP TIP**
>
> The best defence against anxiety, at least in a sizeable production, is to arrange with the DSM to have the daily show report sent to you. This catalogues all the facts of the show – size of audience, running time, who bumped into what, what prop needs repair, etc. – and provides enough news to help the suffering writer feel 'connected' without recourse to the theatre pages.

Even the show report may not be enough. The playwright with a show in production is so caught up in the fate of the play, so keenly aware of its longer-term implications, that it can be hard not to scan every newspaper for reaction. This is probably a form of madness; basically, you are trying to read your own palm. You can avoid the reviews for a while, bury yourself in other work, pick up a few of the domestic duties you've dodged for the last many weeks, but the ripples will soon reach you; one way or another, a view of your play is steadily being formed.

How should critical approval, or condemnation, be assessed?

Below are two possible strategies, represented by writer Michael Frayn and composer and writer Stephen Sondheim.

Coping with critics

As Maddy Costa wrote in the *Guardian* newspaper in 2012, Michael Frayn's career demonstrates that success and failure can prove remarkably transient conditions:

> Frayn's reputation as a playwright is now so secure it's hard to remember it wasn't ever thus. For every hit, such as *Noises Off* or *Copenhagen*, there has been an equally substantial flop, the nadir being 1990's *Look Look*, which is not included in Frayn's four volumes of

> collected plays. His very first show, a Footlights review [*sic*] written as a student at Cambridge in the mid-1950s, was received so badly that he went into a sulk with the theatre that lasted several years.

Despite this, Frayn's interviewer found that Frayn himself was 'surprisingly puckish about critical crushings', as his own words reveal:

> It's very painful reading bad reviews but you can learn from them. You can see what put the reviewer's back up – and with a play you've got the chance to do another version.[4]

In fact, as seen in *Drafting and Redrafting*, Frayn has to be counted one of contemporary theatre's great rewriters – even prepared to engage in redrafting a play post-production. His willingness to learn from reviewers shows an appreciation of, and respect for, the genuine critic's craft, as well as an impressive commitment to his own.

The alternative view of the impact of critics is represented by Stephen Sondheim:

> For the young writer, critics have a number of destructive effects … […] praise makes you overestimate yourself, whereas anything less often leaves you disappointed or angry – and impotent […]. You subsequently find yourself brooding, briefly but often, over the unjustified indignities you've suffered, dwelling on everything negative published about you in the past – especially when you hit a snag while working. That's the most pernicious thing about critics; they cause you to waste your time.[5]

There are a couple of things to note here:

- A play in production is unavoidably an exposing experience. A playwright committing the act of playwriting puts themselves out there, making secret things

[4] Maddy Costa, *The Guardian G2* 7 March 2012, http://www.guardian.co.uk/stage/2012/mar/06 (accessed: 9 March 2012).

[5] 'Critics and their uses' in Sondheim, S. (2011) *Look, I Made a Hat* (London: Virgin Books).

public. Whether the response is positive or negative, you have made yourself vulnerable, and in the most public way.

- Even the best of critics are offering an educated but still subjective opinion. Not only do they sometimes trash a play that goes on to be a great success (think of Michael Billington's toxic reaction, later retracted, to Sarah Kane's play *Blasted*), they can and possibly should disagree among themselves.

If you doubt this last point, try spotting the difference between the following reviews of a single production of my play, *Frobisher's Gold*. The first comes from Lucy Powell in *Time Out*:[6]

> As in his earlier, implosive 'Breakfast with Mugabe', Grace searches in the most personal of debris for the elusive causes of imperialism, and the uncharted casualties it inflicts on the human heart [...] The early scenes, where [Janet] Suzman holds unshakeable sway are enthralling, but all too soon we veer wildly off course ... Much dreary silliness ensues.

Compare that with this, from Lyn Gardner in the *Guardian*:[7]

> Peerlessly acted by a superb cast led by Janet Suzman, this is a rare play that gets better the longer it chunters on. Up to the interval it is a tedious historical drama. But with the arrival of Elizabeth in the Arctic wastes, the whole thing suddenly bursts into surreal life. In the second half the play dazzles with its wit and wordplay.

We shouldn't conclude from this that neither critic is worth listening to. The major points are, after all, quite clear:

- The playwright has failed to create a convincing, cohesive whole.
- Janet Suzman turns in a typically stellar performance.

But which to listen to most?

[6] Powell, Lucy, *Time Out London*, 1–8 November 2006.

[7] Gardner, Lyn, *The Guardian*, 31 October 2006.

TOP TIP

Critics are good at skewering frailty, but should not be expected to provide a fix. That remains the job of the beleaguered playwright.

Success and failure

As history shows, each of what Kipling called the 'two imposters' can bring their own problems:

- Tennessee Williams is said never to have recovered from the standing ovations that *A Streetcar Named Desire* earned on Broadway: how could he ever match it?
- The novelist William Golding had such a shock when his new novel was trashed in a radio programme that he was plunged into a deep depression which, according to his daughter, lasted almost a decade.[8]

What's clear from all the above is that in a sustained career any playwright will need to recover from both critical success and failure – and possibly from that even worse fate, indifference.

TOP TIP

Getting as far as press night and drawing the critics to see your play is a triumph in itself.

Enjoy the moment, then get back to work. Whether anything you read about your work is of lasting value, only time will tell.

EXERCISE:

- In preparation for your next Press Night, ask yourself what success for your new play would look like. Try creating two versions of the list; label them Dream Scenario and Genuine Progress.

[8] Robert McCrum, *William Golding's Crisis, Observer Magazine*, 11 March 2012.

- Make sure you consider the question using several categories:

  Creative (short term) – I've started to understand my play much better.

  Creative (long-term) – part way through rehearsal, it struck me there was another play I should write.

  Commercial – numbers were good, so there should be some money to come back/I've got a meeting with an agent.

  Critical – one paper liked the play/the internet was on fire.

  Personal – my marriage survived/ I have never felt more like myself.

– add any other categories you can think of.

TOP TIP

- A good working relationship with a director and/or actors you trust is a great outcome from any production.
- After a production, if there is anything at all in the Genuine Progress column, there is reason to be cheerful.
- An invitation to write your next play is the best result of all.

Reviews and reviewers note from a former critic

Clare Bayley

In traditional publications – newspapers and magazines – the space allowed for reviews is decreasing all the time, and editors put pressure on critics to declare something either a five-star hit or a one-star flop. Some editors refuse to print reviews awarded three stars, and they aren't interested in measured reviews which provide a context to the work. However ambivalent many theatre practitioners feel about the national critics, the decline of formal theatre criticism is a loss for theatre. It may now be easier to see videos of performances on YouTube, but what we lack is analysis of how it affected its first audiences, what was challenging or groundbreaking about it, where it fits in with that artist's body of work.

Artists always remember the negative parts of reviews, over and above the positive ones. This is because they hurt. But as an artist you have to train yourself to see the good parts too.

True story

I once wrote a very positive review of a show I'd enjoyed and admired, except for some really awful wigs which had clearly cost a fortune and looked ridiculous. I made passing reference to the wigs. When I met the director some time later, all she remembered of what I'd written was the bit about the wigs.

Bibliography

Books referenced

Ayckbourn, A., *The Crafty Art of Playmaking* London: Faber and Faber, 2003.

Bentley, E., *The Life of the Drama* New York: Applause Theatre Books, 1964.

Bentley, E., (ed.) *The Theory of the Modern Stage* London: Penguin Books, 1992.

Bigsby, C., (ed.) *The Cambridge Companion to August Wilson*

Billington, M., *The Life and Work of Harold Pinter* London: Faber and Faber, 2007. Cambridge: Cambridge University Press, 2007.

Blakemore, M., *Stage Blood: Five Tempestuous Years in the Early Life of the National Theatre* London: Faber and Faber, 2013.

Boardman, J., Griffin, J. and Murray, O., (eds) *The Oxford History of the Classical World* Oxford: Oxford University Press, 1986.

Bolton, W. F., (ed.) *Sphere History of Literature: The Middle Ages* London: Sphere Books, 1987.

Branigan, K., *Roman Britain: Life in an Imperial Province* London: Reader's Digest, 1980.

Brennan, E. M., (ed.) *The Duchess of Malfi* London: New Mermaids Edition, 1977.

Brewer, J., *The Pleasures of the Imagination: English Culture in the Eighteenth Century* London: Harper Collins, 1997.

British Theatre Repertoire 2013, Interim Report, www.britishtheatreconference.co.uk/british-theatre-repertoire-2013 p2, accessed 11 May 2015.

Brown, J. R., (ed.) *The White Devil* Manchester: Manchester University Press, 1966.

Brown, J. R., (ed.) *The Oxford Illustrated History of the Theatre* Oxford: Oxford University Press, 2001.

Cardullo, B., *What Is Dramaturgy?* New York: Peter Lang Publishing, 2008.

Chadwick, O., *The Pelican History of the Church, Vol 3: The Reformation* London: Pelican Books, 1972.

Coffelt, N. and Hall, E., *Inventing the Barbarian: Greek Self-Definition through Tragedy* Oxford: Oxford Classical Monographs, 1989.

Dillon, J., *The Cambridge Introduction to Early English Theatre* Cambridge: Cambridge University Press, 2006.

D'Monte, R. and Saunders, G., (eds) *Cool Britannia? British Political Drama in the 1990s*, Basingstoke: Palgrave Macmillan, 2008.

Drabble, M., (ed.) *Oxford Companion to English Literature*, London: Oxford University Press. 1985.

Dromgoole, D., *The Full Room: An A–Z of Contemporary Playwriting* London: Methuen, 2002.

Edgar, D., *State of Play: Playwrights on Playwriting* London: Faber and Faber, 1999.

Edgar, D., *How Plays Work* London: Nick Hern Books, 2010.

Egri, L., *The Art of Dramatic Writing* 2nd edn New York: Simon & Schuster, 1960.

Esslin, M., *Theatre of the Absurd* London: Eyre and Spottiswood, 1962.

Esslin, M., *Pinter: A Study of His Plays* London: Methuen, 1970.

Esslin, M., *The Field of Drama: How the Signs of Drama Create Meaning on Stage and Screen* London: Methuen, 1987.

Findlater, R., *25 Years of the English Stage Company at the Royal Court* Derbyshire: Amber Lane Press, 1981.

Ford, B., (ed.) *The Cambridge Cultural History Vol 4: 17th Century Britain* Cambridge: Cambridge University Press, 1992.

Gooch, S., *Writing a Play* London: A&C Black, 1988.

Greig, N., *Playwriting: A Practical Guide* Abingdon Oxon: Routledge, 2005.

Griffiths, T. R. and Woddis, C., (eds) *Bloomsbury Theatre Guide* London: Bloomsbury, 1991.

Hall, H. R., *The Ramesseum 'Dramatic' Papyrus*, The British Museum Quarterly, Vol. 4, No. 2, London: British Museum, pp. 37–38 (1929), http://www.jstor.org/stable/4421050 (accessed: 17 December 2014).

Hare, D., *Writing Left Handed* London: Faber and Faber, 1991.

Hartnoll, P., (ed.) *The Concise Oxford Companion to the Theatre* Oxford: Oxford University Press, 1981.

Hartnoll, P., (ed.) *The Oxford Companion to the Theatre* 4th edn Oxford: Oxford University Press, 1998.

Hellman L., (ed.), *Selected Letters of Anton Chekhov* Bungay, Suffolk: Picador, 1984.

Hern, N., (ed.) *My First Play: An Anthology of Theatrical Beginnings* London: Nick Hern Books, 2013.

Hibbert, C. *The English: A Social History 1066–1984* London: Paladin, 1988.

Law, J., (ed.) *The Methuen Drama Dictionary of the Theatre London*: Methuen Drama, 2013.

Letzler Cole, S., *Playwrights in Rehearsal: The Seduction of Company* New York: Routledge, 2001.

Loughrey, B. and Taylor, N., (eds) *Thomas Middleton: Five Plays* London: Penguin Classics, 1988.

Luckhurst, M., *Dramaturgy: A Revolution in Theatre* Cambridge: Cambridge University Press, 2006.

Mangan, M., *The Drama, Theatre and Performance Companion* Basingstoke: Palgrave Macmillan, 2013.

Meisel, M., *How Plays Work: Reading and Performance* Oxford: Oxford University Press, 2007.

Miller, A., *Timebends: A Life* London: Methuen, 1987.

Moore, C. A., *Twelve Famous Plays of the Restoration and Eighteenth Century* New York: The Modern Library, 1933.

Murray, P. and Dorsch, T., (trans.) *Classical Literary Criticism* London: Penguin Classics, 2004.

Nicoll, A., *The Development of the Theatre* London: George G. Harrap & Company, 1966.

Pallin, G., *Stage Management: The Essential Handbook* London: Nick Hern Books, 2003.

Pearson, M., *Site-Specific Performance* London: Palgrave Macmillan, 2010.

Plimpton, G., (ed.) *The Paris Review Interviews: Playwrights at Work* London: Harvill, 2000.

Sierz, A., *In-Yer-Face Theatre: British Drama Today.* London: Faber and Faber, 2001

Sillick, A. and McCormick, M., *The Critics Were Wrong: Misguided Movie Reviews and Film Criticism Gone Awry* New York: Citadel Press Books, 1996.

Simon, S., *The Cambridge Introduction to Modern British Theatre* Cambridge: Cambridge University Press, 2009.

Smiley, S., *Playwriting: The Structure of Action.* New Haven, CT: Yale University Press, 2005.

Sommerstein, A. H., *Aristophanes: Lysistrata/The Archarnians/The Clouds,* Introduction London: Penguin Classics, 1973.

Sondheim, S., *Look: I Made a Hat* New York: Virgin Books, 2011.

Speake, G., (ed.) *Penguin Dictionary of Ancient History* London: Penguin Books, 1994.

Spencer, S., *The Playwright's Guidebook* New York: Faber & Faber, 2002.

Taylor, J. R., *Anger and After* Middlesex: Penguin, 1963.

Thomas, C., 'Negotiating the Interregnum: The Political Works of Davenant and Tatham' in *1650-1850: Ideas, Aesthetics, and Inquiries in the Early Modern Period*, 2004, https://www.academia.edu/530241/ (accessed: 4 June 2014).

Thomson, P., *The Cambridge Introduction to English Theatre, 1660–1900* Cambridge: Cambridge University Press, 2006.

Trussler, S., *The Cambridge Illustrated History of British Theatre* Cambridge: Cambridge University Press, 1994.

Tynan, K., *Tynan on Theatre* Middlesex: Penguin, 1964.

Wandor, M., *Drama Today: A Critical Guide to British Drama 1970–90* Essex: Longman, 1993.

Waters, S., *The Secret Life of Plays* London: Nick Hern Books, 2010.

Webster, T. B. L., *Life in Classical Athens* London: B. T. Batsford Ltd, 1969.

Wells, S. and Taylor, G., (eds) *Complete Oxford Shakespeare* London: Oxford University Press, 1986.

Wickham, G., *Early English Stages 1300–1660, Vol 2 1567–1660, Parts 1&2* London: Routledge and Kegan Paul, 1963.

Williams, R., *Drama from Ibsen to Brecht* Middlesex: Penguin Books, 1983.

Woolf, R., 'Later Poetry: The Popular Tradition' in Bolton, W. F. (ed.) *Sphere History of Literature: The Middle Ages* London: Sphere Books, 1970.

Yapp, N., *The Write Stuff: A History of the Writers' Guild of Great Britain 1959–2009* London: The Writers' Guild, 2009.

Zarilli, P., (ed.) *Theatre Histories: An Introduction*, Abingdon, Oxon: Routledge, 2006.

Plays referenced

Ayckbourn, Alan – *Just Between Ourselves, Season's Greetings*

Bartlett, Mike – *Love Love Love*

Bayley, Clare – *The Container*

Beckett, Samuel – *Endgame, Footfalls, Krapp's Last Tape, Waiting for Godot*

Bennett, Alan – *Talking Heads*
Butterworth, Jez – *Jerusalem*
Cartwright, Jim – *Road*
Chekhov, Anton – *The Cherry Orchard, The Seagull, Three Sisters*
Churchill, Caryl – *Top Girls, Love and Information*
Delaney, Shelagh – *A Taste of Honey*
Friel, Brian – *Faith Healer, Translations*
Frisch, Max – *The Fire Raisers*
Grace, Fraser – *Breakfast with Mugabe, Frobisher's Gold*
Hall, Katori – *The Mountaintop*
Harris, Zinnie – *Further from the Furthest Thing*
Kane, Sarah – *Blasted*
Kirkwood, Lucy – *It Felt Empty When the Heart Went at First but It Is Alright Now; Chimerica*
Lindsay-Abaire, David – *Good People*
Mamet, David – *Edmond, Glengarry Glen Ross, Oleanna, Speed the Plow*
McDonagh, Martin – *The Beauty Queen of Leenane*
Morgan, Abi – *Splendour*
Munro, Rona – *Iron*
Nottage, Lynn – *Ruined*
Payne, Nick – *Constellations*
Penhall, Joe – *Blue/Orange*
Prebble, Lucy – *Enron*
Shaffer, Peter – *The Royal Hunt of the Sun*
Shakespeare, William – *Hamlet, Henry IV Part II, MacBeth, The Merchant of Venice, King Lear*
Sophocles – *The Theban Plays* (various translations including E. F. Watling, Don Taylor)
Stoppard, Tom – *Jumpers*
tucker green, debbie – *Random*
Waters, Steve – *The Contingency Plan*
Wertenbaker, Timberlake – *Our Country's Good*
Williams, Roy – *Sucker Punch*
Williams, Tennessee – *Cat on a Hot Tin Roof*

Index

Note: locators followed by 'n' refer to the note numbers.